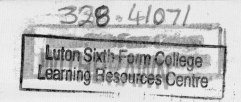

Royal Commission on the Reform of the House of Lords
Chairman: The Rt Hon Lord Wakeham DL

A House for the Future

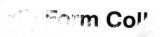

Presented to Parliament by Command of Her Majesty
January 2000

Cm 4534 £24 (inc VAT in UK)

Baroness Dean   Lord Butler   Professor Dawn Oliver   Professor Anthony King

Bill Morris   Kenneth Munro   Lord Hurd   Sir Michael Wheeler-Booth

Ann Beynon   Gerald Kaufman MP   Lord Wakeham   Richard Harries, Bishop of Oxford

To the Queen's Most Excellent Majesty

MAY IT PLEASE YOUR MAJESTY

We, the undersigned Commissioners, having been appointed by Royal Warrant incorporating the following terms of reference:

"Having regard to the need to maintain the position of the House of Commons as the pre-eminent chamber of Parliament and taking particular account of the present nature of the constitutional settlement, including the newly devolved institutions, the impact of the Human Rights Act 1998 and developing relations with the European Union:

- to consider and make recommendations on the role and functions of the second chamber;

- to make recommendations on the method or combination of methods of composition required to constitute a second chamber fit for that role and those functions;

- to report by 31 December 1999."

HUMBLY SUBMIT TO YOUR MAJESTY THE FOLLOWING REPORT.

Contents

Executive Summary

1.   Reform of the House of Lords raises many complex and interrelated issues which have defied resolution for more than 100 years. But there has never been a better time to make progress.

2.   The departure of most of the hereditary peers from the House of Lords has made it necessary to focus on the basic questions. What is the role of the second chamber? What contribution could it make to the political life of the United Kingdom in the 21st century? What is the modern rational basis on which it should be constituted?

3.   The United Kingdom's constitution has been evolving – and fast. Devolution and decentralisation, the impact of the Human Rights Act 1998, developing relations with the European Union – all these factors need to be taken into account in deciding the shape of the new second chamber.

4.   Our report points the way to a new second chamber for the United Kingdom Parliament. It traces the arguments which led to our conclusions. It defines the roles and functions that we recommend the new second chamber should perform. We show how the second chamber can complement and support the decisive political role of the House of Commons while increasing the effectiveness of Parliament as a whole in scrutinising proposed legislation and holding the Government to account. We examine the various suggestions for creating a second chamber fit to carry out this enhanced role. We make a number of proposals which represent a clear break from the past. The second chamber we envisage will build upon the strengths of the present House of Lords but it will also have important new sources of authority. If our recommendations are accepted the link between the possession of a peerage and membership of the second chamber will be broken.

5.   We began our work by looking at the *roles* which the reformed second chamber could play. We then considered the *powers* it should have and the specific *functions* it should perform. Our conclusions on these matters gave us the basis for determining the *characteristics* which the reformed second chamber should possess and it was this assessment that shaped our recommendations on how the second chamber should be *constituted*.

The challenges

6.   We needed to find a way of building on the strengths of the existing House of Lords while creating a new second chamber better adapted to modern circumstances. Change must be in a direction, and at a pace, which goes with the grain of the traditional British evolutionary approach to constitutional reform, while taking this once-in-a-lifetime opportunity to produce a coherent blueprint for the second chamber of Parliament.

7.   We were also determined to define the role and functions of the new second chamber in terms which demonstrated that it has a real and important part to play in the political life of the country. At the same time we needed to allay fears that it could undermine the pre-eminence of the House of Commons as the United Kingdom's primary democratic forum.

8.   In particular, we wanted to produce recommendations which would illustrate the crucial trilateral relationship between the Government, the House of Commons and the new second chamber. We took into account the fact that the stability of the trilateral relationship could be affected by the powers of the new second chamber and also by the way its members are selected.

9.   We saw the need for a new second chamber with the authority and confidence to function effectively and to use its powers wisely. At the same time we recognised the danger of setting up an institution which could threaten the status of the House of Commons and cause constitutional conflict or whose members could rival those of the House of Commons (for example in the discharge of their constituency representative role).

10.   Above all, we were keen to make proposals that would produce a new second chamber distinctively different from the House of Commons, whose members were more representative of the whole of British society and who could bring a wider range of expertise and experience to bear on the consideration of public policy questions.

11.   We acknowledged from the outset that it would be wrong – as well as futile – to try to make the second chamber a politician-free zone. Parliament is a place where political issues are debated and fought over, and the second chamber cannot and should not be disengaged from that process. It will need a cadre of men and women with appropriate political experience to help it play a constructive role. But the new second chamber should not simply be a creature of the political parties, and the influence of the parties on individual members should be minimised. We wanted to create a new second chamber which was politically astute but not a home for yet another group of professional politicians; which provided an appropriate role for the political parties but discouraged sterile partisan confrontation; and which included members of the political parties but was designed to limit the parties' influence and foster the exercise of independent judgement.

Roles

12.   The new second chamber should have four main roles:

- It should bring a range of different perspectives to bear on the development of public policy.

- It should be broadly representative of British society. People should be able to feel that there is a voice in Parliament for the different aspects of their personalities, whether regional, vocational, ethnic, professional, cultural or religious, expressed by a person or persons with whom they can identify.

- It should play a vital role as one of the main 'checks and balances' within the unwritten British constitution. Its role should be complementary to that of the House of Commons in identifying points of concern and requiring the Government to reconsider or justify its policy intentions. If necessary, it should cause the House of Commons to think again. The second chamber should engender second thoughts.

- It should provide a voice for the nations and regions of the United Kingdom at the centre of public affairs.

Powers

13.   No radical change is needed in the balance of power between the two Houses of Parliament. The new second chamber should retain the 'suspensory veto' set out in the Parliament Acts. This will give it the power to delay the enactment of proposed legislation but not to prevent the passage of a Commons Bill which has been approved by the House of Commons in two successive sessions of Parliament.

14.   The corollary of recommending that the new second chamber should have the same powers as the present House of Lords is that it should continue to consider all Government business within a reasonable time and that the principles underlying the 'Salisbury Convention' should be maintained. The second chamber should respect a governing party's general election manifesto and be cautious about challenging the clearly expressed views of the House of Commons on major issues of public policy.

15.   The absolute (but unused) power of the House of Lords to veto Statutory Instruments should be adapted so that any vote against a Statutory Instrument in the new second chamber could be overridden by an affirmative vote in the House of Commons. While this would represent a diminution in the formal power of the second chamber, it would give it a mechanism which it could use in order to delay, and demonstrate its concern about, specific Statutory Instruments. The House of Commons should have the last word but would have to take full account of the second chamber's concerns, Ministers' responses and public opinion.

Making law

16.   There should be no significant changes in the second chamber's law-making functions. Parliament should continue to derive the benefits of being bicameral, with a second chamber capable of bringing a distinctive range of perspectives to bear. There should be more pre-legislative scrutiny of draft Bills. The new second chamber should consider how to promote the consideration of law reform Bills drawn up by the Law Commission. The valuable work of the Delegated Powers and Deregulation Committee should continue.

Protecting the constitution

17.   The second chamber's role in protecting the constitution should be maintained and enhanced. It should no longer be possible to amend the Parliament Acts using Parliament Act procedures, as was done in 1949. Such a change would maintain the current balance of power between the two Houses of Parliament and reinforce the second chamber's power of veto over any Bill to extend the life of a Parliament.

18.   There should be no extension of the second chamber's formal powers in respect of any other matter, whether 'constitutional' or concerning human rights. But an authoritative Constitutional Committee should be set up by the second chamber to scrutinise the constitutional implications of all legislation and to keep the operation of the constitution under review.

19. A Human Rights Committee should be set up by the second chamber to scrutinise all Bills and Statutory Instruments for human rights implications. This would enable Parliament as a whole to reach an informed judgement before legislation is enacted. Given the forthcoming implementation of the Human Rights Act 1998, such a procedure is required if Parliament is to discharge effectively its primary responsibility for the protection of human rights. This should reduce the need for points of concern to be adjudicated by the courts.

Giving a voice to the nations and regions

20. The new second chamber should be able to play a valuable role in giving a voice to the nations and regions, whatever pattern of devolution and decentralisation may emerge in future. The chamber must serve the interests of the whole of the United Kingdom and contain people from all over the United Kingdom. It should contain a proportion of 'regional members' to provide a direct voice for the nations and regions of the United Kingdom at the centre of national affairs. These 'regional members' should not be drawn from the devolved administrations, or from the Scottish Parliament and the other devolved Assemblies, but should be able to speak for each national or regional unit of the United Kingdom. Because the 'regional members' would share a regional perspective with MEPs, members of the devolved institutions, the English Regional Chambers and the existing local government groupings, they could encourage and facilitate greater contact across different levels of Government and a stronger 'regional' voice, in Europe as well as at Westminster.

Scrutinising secondary legislation

21. Secondary legislation is increasingly pervasive and voluminous but currently subject to inadequate Parliamentary scrutiny. The House of Lords has shown a conscientious interest in the grant and exercise of delegated powers. The new second chamber should maintain and extend this function, using the new procedure referred to in paragraph 15.

Scrutinising EU business

22. The existing arrangements for scrutinising Ministers' handling of European Union business should be maintained and improved in the new second chamber, with additional resources being made available to its European Union Committee. United Kingdom MEPs should not be represented in the new second chamber, but the chamber should promote greater contact and co-operation between Parliament and the United Kingdom's MEPs.

Holding the Government to account

23.   Some Ministers should continue to be drawn from and be directly accountable to the new second chamber. Senior Ministers based in the House of Commons should make occasional statements to and take questions from an appropriate second chamber Committee.

24.   The new second chamber should continue to be a relatively non-polemical forum for national debate, informed by the range of different perspectives which its members should have. Its specialist investigations (e.g. in respect of scientific and technological issues) should continue, drawing on its members' broad spread of expertise. There is no distinct role for the second chamber to play in scrutinising public appointments.

25.   A Committee should be established to scrutinise Treaties laid before Parliament and draw attention to any implications which merit Parliamentary consideration before ratification takes place.

The Law Lords and the judicial role of the second chamber

26.   It is not for us to say how the superior courts of the United Kingdom should be organised; but we had to reach a view on whether the new second chamber could continue to carry out, through Committees composed exclusively of Law Lords, the judicial functions of the present House of Lords. We conclude that, as long as certain basic conventions (which we recommend should be set out in writing) continue to be observed, there is insufficient reason to change the present arrangements. Indeed, we see some advantage in having senior judges in the legislature where they can be made aware of the social developments and political balances which underlie most legislation.

Continuity with the past

27.   All these recommendations on the roles, powers and functions of the new second chamber build to a considerable extent on those of the existing House of Lords. They broaden the second chamber's role rather than constituting a radical departure from what has gone before. The new second chamber should have a larger role to play in scrutinising the executive, protecting the constitution, safeguarding human rights, deliberating on issues which arise from devolution and decentralisation and examining secondary legislation.

Characteristics

28.   Taking account of the roles and functions we think the new second chamber should perform, we believe it should, above all, be:

- authoritative;
- confident; and
- broadly representative of the whole of British society.

It should also contain members with:

- a breadth of experience outside the world of politics and a broad range of expertise;

- particular skills and knowledge relevant to the careful assessment of constitutional matters and human rights;

- the ability to bring a philosophical, moral or spiritual perspective to bear;

- personal distinction;

- freedom from party domination. A significant proportion of the members should belong to no political party and sit on the Cross Benches, so that no one party is able to dominate the second chamber;

- a non-polemical and courteous style; and

- the ability to take a long-term view.

29.   A new second chamber with these characteristics should remedy the deficiencies of the old House of Lords, which lacked the political legitimacy and confidence to do its job properly, while preserving some of its best features.

Composition

30.   After making a detailed analysis of potential methods of composition and the extent to which they could reliably deliver these characteristics, we do not recommend:

- a wholly or largely directly elected second chamber;

- indirect election from the devolved institutions (or local government electoral colleges) or from among United Kingdom MEPs;

- random selection; or

- co-option.

31.   While the principle of vocational or interest group representation is attractive, the objective would be more effectively achieved through an independent appointments system. On the other hand, total reliance on an independent appointments system to nominate members of the new second chamber would leave no voice for the electorate in its composition. It would be unsatisfactory as a basis for identifying people to provide a voice for the nations and regions of the United Kingdom.

32.   We also believe the proposed arrangements for making appointments to the interim House of Lords through the mechanism of an independent Appointments Commission would not be satisfactory as a long-term solution. They leave too much power in the hands of the Prime Minister of the day and they confine the role of the Appointments Commission to the nomination of Cross Benchers.

33.   We therefore recommend that a new second chamber of around 550 members should be made up as follows:

■ A significant minority of the members of the new second chamber should be 'regional members' chosen on a basis which reflects the balance of political opinion within each of the nations and regions of the United Kingdom. The regional electorates should have a voice in the selection of members of the new second chamber. Those members in turn will provide a voice for the nations and regions.

■ Other members should be appointed on the nomination of a genuinely independent Appointments Commission with a remit to create a second chamber which was broadly representative of British society and possessed all the other characteristics mentioned above.

■ The Appointments Commission should be responsible for maintaining the proportion of independents ('Cross Benchers') in the new second chamber at around 20 per cent of the total membership.

■ Among the politically-affiliated members, the Appointments Commission would be required to secure an overall political balance matching the political opinion of the country as a whole, as expressed in votes cast at the most recent general election.

34.   To facilitate a smooth transition to the new arrangements, the existing life peers should become members of the new second chamber.

35.   Untrammelled party patronage and Prime Ministerial control of the size and balance of the second chamber should cease. The Appointments Commission should ensure that the new second chamber is broadly representative of British society. It should make early progress towards achieving gender balance and proportionate representation for members of minority ethnic groups. In order to identify appropriate candidates for the second chamber it should maintain contacts with vocational, professional, cultural, sporting and other bodies. It should publish criteria for appointment to the chamber and invite nominations from the widest possible range of sources.

36.   We present three possible models for the selection of the regional members. Each model has the support of different members of the Commission. Model B has the support of a substantial majority of the Commission.

Model A – a total of 65 regional members, chosen at the time of each general election by a system of 'complementary' election. Votes cast for party candidates in each constituency at general elections would be accumulated at regional level. The parties would secure the number of regional members for each region proportional to their shares of the vote in that region, drawing the names from a previously published party list. Regional members would be selected for one-third of the regions at each general election.

Model B – a total of 87 regional members, elected at the time of each European Parliament election. One-third of the regions would choose their regional members at each election. The system of election used for electing members of the second chamber should be the same as that used for electing the United Kingdom's members of the European Parliament, although a majority of those supporting this model would prefer a 'partially open' list system of proportional representation (PR).

Model C – a total of 195 regional members elected by thirds, using a 'partially open' list system of PR, at the time of each European Parliament election.

37.   To promote continuity and a longer-term perspective, all members (under all three models) should serve for three electoral cycles or 15-year terms, with the possibility of being reappointed for a further period of up to 15 years at the discretion of the Appointments Commission.

Religious faiths

38.   A substantial majority of the Commission recommends a broadening and deepening of religious representation in the second chamber. Representation should be extended beyond the Church of England to embrace other Christian denominations in all parts of the United Kingdom and representatives of other faiths.

Remuneration

39.   To make participation in the work of the new second chamber possible for people who do not have other sources of income and who come from outside the South East of England, there should be a review of the current system of paying expenses. A modest payment related to attendance in the new second chamber should be introduced.

Conclusion

40.   Our proposals represent a significant change from what has gone before. No new member of the second chamber will arrive there on the same basis as any existing member of the House of Lords. No new member of the second chamber will get there via an Honours List. The new second chamber will be more democratic and representative than the present House of Lords.

More democratic –   The chamber as a whole will reflect the overall balance of political opinion within the country. Regional members will directly reflect the balance of political opinion within the regions.

More representative –   The chamber will contain members from all parts of the country and from all walks of life, broadly equal numbers of men and women and representatives of all the country's main ethnic and religious communities.

41.   We were determined to produce recommendations which were not only persuasive and intellectually coherent but also workable, durable and politically realistic. Our report sets out the case for radical but evolutionary change which will, in our view, contribute to better government for all.

Chapter 1 – Introduction

1.1　　Two primary considerations governed our approach. First, we were determined to produce recommendations which were not only coherent and intellectually persuasive but also realistic, workable and politically achievable. Our aim has been to produce a report that could command a reasonable degree of consensus across the political spectrum and that would therefore stand a good chance of being implemented in the near future. We were aware that if we failed to achieve this aim, another opportunity to reform the House of Lords might not arise for many years. This is the fourth attempt at reforming the House of Lords in the 20th century. The three preceding efforts failed. We did not wish to spend months compiling a report that would gather dust in a pigeonhole.

1.2　　Second, we were very conscious that we had been selected to exercise our collective judgement on the issues raised by our terms of reference. Our task therefore was to put ourselves in a position to make those judgements. As part of that process and before we began to form any conclusions of our own, we sought to secure the widest possible range of views and proposals on the issues raised by Lords reform; but the judgements we reached, having weighed the evidence, are ours alone. We were not appointed merely to reflect other people's views.

1.3　　We identified four key criteria: a modern second chamber should be conducive to a *stable overall constitutional settlement*; *complement* the work of the House of Commons; assist Parliament as a whole to provide *better scrutiny* of the Executive; and thus contribute to *better Government*. There was no challenge to those criteria during our consultation exercise. Our recommendations fulfil them.

Overseas comparisons

1.4　　There are many second chambers around the world and we felt it was important to draw lessons from overseas experience. The Constitution Unit,[1] which had already embarked on a major comparative study, provided useful statistics and analysis. The Foreign and Commonwealth Office also provided helpful reports on the 20 second chambers which seemed to constitute the most likely comparisons for the reformed second chamber. The more we looked into all of them, however, the less it seemed that there were any general lessons to be drawn. It is an interesting feature of second chambers around the world, noted in Patterson and Mughan's *Senates: Bicameralism in the Contemporary World*,[2] that they are nearly all the subject of complaint and criticism and of more or less radical proposals for reform. Furthermore, they are generally very different from each other.

---

[1] At the School of Public Policy, University College London.

[2] S. C. Patterson and A. Mughan, Eds. *Senates: Bicameralism in the Contemporary World*. Ohio State University Press. 1999. ISBN 0 8142 5010 6.

1.5   Our broad conclusion was that the more successful second chambers are those which fit best with the history, traditions and political culture of the country concerned and complement most effectively the characteristics of its 'lower' chamber. We therefore decided to concentrate on identifying what kind of second chamber was needed to fit the unique circumstances of the United Kingdom. We took account of specific overseas comparisons whenever that was appropriate, but we did not consider that any other second chamber provided a sufficiently close parallel to justify making an overseas visit.

The work of the Commission

1.6   Following our first meeting, on 1 March 1999, we started an extensive programme of background reading; organised an academic-led seminar to enhance our knowledge of the main issues; sought additional information from a range of sources; published a consultation paper; and set up a series of public hearings around the country.

1.7   In developing our own understanding of the issues we benefited from the willing assistance of staff in both Houses of Parliament. We received a considerable volume of helpful briefing material from the Clerk of the Parliaments and his staff in the Parliament Office, from the Clerk of the House of Commons and his staff, from the respective Library staffs and from the House of Lords Information Office.[3] We commissioned other analytical papers from a number of sources. Other academics and specialists also responded to our requests for papers and analyses.[4] We were also able to take account of the report of the Conservative Party Constitutional Commission on options for a new second chamber. This became available at an early stage in our own work.[5] We are grateful to all of them. At a later stage in our work we were able to draw on the advice of Sir Christopher Jenkins KCB, retired First Parliamentary Counsel, and Professor Anthony Bradley, both of whom provided expert support for our consideration of specific issues.

1.8   The Commission met formally on 29 occasions, including the public hearings and visits to regional centres. In addition there were numerous informal meetings and discussions, both among members of the Commission and with other interested parties.

The consultation exercise

1.9   We were particularly keen to seek views and opinions from people with a detailed understanding of the specific contributions which a reformed second chamber could make in various fields as well as from members of the public more generally.

Consultation paper

1.10   Our consultation paper was circulated widely within both Houses of Parliament and to MEPs, members of the Northern Ireland Assembly and those active in the

---

[3] We are particularly grateful for the valuable technical advice we received from Sir James Nursaw KCB QC and Mr Derek Rippengal CB QC, Counsel to the Chairman of Committees in the House of Lords, and D.R. Beamish, Principal Clerk of Committees in the House of Lords.

[4] All this material can be found on the CD-ROM enclosed with this report.

[5] The Rt Hon the Lord Mackay of Clashfern KT, Chair. *The Report of the Constitutional Commission on Options for a new Second Chamber.* Douglas Slater. April 1999.

Regional Chambers and Regional Development Agencies. Copies were sent, after the respective elections, to members of the Scottish Parliament and the National Assembly for Wales. The paper was also distributed to a large number of leading academics and other political commentators as well as to people with an interest in particular issues, such as the implications of devolution and regional matters; the scrutiny of European Union institutions; the implications of the Human Rights Act 1998; the judicial role of the House of Lords; and the future of the Lords Spiritual. Copies were also sent to all those members of the public who showed an interest in our work. In all, in addition to making the consultation paper available on the Commission's website, we distributed some 6,000 copies of the consultation paper to more than 4,500 individuals and organisations. We were pleased by the quality of the response we received. In total we received over 1,700 written submissions, many of considerable length. Virtually all of them[6] can be found on the CD-ROM enclosed with this report.

Parliamentary debates

1.11   We also benefited from being able to study the debates which took place in the House of Commons and the House of Lords during the course of our work, both on the White Paper, *Modernising Parliament: Reforming the House of Lords*,[7] published in January 1999, and on the House of Lords Bill. We were particularly assisted by the points made during the House of Commons Second Reading debate on the House of Lords Bill[8] and by the subsequent House of Commons debate on the White Paper.[9] There were major debates in the House of Lords on 14 and 15 October 1998, 17 February 1999, 22 and 23 February 1999 and 29 and 30 March 1999.[10] These focused primarily on the proposals reflected in the House of Lords Bill but also covered a number of issues relevant to our work. We were also interested to read the National Assembly for Wales' debate on our consultation paper.[11]

Private meetings

1.12   During the course of our work, our Chairman met former Prime Ministers The Rt Hon Sir Edward Heath MP, The Rt Hon Lord Callaghan of Cardiff, The Rt Hon Baroness Thatcher and The Rt Hon John Major MP. We are grateful for the insights they provided. At the suggestion of the Speaker of the House of Commons, the Rt Hon Betty Boothroyd MP, our Chairman also had an informal meeting with Nicholas Winterton MP (Chairman) and other members of the House of Commons Procedure Committee. That meeting helped to improve our understanding of the ways in which the reformed second chamber could effectively complement the work of the House of Commons.

---

[6] Some respondents requested that their evidence be treated as confidential.

[7] Cabinet Office. *Modernising Parliament: Reforming the House of Lords* 1999. Cm 4183.

[8] Hansard (HC). 1 and 2 February 1999 (House of Lords Bill, Second Reading Debate).

[9] Hansard (HC). 9 June 1999 (House of Lords Reform, Debate on White Paper).

[10] Hansard (HL). 14 and 15 October 1998 (House of Lords Reform, Motion to Take Note); 17 February 1999 (Separation of Powers); 22 and 23 February 1999 (House of Lords Reform, Debate on White Paper); 29 and 30 March 1999 (House of Lords Bill, Second Reading).

[11] National Assembly for Wales' debate on 22 June 1999, www.wales.gov.uk

1.13   Additionally, the Commission had a series of private meetings with the First Ministers and Presiding Officers of the Scottish Parliament, the National Assembly for Wales and the Northern Ireland Assembly; with the Archbishop of Canterbury and the Bishop of Durham, and with Archbishop Lord Eames of Armagh; with representatives of Churches Together in Britain and Ireland, and with the Chief Rabbi; with two senior Lords of Appeal in Ordinary; with the Rt Hon Chris Patten CH, the former Governor of Hong Kong; with the Rt Hon Lord Neill of Bladen QC, Chairman of the Committee on Standards in Public Life; with the Chairman of the House of Lords' Delegated Powers and Deregulation Committee and his staff; with officials supporting the House of Commons European Scrutiny Committee; and with a number of others. We are grateful to all those who gave us the benefit of their views and their experience in this way.

Public hearings

1.14   We visited Scotland, Wales, Northern Ireland and several of the English regions and had valuable meetings with local politicians and other leading figures. In total we held 21 sessions of public hearings in nine locations around the country, including seven sessions over two and a half days in London.[12] Those hearings gave us an opportunity to probe and test many of the arguments that had already been presented to

us in written evidence and to explore the implications of various proposals. They also stimulated considerable media interest throughout the United Kingdom and gave members of the audience the opportunity to register their views, both directly and by completing a brief questionnaire. In total some 900 copies of the questionnaire, which was also available on the Commission's website, were completed. Although it could not be regarded as providing an authoritative reflection of public opinion, the data it provided (see Appendix A for details) were very much in line with the arguments presented to us in both written and oral evidence.

1.15   The public hearings, and the consultation exercise more generally, turned out to be an important aspect of our work. They enabled us to assess the relative strength of different arguments for and against particular propositions, and to see how robust they were to vigorous cross-examination. Members of the public made some significant contributions. Our recommendations are not in line with any individual set of proposals put to us, but they take fully into account those arguments that emerged most clearly from the consultation exercise and meet those criticisms that we felt were most valid. Our recommendations have been significantly influenced by the consultation exercise and we are grateful to all who put their views in writing, responded to our questions, attended the public hearings and completed the questionnaire. All of them contributed to the formulation of this report.

---

[12] The transcripts of all these public hearings can be found on the CD-ROM enclosed with this report.

The structure of the report

1.16   Our report follows a logical sequence. After a brief review of the historical background and recent developments (Chapter 2) we discuss the overall role of the reformed second chamber (Chapter 3) and then, in turn, the part it could play in:

■ making the law (Chapter 4);

■ protecting the constitution (Chapter 5);

■ giving a voice to the nations and regions (Chapter 6);

■ scrutinising secondary legislation (Chapter 7); and

■ holding the Government to account (Chapter 8).

The powers of the second chamber are discussed in Chapters 4 and 7. Chapter 9 discusses the judicial functions of the present House of Lords and the role of the Law Lords.

1.17   The next part of the report considers what method or methods of composition would produce a second chamber with the characteristics necessary to enable it to carry out the overall role and specific functions which we recommend. Chapter 10 sets out the characteristics which the second chamber should possess. Chapter 11 sets out our broad overall conclusions on composition. Chapters 12 and 13 discuss specific practical points arising from those conclusions. These include the arrangements we envisage for the selection of 'regional' members for the second chamber and the establishment, role and working practices of an independent Appointments Commission.

1.18   Chapter 14 explains our proposals regarding the existing life peers and Chapter 15 deals with the representation of religious faiths in the second chamber.

1.19   Chapters 16 to 18 incorporate our recommendations on a series of essentially subsidiary points, including the procedural style appropriate to the role and functions of the reformed second chamber; the principles that should be followed in setting a structure of expenses and allowances; and the future relationship between the peerage and membership of the reformed second chamber. We also discuss the name of the new chamber and the title by which its members should be known.

1.20   Chapter 19 describes how our recommendations could be implemented.

Conclusion

1.21   The issues raised by our terms of reference are individually difficult and interconnected in a variety of often subtle ways. The evidence we received, while helpful, was conflicting and frequently internally inconsistent. For example, widespread support for elections to the second chamber was combined with near-universal cynicism about the role of political parties and a desire to limit their influence in the second chamber. That said, we found the process of reaching our conclusions both challenging and stimulating. While we naturally all came to the subject with our own views, we found that our thinking developed along new lines as we became immersed in the issues and came to weigh the balances between the various factors. Our recommendations provide a coherent response to the complex and interrelated issues raised by our terms of reference. This report sets out the arguments which have led us to those conclusions.

Thanks to the Secretariat

We owe a great debt to our Secretary, David Hill, his Deputy, Dr Martin Samuels, and the rest of the Secretariat. We were extremely well looked after: all the practical arrangements went like clockwork. But it was the quality of their supporting papers, both their factual content and the clear analysis of the many issues, which was so invaluable. Without this and their skill with words the Commission simply could not have completed its work in time and that work would have been greatly impoverished.

Chapter 2 – Development of the House of Lords

Historical background

2.1   With its origins in the medieval royal practice of summoning the great landowners (both lay and ecclesiastical) to offer counsel and provide resources, the House of Lords pre-dates the House of Commons by some centuries and it was long the pre-eminent House of Parliament. The House of Commons' power over financial resources was evident as early as the 14th century, and it asserted its sole privilege in financial matters from the 17th century onwards. This change in the balance of power between the two Houses was given further impetus through the growing linkage between a Government's perceived legitimacy and its popular support, as expressed through the ballot box. The significance of electoral support was underlined by the Reform Acts of 1832, 1867 and 1884 which together increased the size of the electorate by a factor of ten, to around 8 million. At the same time, the issue of Home Rule for Ireland led to a split in the Liberal Party, which gave the Unionists a permanent majority in the House of Lords. The contrast between a House of Commons which reflected changes in the political will of the electorate and a House of Lords under the permanent control of one of the major political parties inevitably led to conflict and to pressure for reform.

The House of Lords rejecting the 1909 Budget

Previous reforms

2.2   While motions proposing reform were debated from the mid–1880s onwards, the first major consideration of the issue was precipitated by the clashes between the Unionist-dominated Lords and the Liberal Government which came to office in 1905. In 1908, the all-party Rosebery Committee agreed that heredity should no longer of itself entail the right to membership of the House. Instead, it recommended that eminent independents should be appointed to life peerages. No agreement was reached on the powers that the House of Lords should wield. These powers became the central consideration during the constitutional crisis which followed the Lords' rejection of Lloyd George's 1909 Budget. The Government decided to leave the issue of how the House of Lords should be constituted for a later date and eventually secured the passage of the Parliament Act 1911. The Act gave the House of Commons the right to overrule the House of Lords' rejection of a Bill if the Bill was passed by the House of Commons in three successive sessions over a period of at least two years.[1]

---

[1] See R. Jenkins. *Mr Balfour's Poodle* 1968. There is a fuller discussion of the Parliament Acts in Chapter 4 of this report.

2.3   The Bryce Conference 1917–18[2] set out the powers considered appropriate to the second chamber but failed to reach full agreement on composition. It did, however, agree that members should include "persons of experience in various forms of public work". It also emphasised that the chamber should include "a certain proportion of persons who are not extreme partisans" and that every precaution should be taken to ensure that "no one set of political opinions should be likely to have a marked and permanent predominance". The members agreed that heredity alone was not an appropriate basis for membership of the second chamber but were unable to agree on what should replace it. A substantial majority proposed that most of the members should be elected by regional groups of MPs, with the full complement made up by a number of hereditary peers chosen by a Committee of Selection. However, the fire had gone out of the reform movement and the First World War meant that other matters had become more pressing. None of the Bryce Report's recommendations was implemented.

2.4   The second phase of reform came after Labour's landslide victory in the 1945 election. Although the Conservative majority in the Lords adopted the self-denying ordinance of the 'Salisbury Convention'[3] – under which they did not reject Bills fulfilling manifesto commitments – the Government decided to reduce the length of the Lords' delaying power. An inter-party conference[4] again agreed that heredity should not be sufficient grounds for membership of the House of Lords and that no one political party should enjoy a permanent majority. It proposed that individuals, including women, should be appointed as life peers on the basis of their "personal distinction or public service" and that some remuneration should be payable so as not to exclude people who had no private income. No agreement was reached on reducing the powers of the House of Lords. The Government accordingly used the procedures of the existing Parliament Act to secure the passage of the Parliament Act 1949. This Act reduced the Lords' delaying power from a minimum of two years to a minimum of one. The issue of composition was again deferred, though Conservative Governments subsequently introduced a system of expenses in 1957 and life peerages in 1958.[5] The introduction of life peerages (for men and women) enabled the number of Labour peers – then only a handful – to be increased without requiring those concerned to accept a hereditary peerage. The right to disclaim a hereditary peerage and the right of hereditary peeresses to sit in the House of Lords followed in 1963.[6]

Baroness Wooten of Abinger, one of the four women life peers created in 1958.

---

[2] *Conference on the Reform of the Second Chamber.* Letter from Viscount Bryce to the Prime Minister. April 1918. Published as Cd 9038.
[3] There is a fuller discussion of the Salisbury Convention in Chapter 4 of this report.
[4] *Parliament Bill 1947: Agreed Statement on Conclusions of Conference of Party Leaders.* February–April 1948. Cmd 7380.
[5] Life Peerages Act 1958.
[6] Peerage Act 1963.

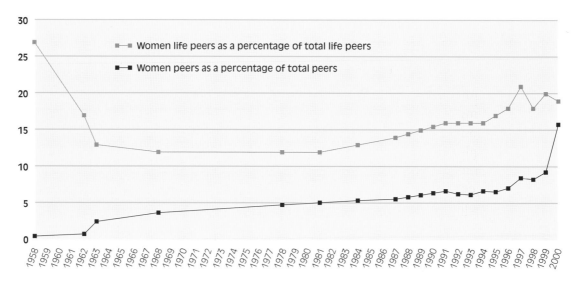

Percentage of women in the House of Lords 1958–2000

2.5   A third phase of reform was attempted in 1967, when the Wilson Government opened inter-party talks. These broke down following the House of Lords' rejection of the Southern Rhodesia (United Nations Sanctions) Order in June 1968. The Government then put forward proposals based on the emerging conclusions of the inter-party talks.[7] These proposals envisaged that the voting rights of both hereditary and infrequently-attending life peers should be removed. They also argued that the governing party should have a small majority over the other political parties, while the continued presence of independent members would prevent it securing an absolute majority. In addition, the House of Lords' power to delay Bills would be reduced to six months and its power to veto secondary legislation abolished. The resulting Bill, however, was talked out by a combination of backbenchers from both sides of the Commons, some of whom feared the proposals would give the Prime Minister too much power of patronage while others were concerned about the risk of changing the relationship between the two Houses.

Changes since 1958

2.6   The years since the introduction of life peerages have seen considerable changes in the composition of the House of Lords; in its workload and work rate; and in the way it has gone about discharging its responsibilities. Bagehot divided the institutions of the British state into two categories: the "*dignified* parts…, which excite and preserve the reverence of the population" and the "*efficient* parts… those by which it, in fact, works and rules."[8] In many respects, the House of Lords has over the past 40 years made the transition from the first to the second.

---

[7] *House of Lords Reform*, November 1968, Cmnd 3799.

[8] Walter Bagehot, *The English Constitution*, first published in 1867, Chapter 1.

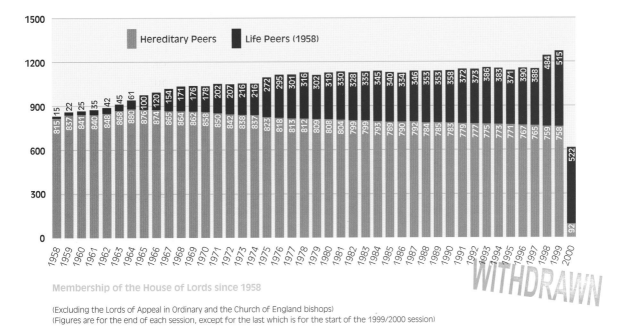

Membership of the House of Lords since 1958

(Excluding the Lords of Appeal in Ordinary and the Church of England bishops)
(Figures are for the end of each session, except for the last which is for the start of the 1999/2000 session)

2.7   Since the arrival of life peers in the House of Lords, there have been significant changes in its characteristics and working practices. While these have not been exclusively due to the introduction of life peers, their impact has been considerable. The changes may be illustrated by considering developments in a number of key areas.

2.8   The average daily attendance has more than trebled, from 136 in 1959/60 to 446 in 1998/99. The proportion of regular attenders has also grown. Although there is no formal distinction between 'working' peers and others, the increased level of attendance reflects a change from the largely part-time and amateur nature of the House in the 1960s to the more professional approach we see today. This trend has been supported and reinforced by the introduction of a system of modest expenses related to participation in the work of the House of Lords.

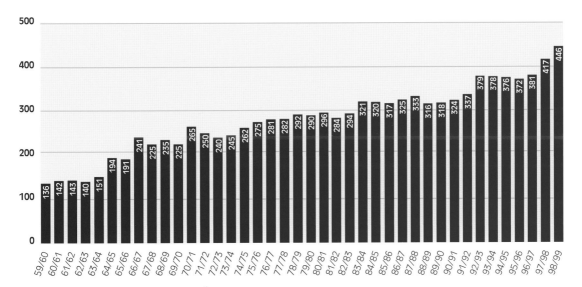

Average daily attendance by session

2.9   The number of sitting days per session and the amount of time spent considering public Bills have also risen substantially. From the 1970s onwards, the tempo of work in the House has risen steadily, with the number of sitting hours almost doubling by 1998. Accompanying this increase, the time spent by the whole House on public Bills has more than trebled.

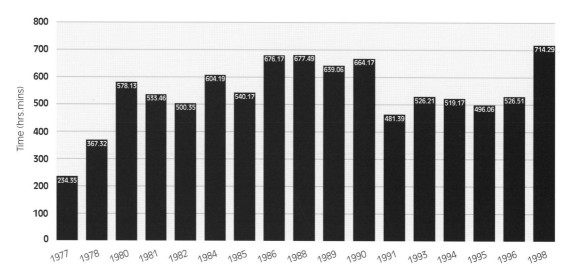

Time spent on public Bills (excluding election years)

2.10   The introduction of life peers, and the increasingly wide range of occupations followed by hereditary peers, has broadened the areas of expertise of the House's members beyond the traditional fields of agriculture, the armed forces and the law. Life peers have included, for example, university vice-chancellors, economists, businessmen and women, trade unionists, social welfare workers, environmentalists, people active in local government and authors. In its consideration of public policy issues, the House of Lords has also increasingly been able to draw on the political experience of former Cabinet Ministers, other senior politicians, retired public servants and people eminent in a range of spheres of public life. As a result, debates have been better informed and questioning of Ministers has become more thorough. This has been reflected in the increased range and number of questions Ministers are asked. The number of Questions for Written Answer has increased 80-fold and in 1998/99 Questions for Oral Answer took up over 14 per cent of the time of the House of Lords.

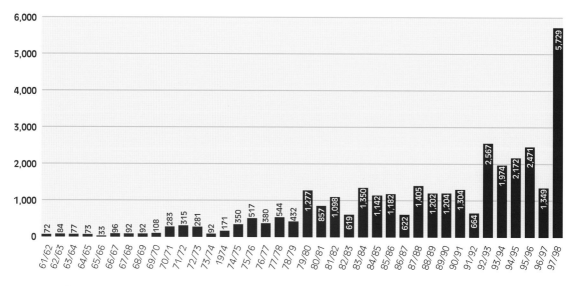

Questions for Written Answer by session

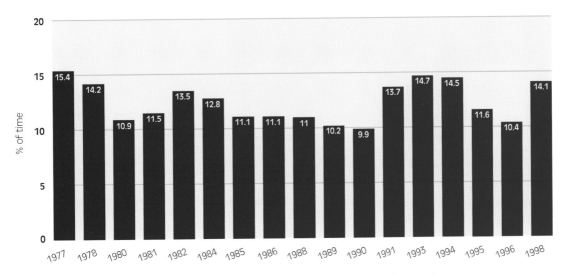

Percentage of time spent on Questions for Oral Answers (excluding election years)

2.11   A further trend has been observable in changes in the House of Lords' social and political attitudes. In 1956, the House rejected a Bill to abolish the death penalty by 238 votes to 95 – a huge majority by the standards of that time. Ten years later, the House passed a Bill to abolish the death penalty, this time by a majority almost as large as that against the Bill of ten years earlier (204-104). It also initiated legislation on homosexual relations and on divorce and abortion. During the 1960s, the House began to gain a reputation as a liberal political force on social matters. Again, this change was due not simply to the arrival of life peers in increasing numbers but also to a change in the attitudes of hereditary peers, many of whom voted in the reformist lobbies.

New areas of scrutiny

2.12   All these changes seem to have been reinforced by the failure of the 1968 scheme to reform the powers and composition of the House of Lords, a scheme which the House of Lords supported, but which was vigorously and successfully opposed by Labour and Conservative backbenchers in the House of Commons. The House seemed to find a new sense of purpose and direction through developing its ability to hold the Government to account in various ways which did not run the risk of triggering any constitutional confrontation with either the Government or the House of Commons.

2.13   In response to the United Kingdom's accession to the European Economic Community in 1972, the House of Lords established the European Communities Committee[9] to scrutinise proposals emanating from Brussels. The Committee has absorbed a large part of the staff resources of the House. A considerable number of peers serve as members of its six sub-committees, which have a well deserved reputation throughout the European Union for the quality of their reports. The House also responded to the abolition of the Commons Science and Technology Committee in 1979 by establishing its own Committee. This Committee, and other *ad hoc* committees on specific issues, conduct specialist investigations and produce a large number of authoritative reports.

[9] Now the European Union Committee.

2.14 Innovations have been made in the consideration of legislation, such as the use of a Grand Committee procedure to relieve pressure on the floor of the House and the establishment of Special Public Bill Committees able to take evidence on Bills before subjecting them to detailed scrutiny. Alongside these developments there has been a considerable rise in the number of amendments made by the House of Lords, especially to Government Bills. While a high proportion of these are Government amendments, they frequently arise from points made during House of Lords proceedings and in general reflect the constructive role which the House of Lords plays in the technical consideration of proposed legislation. The greater importance of the House of Lords' consideration of primary legislation has also been reflected in changes in the scheduling of Government business. A larger number of Government Bills now start in the Lords. This allows for a more even distribution of legislative work between the two chambers throughout the Parliamentary year.

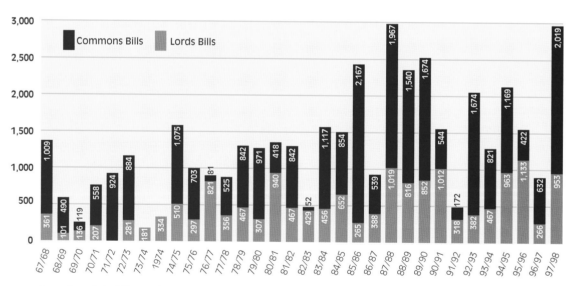

Amendments to Bills considered by the House of Lords by session

2.15 Finally, the House of Lords has conscientiously examined the grant of delegated powers and the subsequent exercise of powers to make secondary legislation. This work was given focus by the establishment of a Delegated Powers Scrutiny Committee in 1992.

2.16 Alongside these developments, there has been an improvement in the range and quality of facilities available to members of the House of Lords, although these are still well below the standards enjoyed by the House of Commons or other legislatures. The House also took the lead, in 1984, in allowing the broadcasting of its proceedings on television, five years before the Commons.

Key features

2.17 Several features of the present House of Lords, which have contributed to the relative success it has made of its new role, were highlighted with approval by respondents to our consultation exercise:

A debate in the House of Lords

- **procedural freedom** – The House of Lords is self-regulating, with proceedings regulated by consensus rather than being dictated by the Speaker or the Government. All members have equal rights and there are virtually no formal restrictions on the ability of members to raise issues of concern. The growing volume of business has led to the development of conventions and other 'guidance', which have restricted these freedoms to some extent, but have not altered the underlying spirit of the House;

- **expertise** – The breadth of expertise among members means that many speakers and members of Select Committees will have significant practical understanding of the subject under consideration. This allows the House as a whole to consider proposals with the benefit of knowledge and so make informed decisions;

- **time** – The absence of constituency duties and of the need to sustain a Government in office means that the House of Lords and its members can devote their time to the detailed consideration of legislation and other issues of public importance. This provides the opportunity for a significant level of scrutiny, often of technical areas which may be of limited public interest despite their practical importance;

- **independence** – Members of the House of Lords have considerable independence; they are relatively immune from any pressure from the Government or the political parties. Most members have a degree of personal standing which makes it unlikely that they will subordinate their personal judgement to the views of their party. Few have further political ambitions. They also have security of tenure. Also, the presence of the Cross Benchers, comprising at least 20 per cent of the membership of the House of Lords, is important in ensuring that independent judgement is brought to bear on the issues; and

- **non-partisan style** – The presence of the Cross Benchers also means that a partisan appeal will rarely strike a chord in the House of Lords. Reasoned and courteous argument is more likely to secure support, as well as being consistent with the self-regulating nature of the chamber. The contrast with the more combative style of the House of Commons is noticeable.

2.18 The House of Lords has developed considerably over the past four decades. Further significant changes are required if the second chamber is to play an effective role in the new century. The departure of a majority of the hereditary peers and the consequent need to determine a new basis of composition provide a rare opportunity to make these changes. For the moment, we simply note that over the past 40 years the House of Lords has developed, or maintained, characteristics which have won widespread approval and are well suited to the various roles and functions which a reformed second chamber could play. We return, in Chapter 10, to a consideration of what characteristics the reformed second chamber should possess after reviewing those roles and functions in more detail.

Chapter 3 – The overall role of the second chamber

3.1   Our terms of reference require us to proceed on the assumption that there will continue to be a second chamber of Parliament. We believe this to be right. We have therefore focused our efforts on considering what the second chamber should do and how it should be constituted.

3.2   We began by stepping back to consider what the overall role of the second chamber should be, given the present nature of the constitutional settlement. The answer to the question 'Why have a second chamber?' provides a firm rationale for the various *functions* which we believe the reformed second chamber should perform. It also implies a number of things about the *powers* it should have, the *characteristics* its members should possess and how it should be *constituted*.

The constitutional context

3.3   Two central features of the present constitutional settlement in the United Kingdom are simple, at least in theory, and well-known. One is the sovereignty of Parliament. The other is the absence of a written constitution.

3.4   Legislation in the United Kingdom can be passed only with the authority of the Crown in Parliament.[1] Moreover, although elements of the constitution have been progressively set out in legislation,[2] there remains no formal constitutional check on Parliament's sovereign authority. The Human Rights Act 1998, for example, is carefully drafted to preserve Parliamentary sovereignty: judicial declarations of incompatibility do not strike down primary legislation and the fast-track procedure for passing remedial orders requires the authority of Parliament. There is therefore no judicial remedy against Parliament's clearly expressed will. It follows that the will of Parliament must be the product of careful consideration and debate. Procedures need to be in place to ensure that when Parliament acts with a will it does not act wilfully.

3.5   Several other features of the present constitutional settlement are also relevant. The House of Commons, because it is directly elected by the whole people, is the ultimate repository of democratic authority in the United Kingdom. It alone can make and unmake Governments and call the Prime Minister and the Government fully to account. It authorises taxation and supply and can, if it wishes, achieve its legislative objectives in the face of opposition from the House of Lords. In other words, whatever the theory, Parliamentary sovereignty in the United Kingdom ultimately resides, in practice, in the House of Commons. As things stand, the House of Commons could, if it insisted and subject to a delay of only about 13 months, achieve almost any result it desired, including the further amendment of the Parliament Acts. Here, we believe, is another reason for the existence of a second chamber sufficiently confident and authoritative to require the House of Commons, at the very least, to think again.

---

[1] Directly applicable European Union law is consistent with this doctrine of Parliamentary sovereignty because it is made possible by virtue of the European Communities Act 1972 which could be repealed or amended.

[2] For example, by the Scotland Act, the Government of Wales Act and the Northern Ireland Act 1998, and arguably by the Human Rights Act 1998.

3.6   Moreover, within the House of Commons, the Government of the day is normally in a dominant position. It must of course retain the support of its Parliamentary followers and therefore has every incentive to be alert to their opinions. In practice, Governments are also constrained by the media, public opinion and the fear of defeat at the next general election. Nevertheless, Governments in the United Kingdom can usually get their way. Their Budgets are implemented. So is the great bulk of their legislative programme. In addition, the Government of the day exercises extensive executive powers by right of the Royal Prerogative, including the power to make appointments and enter into treaties. Given the Government's enormous power in our system, it seems to us important to have a second chamber able and willing to complement the House of Commons in its essential work of scrutinising the executive and holding the Government to account.

3.7   This need is reinforced by the fact that Governments in the United Kingdom are normally one-party Governments, backed by absolute majorities in the House of Commons. There is no need for Governments in the United Kingdom, as there is for governments in many other countries, to negotiate with coalition partners over their Budgets and legislative programmes. Moreover, although Governments in this country must be alert to the views of their backbench supporters, the fact remains that, thanks to the high level of party discipline that obtains, the Government's will usually prevails.

3.8   It was all these considerations that led The Rt Hon Lord Hailsham of Saint Marylebone a generation ago to describe the United Kingdom's system of government as amounting to an 'elective dictatorship'.[3]

3.9   The further point is sometimes made that there is something inherently unsatisfactory about the fact that strong Governments in the United Kingdom, usually with secure Parliamentary majorities, are in fact typically elected on the basis of only a minority of the popular vote. Not since 1935 has any single party in the United Kingdom won more than 50 per cent of the vote. Our own concern, however, is somewhat different. Our concern is with creating a second chamber sufficiently robust to act, alongside the House of Commons, as a check on the Government of the day, whatever its basis of electoral support. If Governments were typically elected on the basis of majority support, the need for such a constitutional check might well be greater, not less.

3.10   While we recognise the numerous informal constraints which restrict any Government's freedom of action (and which can frequently make life difficult for a Government), we are also concerned that the number of formal constraints on Governments is so limited under our constitution. In particular, we are concerned that the House of Commons often finds it difficult to balance its twin responsibilities of sustaining a Government in office and at the same time holding it effectively to account. Backbenchers on the Government side frequently speak out, and there are occasional Parliamentary revolts, some of them significant. But our view is that the country's new constitutional arrangements should provide for a second chamber which does not pose a threat to the House of Commons' pre-eminence but which is nevertheless able to augment and complement the Commons' work. It should enhance the ability of Parliament as a whole to scrutinise the executive and act as a check upon it.

---

[3] The Richard Dimbleby Lecture, broadcast 14 October 1976, published by the BBC.

The nature of the second chamber

3.11   In determining what the roles of the second chamber should be, we have taken a number of considerations into account. One has already been referred to and is implicit in our terms of reference: it should *not* be the role of the second chamber to substitute its own opinion for that of the House of Commons. The House of Commons should continue to be the pre-eminent chamber of Parliament and should remain the principal forum for the resolution of political differences. Nothing in what follows should be construed – or *could* reasonably be construed – as seeking to undermine the House of Commons as the final political authority under our constitution.

3.12   That said, the new second chamber, whatever precise form it takes, will inevitably be a political chamber. Some of our witnesses and a number of those who wrote to us seemed to imagine that the new second chamber should be, and could be, a sort of council of tribal elders: a body of wise men and women capable of determining, in a wholly detached manner and in the light of an entirely dispassionate examination of all the available evidence, what was in the nation's best interests. Such a vision is, in our view, pure fantasy. Politics exists because people disagree, often passionately. The new second chamber, like the old, will be and should be one of the principal forums in which these disagreements are expressed. Largely for that reason but also because the new second chamber, like any other legislative chamber, will require a degree of discipline and organisation, we take it for granted that the political parties will continue to have, as they have in the existing House of Lords, a central role to play.

Lord Wakeham

3.13   The new second chamber will be a political body, and practical politics requires political parties. Nevertheless, a central part of the rationale for having a second chamber in a political system like the United Kingdom's is that the second chamber should to some extent counterbalance the dominance of the governing party in the House of Commons. We believe, therefore, that the new second chamber should be composed in a way which both ensures that no one party is ever in a position to control it and also limits the influence of political parties upon its individual members.

3.14   By the same token, and for reasons spelled out below, we also believe that the new second chamber should differ from the House of Commons in not being composed primarily or largely of professional politicians. The general public would almost certainly resent the idea that the successor body to the existing House of Lords should provide a hunting ground for yet another 'tribe of professional politicians'. We also believe that, in a body which is meant to complement rather than compete with the House of Commons, a different set of attributes and qualities is required.

3.15   Given the dominant position of the House of Commons in the United Kingdom system, and given the normally dominant position of the Government within the House of Commons, we might have been tempted, in an earlier age, to recommend the creation of a more powerful second chamber than the one to be proposed here. We recognise, however, that the present Government's programme of constitutional reform is already bringing about, as one of its inevitable effects, a reduction in the centralised power of Westminster and Whitehall. The number of formal as well as informal constraints on the executive is already increasing substantially. It is therefore a good deal harder today than it was a generation ago to argue the case for radically altering the existing balance of power between the Commons and the second chamber. The concentration of power in our system of government is already considerably less than it was.

3.16   Membership of the European Union means that European legislation has the force of law in the United Kingdom. The creation of a new Scottish Parliament, a new National Assembly in Wales, a new Northern Ireland Assembly, and a new Mayor and Assembly for Greater London marks a significant transfer of power away from Westminster and Whitehall to sources of political authority closer to the people. The new Regional Chambers in England will soon be able to play a part in holding the new Regional Development Agencies to account and there may in time be elected assemblies in the English regions. In addition, the Human Rights Act 1998 will undoubtedly strengthen the position of the individual vis-à-vis the state. Strictly, none of these developments offends against the traditional principle of Parliamentary sovereignty. Each of them could, in theory, be abrogated by the Westminster Parliament but, in practice, this is unlikely. Each is now very firmly entrenched, politically if not legally.

3.17   Against this background, one of our principal aims in recommending the creation of a new second chamber has been to devise a chamber that goes with the grain of the other constitutional changes currently taking place.

The roles of the second chamber

3.18 As well as considering the roles which a new second chamber *should* play, we need to consider the roles which it *might* play. Four separate strands of thinking have long dominated discussions about the possible roles of second chambers. We consider each in turn.

Counsel from a range of sources

3.19 The view of the classical world, as expressed by Aristotle and reflected in the constitution of republican Rome, was that good governance required those in power to take 'counsel from a range of sources'. One potentially important role for a reformed second chamber might therefore be to provide a means whereby a range of different experiences and points of view – different, not least, from those of the House of Commons – could be brought to bear on proposed legislation and on public affairs more generally. The old House of Lords clearly played such a role, often successfully. We believe that the new second chamber should continue to play such a role. Its demonstrated ability to do so, and to do so effectively, would clearly add considerably to its overall authority.

Estates of the realm

3.20 The medieval view, not just in this country but throughout most of Europe, was that the principal 'estates of the realm' needed to be represented separately in any national assembly. Power in the state effectively resided in the estates; the structure of the national assemblies was organised to reflect that. The institution of Parliament in England and Wales and later in the whole United Kingdom originally embodied such a conception. The commoners were represented in the House of Commons; the lords, both temporal and spiritual, in the House of Lords. No commoner could sit in the House of Lords; no lord (except the bearer of a courtesy title) could sit in the House of Commons. The notion of strictly defined estates of the realm makes no sense in the context of today's far more heterogeneous, far more fluid society. Nevertheless, we believe that the new second chamber does have a role to play in being broadly representative of United Kingdom society as it is now – ideally, considerably more representative than are the members of the present House of Commons – and in reflecting the diverse experiences and traditions of that society.

Checks and balances

3.21 A third strand of historical thinking about second chambers has been concerned with what the authors of the United States Constitution, the Founding Fathers, thought of as 'checks and balances'. The Founding Fathers' view, as expressed in *The Federalist Papers*, was that a second chamber was desirable in a legislative assembly to "double the security of the people by requiring the concurrence of two distinct bodies". As the House of Representatives in the United States was to be popularly elected, a powerful Senate, chosen on a different basis, was essential to act as a brake on the tendency of popular assemblies, "stimulated by some irregular passion .., or misled by the artful representations of interested men, [to] call for measures which they themselves will afterwards be most ready to lament and condemn".[4] We would not want to go that far but, as we have already indicated, we believe there is a role for the reformed second chamber to play as a check on the Government, with its majority in the House of Commons (the 'popular assembly').

---

[4] *The Federalist.* Paper 62. Alexander Hamilton and James Madison.

3.22 The American notion of checks and balances, carried over into the United Kingdom system of government, could express itself in three areas: scrutinising the actions of the executive and holding it to account; participating in the legislative process; and playing a role in connection with proposed constitutional change.

3.23 For the reasons already given in paragraph 3.10 above, we believe the new second chamber should play an active role, complementary to that of the House of Commons, in scrutinising the executive and holding it to account. The House of Commons often finds it difficult *both* to sustain in power the Government of the day *and* to act as an effective check upon it. A revitalised second chamber could enhance the ability of Parliament as a whole to provide an effective check on the executive.

3.24 This conclusion is reinforced by the findings of a study of unicameral (single chamber) parliaments around the world, commissioned by the Scottish Office in preparation for the establishment of the Scottish Parliament.[5] The study found that the few successful unicameral parliaments that exist in the world, far from being dominated by an untrammelled executive, incorporate alternative checking and balancing devices. These include proportional representation, usually leading to minority or coalition governments; significant rights for minority parties; powerful backbench and other external scrutiny arrangements; and constitutional and/or judicial controls on the power of the executive. Given the present nature of the constitutional settlement in the United Kingdom and in the absence of the kinds of constraints to be found in countries with unicameral systems, it falls to the second chamber in this country to assist Parliament as a whole to play its checking and balancing role.

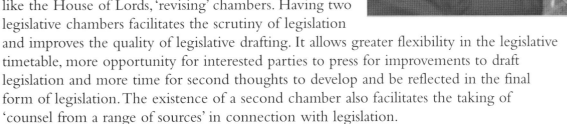

3.25 The House of Lords already plays an active part in the legislative process in the United Kingdom, and many second chambers overseas are referred to as being, like the House of Lords, 'revising' chambers. Having two legislative chambers facilitates the scrutiny of legislation and improves the quality of legislative drafting. It allows greater flexibility in the legislative timetable, more opportunity for interested parties to press for improvements to draft legislation and more time for second thoughts to develop and be reflected in the final form of legislation. The existence of a second chamber also facilitates the taking of 'counsel from a range of sources' in connection with legislation.

3.26 It is not enough, however, for the second chamber merely to add its own voice to the other voices raised in legislative debates. It must, in addition, have the formal power to require those who initiate legislation to justify their proposals to the public and to both Houses of Parliament – if need be for a second time. Using this power, the second chamber can raise issues which the House of Commons has neglected and can bring considerable political pressure to bear on both the House of Commons and the Government. We discuss the powers which should be available to the reformed second chamber in Chapters 4 and 7. But we take the general view that even limited powers to

---

[5] *Checks and Balances in Single Chamber Parliaments* (Stage 1) (February 1998) and *Single Chamber Parliaments: A Comparative Study* (Stage 2) (September 1998). Constitution Unit.

refer issues back for consideration or to impose a delay could, if exercised with restraint and only when occasion clearly demanded it, have a substantial political impact. If a reformed second chamber were to express concern about a particular Government proposal and exercise whatever powers of delay or referral were available, that would lead to (renewed) public and media interest in the issue, with opportunities for the causes of concern to be set out. It would force the Government to reconsider the issues in the light of that interest, and it would give members of the House of Commons an opportunity to revisit the issues and make the final determination in the light of all the relevant information. The Government of the day would have to take such powers and their consequences into account in drafting its legislation in the first place as well as in seeking to put it on the statute book.

3.27   As regards proposed constitutional changes, we merely note at this stage that many second chambers overseas have an explicit role to play in safeguarding their country's constitution. Many are accorded enhanced powers in connection with constitutional issues. However, because of the absence of a written constitution, the position in the United Kingdom is more complicated. On the one hand, a case can be made out that the new second chamber in this country should play a more clearly defined role with regard to constitutional matters and issues relating to human rights. On the other, there are a number of substantial difficulties in the idea of assigning the second chamber a significant formal role as 'guardian of the constitution'. We discuss these questions further in Chapter 5.

3.28   Our view is that the new second chamber should have the ability effectively to scrutinise the actions of the executive, including its legislative proposals; that it should have sufficient authority to ensure that it will be listened to when it draws attention to issues of concern; and that it should have sufficient power to require the Government of the day to consider its legitimate concerns. It should, in short, have the power to make the Government of the day think again, even against its will.

The representation of regions

3.29   The fourth strand in most thinking about the role of second chambers is the representation of regions, provinces, states and other territorial units. The United States Constitution, to take the obvious case, requires the United States Senate to provide equality of representation for each state, whatever its size. Not only in countries with federal systems but also in some countries with unitary systems, the second chamber is seen as a suitable vehicle for representing regions and other territorial units as distinct from simply representing population. As will emerge in Chapter 6, we do not under present circumstances believe that the representation of the nations and regions should constitute one of the primary roles of the new second chamber in this country. In other words, we do not see the new second chamber playing the role of the United States Senate, the Australian Senate or the German Bundesrat. However, the reformed second chamber could have an important role in giving this country's nations and regions a direct voice at Westminster which they currently lack.

Conclusion

3.30   As we have indicated, we believe that the reformed second chamber can and should play many of the roles traditionally played by second chambers – and can and should play some of them better than the existing House of Lords has done.

> **Recommendation 1:** The new second chamber should have the capacity to offer counsel from a range of sources. It should be broadly representative of society in the United Kingdom at the beginning of the 21st century. It should work with the House of Commons to provide an effective check upon the Government. It should give the United Kingdom's constituent nations and regions, for the first time, a formally constituted voice in the Westminster Parliament.

3.31   It is against this background that in the remainder of this report we consider what the precise powers and functions of the new second chamber should be and how it should be constituted.

Chapter 4 – Making the law

4.1   It is not surprising that the House of Lords, as one chamber of a bicameral legislature, spends roughly half its time considering primary legislation. Such legislation is the main vehicle for introducing significant changes of policy in all areas except foreign affairs. It therefore follows that the scrutiny and revision of primary legislation is also a central part of holding the executive to account, by requiring it to explain and justify its policy choices.

4.2   The relative power of the two Houses of Parliament in relation to primary legislation is of fundamental political and constitutional significance. In this chapter we consider how the reformed second chamber could help to improve the quality of primary legislation but we start by reviewing the powers which we believe the second chamber should have in this key area.

Powers

4.3   Until 1911, the United Kingdom Parliament was fully bicameral, except in respect of the Commons' financial privilege. Following the House of Lords' effective destruction of much of the Liberal Government's 1906–1908 legislative programme, capped by the rejection of Lloyd George's Budget in 1909, the Parliament Act 1911 restricted the House of Lords' powers in two ways. First, the House of Lords formally lost the power to delay certified Money Bills for more than a month, except with the consent of the Commons. Second, any other public Bill passed by the Commons in three successive sessions, with at least two years between Commons' Second Reading in the first session and Commons' Third Reading in the third session, could be presented for Royal Assent once it had been 'rejected' by the Lords in the third session. (The only exception was a Bill to extend the maximum duration of a Parliament beyond five years: in respect of any such Bill the House of Lords retained its original absolute veto.) The Parliament Act 1949 reduced the operative period of a Lords veto from three sessions to two and from at least two years (between Commons' Second Reading in the first session and Commons' Third Reading in the last) to at least one.

4.4   In the event, only five Bills have been enacted under Parliament Act procedures.[1] However, other Bills have been rejected by the House of Lords and not subsequently reintroduced.[2] Others have eventually been agreed to by the House of Lords after having been passed by the House of Commons for a second time.[3] Overall, it is probable that decisions – by both the Government and the House of Lords – about the handling of most contentious Bills over the past 88 years have been influenced by the existence of the Parliament Acts. The threat of using, or the ability to override, the House of Lords' power of veto has influenced attitudes towards individual amendments to Bills as well as their overall principle. The Parliament Acts have been an important part of the political calculus.

---

[1] The Government of Ireland Act 1914, which was suspended on the outbreak of war and repealed by the Government of Ireland Act 1920; the Welsh Church Act 1914, which was also suspended on the outbreak of war and given effect by the Welsh Church (Temporalities) Act 1919; the Parliament Act 1949; the War Crimes Act 1991; and the European Parliamentary Elections Act 1999.

[2] For example, the Representation of the People Bills 1917 and 1931.

[3] For example, the Trade Union and Labour Relations (Amendment) Act 1976 and the Aircraft and Shipbuilding Industries Act 1977.

4.5   The most important questions to be considered are: whether the formal relationship between the two chambers of Parliament (as reflected in the terms of the Parliament Acts) is right or whether it should be adjusted; and whether the device of leaving the second chamber with a 'suspensory veto' over most primary legislation is necessarily the best way to express that relationship. The answer to these questions is complicated by the fact that the formal balance of power between the two Houses is only part of the story. The present House of Lords has consciously observed a series of conventions, including, in particular, the so-called 'Salisbury Convention'. These have constrained the House of Lords' use of the formal powers which it retains; but a second chamber which had greater political legitimacy might feel free to exercise its powers more robustly in ways which would alter the *de facto* situation.

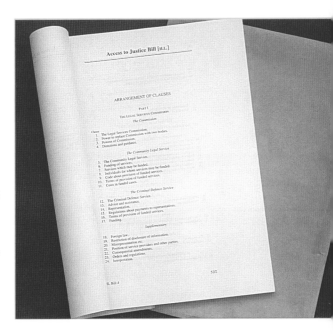

4.6   In practice, the issue is not the resolution of conflicts between the two Houses of Parliament but the relationship between both of them and the Government, which still initiates most legislation. It is that trilateral relationship which needs to work properly. For the reasons set out in Chapter 3, we believe it is important that the second chamber should continue to be in a position to challenge the Government's legislative proposals and force it to justify them to the House of Commons for at least a second time. It is against that background that we have considered the balance of formal power between the two Houses in respect of primary legislation.

4.7   Our conclusion is that the current balance is about right and should not be radically disturbed. It would be wrong to move in the direction of a basically unicameral system with the second chamber able to play only a 'revising' role in suggesting detailed amendments. Equally, although the original impetus behind the Parliament Act 1911 – the domination of the second chamber by one political party – is now a thing of the past, it would be wrong to restore the fully bicameral nature of the pre-1911 Parliament. It is right that the House of Commons should be the principal political forum and have the final say in respect of all major public policy issues, including those expressed in the form of proposed legislation. Equally, it is right that the second chamber should have sufficient power, and the associated authority, to require the Government and the House of Commons to reconsider proposed legislation and take account of any cogent objections to it.

Recommendation 2: The House of Commons, as the principal political forum, should have the final say in respect of all major public policy issues, including those expressed in the form of proposed legislation. Equally, the second chamber should have sufficient power, and the associated authority, to require the Government and the House of Commons to reconsider proposed legislation and take account of any cogent objections to it.

4.8   We received no significant proposals during our consultation exercise that this balance should be altered. On the contrary, there was general support for the *modus vivendi* which has been reached. It is, however, necessary to work through the issues quite carefully because the ending of the right of most hereditary peers to sit in the House of Lords will subtly alter the situation. Our own conclusions on the composition of the reformed second chamber will also need to be consistent with achieving the right balance of power and authority in the trilateral relationship.

The 'suspensory veto'

4.9   One question is whether the 'suspensory veto' arrangement which emerged from the constitutional crisis of 1909–11 (as amended in 1949) is the best way of achieving the right balance between the two Houses. Several other approaches were suggested during the debates which led up to the Parliament Act 1911.[4] Joint sittings of the two Houses, or of the House of Commons and 100 peers, selected in proportion to the balance of opinion within the House of Lords, were proposed. Other suggestions included requiring a 'super majority' (of 50, 100 or two-thirds) in the Commons to overturn a Lords veto; distinguishing between different categories of legislation (see Chapter 5); or putting the issue to a referendum. None of these proved a match for the simplicity of the suspensory veto. The Bryce Conference, which reported in 1918, explored the concept of a Free Conference of 20 of the most experienced members of each House, plus up to ten further members of each House with an interest in or knowledge of the subject. This Committee would work in secret 'by friendly methods' to reach an agreed report which would be put to both Houses. If the Lords did not agree to the report in two consecutive sessions, it could be passed by the Commons alone – otherwise the Bill would fall. Like the rest of the Bryce Report, the proposal was never implemented. The party leaders' conference of 1948 and the inter-party talks of 1968 both limited themselves to considering the duration of the suspensory veto.

4.10   Other countries with bicameral legislatures use a range of methods for dealing with disagreements[5] including:

- arrangements whereby the lower chamber can achieve its wishes regardless of the views of the second chamber. Usually some **delay** or disruption is incurred as an incentive to compromise (Poland, Belgium, Austria, Ireland);

- provision for the lower chamber to override any decision of the second chamber with a **'super majority'** vote (Japan and Spain);

- the initiation of a **'shuttle'** between the two chambers until agreement is reached, although this does not in itself provide a means for resolving any deadlock. A joint committee may be convened after three shuttles (France) or shuttles may continue indefinitely until the Bill is withdrawn or the chambers finally agree (Italy);

- provision for the second chamber to request, or the Parliament to initiate, a **referendum** on an issue where there is disagreement between the two chambers (Spain, Italy, Ireland);[6]

---

[4] J. Jaconelli. *The Parliament Bill 1910–1911: The Mechanics of Constitutional Protection.* In: *Parliamentary History, Vol 10.* 1991.

[5] M. Russell. *Resolving disputes between the chambers.* Constitution Unit, the original text of which can be found on the CD-ROM enclosed with this report.

[6] In practice such powers are resorted to very infrequently. The Irish Seanad has the right to petition the President for a referendum on a Bill 'of national importance' passed against their will, but has never exercised that power.

- an option for **both chambers to be dissolved**, even when the second chamber is normally elected by fractions, allowing the issue to be presented to the electorate and possibly leading to a change in the political balance of either or both chambers (Australia);

- calling a **joint session** of the two chambers, with the outcome determined by a simple majority vote (India, Australia); and

- referring the issue to a **joint committee**, meeting off the floor of the two chambers and perhaps allowing a less confrontational atmosphere to develop (France, Germany, Japan, Russia, South Africa and the United States).

The success of this last method appears to vary. Key factors may include:

- whether the lower chamber can insist on its view after the committee has reported;

- whether the members of the committee are permanent, and whether they are senior members of the respective chambers;

- whether the political balance on the committee is the same as in the two chambers; and

- whether the committee's proposals can subsequently be amended.

4.11   The idea of establishing a joint committee to help promote agreement between the two chambers has some attractions, although it might not in itself provide a means of resolving a fundamental disagreement. We consider it further below. The options considered in the past or used elsewhere for resolving disputes between the two chambers of Parliament do not seem to us to offer any significant advantages over the suspensory veto. Referring the point of disagreement to a joint session of both chambers would be inconsistent with acknowledging the pre-eminence of the House of Commons and could generate a range of practical problems. Dissolution of either or both Houses, as happened in Australia six times in the 20th century, seems unduly drastic and would only be appropriate if the second chamber were wholly elected. It would be difficult to reconcile the introduction of decisive referendums on issues of such significance with the doctrine of Parliamentary sovereignty, quite apart from the difficulty of encapsulating the issues in a simple referendum question and the risk of voter fatigue or lack of interest.

> **Conclusion:** Other ways of resolving disputes between the two chambers of Parliament which have been considered in the past, or which are used in other countries, do not seem to offer any significant advantages over the suspensory veto.

4.12   We therefore conclude that the second chamber should continue to have a suspensory veto of the present length in respect of most primary legislation. This has the advantage of being a familiar and established part of the United Kingdom's constitution. There was no significant support for any other approach during our consultation exercise. It strikes a generally acceptable balance between the pre-eminence of the House of Commons (and the ability of the Government to get its business through) and the ability of the second chamber to exercise a restraining influence. While its formal effect may be limited, it allows for the issues to be properly aired. It also ensures that pressure from public and media opinion, and from within the House of Commons, can be brought to bear to make the Government reconsider and adequately justify its position. We are reinforced in this conclusion by the fact that the Parliament Act 1911 emerged from a major constitutional crisis. Any proposal to reopen the extremely difficult and sensitive issues involved could well give rise to considerable debate without, in our judgement, any compensating benefit.

> **Recommendation 3:** The second chamber should continue to have a suspensory veto of the present length in respect of most primary legislation.

4.13   That said, we do propose one limited amendment to the Parliament Acts, which we discuss in Chapter 5. We also note that the Parliament Acts contain a number of technical weaknesses; there are other proposals to clarify their effect; and it has been suggested that the Parliament Acts be extended to cover Lords Bills as well as Commons Bills. We deal with each of these matters here.

Technical weaknesses of the Parliament Acts

4.14   The Clerk of the House of Commons, Mr W R McKay CB, has drawn our attention to some of the technical weaknesses in the Acts. There is, for example, no satisfactory definition of what changes to a Bill's text are "necessary owing to the time which has elapsed since the date of the former Bill". The Acts also contain the conundrum that a Bill can be presented for Royal Assent if the House of Lords has not agreed to it by the end of the second session but that it is not possible to get Royal Assent once the session has ended. However, these difficulties have had little practical effect and ways have been found of getting round them. There would be no point in seeking to tackle them unless wider substantive changes were proposed.

4.15   It has been argued that it should be possible to amend a Bill being reconsidered by the Commons in a second session without losing the protection of the Parliament Acts and/or that, if the Commons have to pass it in an identical form to the previous Bill, a shortened procedure would be appropriate. In fact the Parliament Act 1911 does provide a mechanism by which the House of Commons may 'suggest' amendments to a Bill which is being reconsidered in a second session. On the procedural issue, we are not convinced that any change to the present rules is needed to enable the House of Commons to adopt an accelerated timetable if it wished to do so. However, if desirable changes are identified they might best be achieved by changes to the procedures of the two chambers.

> **Conclusion:** The technical weaknesses of the Parliament Acts have not given rise to any real difficulty in practice and there would be no point in seeking to tackle them unless wider substantive changes were proposed.

Timing consequences

4.16 Of more significant concern is the lack of clarity regarding the timing consequences of using Parliament Act procedures. At least one year must elapse between the Commons' Second Reading of the relevant Bill in the first session and the Commons' Third Reading in the second session; it must be sent up to the Lords at least a month before the end of each session; and it may be presented for Royal Assent if the Lords 'reject' it in the second session or if they do not approve it by the end of that session.

4.17 A Bill subject to Parliament Act procedure could therefore be presented for Royal Assent 13 months and a day after its Second Reading in the first session, but the delay could be much longer. The only way for the Government to guarantee the minimum delay is to bring the second session to an early end, as was done in 1948 to facilitate the passage of the Parliament Act 1949; but this could severely disrupt the rest of its legislative programme. From one point of view all this may be unsatisfactory and it might be preferable to adopt a more straightforward calendar-based system. However, we see the awkwardnesses in the arrangement as part of the current delicate balance. A calendar-based system would alter the trilateral balance of power in favour of the Government and reduce the incentive for it to seek a satisfactory resolution of the issues raised by the second chamber. In addition, any attempt to resolve the timing point would also require the whole of the Parliament Acts to be opened up for debate and amendment. As we have already said, we do not believe this would be wise. Overall, we conclude that no attempt should be made to impose what would amount to a time limit on the second chamber's consideration of 'Parliament Act' Bills in the second session.

> **Recommendation 4:** No attempt should be made to impose a time limit on the second chamber's consideration of 'Parliament Act' Bills in the second session.

Extension to Lords Bills

4.18 A more substantial case can be made that the scope of the Parliament Acts should be extended to cover Bills introduced into the second chamber, as well as those introduced into the Commons. As things stand, a Government Bill starting in the House of Lords which is the subject of a disagreement between the two Houses cannot be presented for Royal Assent under Parliament Act procedures, even if the House of Commons were to approve it for a second time in the second session. We agree that, in principle, in the event of such a disagreement, the views of the House of Commons should prevail, after a suitable period for reflection and reconsideration. It might also make it easier for the business managers scheduling Government business to allow a more even distribution of work between the two chambers and a more balanced workload for each chamber throughout the year. However, other considerations point a different way:

- the extension of the Parliament Acts to cover Bills introduced into the second chamber could often be side-stepped. If the members of the second chamber knew that the House of Commons was likely to make unacceptable amendments to a second chamber Bill, and suspected that the Government would then seek to push the Bill through under the Parliament Acts, they could refrain from giving it a Third Reading, ensuring that it would never reach the House of Commons;

- the extension is unnecessary as its purpose can already be achieved by another route. If a Government Bill, introduced in the second chamber, runs into such serious trouble there that the Government contemplates using the Parliament Acts to get it enacted, they can at present introduce a virtually identical Bill in the House of Commons and send it up to the House of Lords, if they do so at least a month before the end of the first session. This enables the Government to secure the Bill's enactment under the terms of the Parliament Acts in the second session;

- the present arrangements tend not to cause problems in practice. Ministers, especially Commons Ministers, tend to prefer to take major Bills in the House of Commons first and they see a tactical advantage in securing Commons endorsement for any controversial Bills before sending them to the House of Lords;

- the extension could create a situation in which the Government could force legislation through without proper scrutiny by the second chamber. A second chamber Bill sent down to the Commons could be radically amended there to produce results which conflicted with the intentions of the second chamber. The amendments would have to be considered by the second chamber but, even if it rejected them, under this proposal the amended Bill could be enacted in the next session without the second chamber's agreement. In effect, the second chamber would have had only one opportunity to look at the amendments. This is in strong contrast with the usual stages of a Bill and would clearly be inadequate;

- it would subtly alter the balance between the two Houses of Parliament, extending the pre-eminence of the House of Commons; and

- it would remove a marginal restraint on the proportion of controversial Government Bills per session.

4.19   On balance, we therefore recommend against extending the scope of the Parliament Acts to cover Bills which are introduced into the second chamber. The basic problem is that the 1911 Act is couched exclusively in terms which deal with the problem which its proponents then faced – a second chamber which had vetoed or amended a whole series of Commons Bills. If the Parliament Acts were ever to be radically overhauled it might well be appropriate to construct them in a way which secured equivalent protection for all Bills introduced by Government Ministers, whichever chamber they started in; but unless and until that point is reached, the present position in respect of second chamber Bills should be left unaltered.

> **Recommendation 5:** The scope of the Parliament Acts should not be extended to cover Bills which are introduced into the second chamber, unless the Acts are to be subjected to a radical overhaul.

Conventions

4.20   All the above conclusions in relation to the Parliament Acts are subject to two important provisos. First, that the reformed second chamber should maintain the House of Lords convention that all Government business is considered within a reasonable time. Traditionally, the convention applies to all business, but it is particularly important that there should be no question of Government business being deliberately overlooked.

> **Recommendation 6:** The reformed second chamber should maintain the House of Lords' convention that all Government business is considered within a reasonable time.

4.21   Second, we agree with those who argue that the principles underlying the Salisbury Convention[7] remain valid and should be maintained. The convention amounts to an understanding that a 'manifesto' Bill, foreshadowed in the governing party's most recent election manifesto and passed by the House of Commons, should not be opposed by the second chamber on Second or Third Reading. This convention has sometimes been extended to cover 'wrecking amendments' which "destroy or alter beyond recognition"[8] such a Bill. It has played a key part in preventing conflict between the two Houses of Parliament during periods of Labour Government. Some have argued that its main effect has been to provide a rationale for Conservative peers to acquiesce in legislation which they found repugnant; and that once the situation had been reached in which no one party could command a working majority in the second chamber there would be no need to maintain the Salisbury Convention. In our view, however, there is a deeper philosophical underpinning for the Salisbury Convention which remains valid. This arises from the status of the House of Commons as the United Kingdom's pre-eminent political forum and from the fact that general elections are the most significant expression of the political will of the electorate. A version of the 'mandate' doctrine should continue to be observed: where the electorate has chosen a party to form a Government, the elements of that party's general election manifesto should be respected by the second chamber. More generally, the second chamber should think very carefully before challenging the clearly expressed views of the House of Commons on any issue of public policy.

4.22   There is an important and delicate balance to strike here. Our proposals envisage a reformed second chamber with the authority and self-confidence to take a stand on any issue where it believes that the Government and the House of Commons should be required to think again. But the value of the reformed second chamber will be undermined if it exercises its powers indiscriminately or too frequently.

4.23   As to how the convention should be expressed, there are substantial theoretical and practical obstacles to putting any formal weight on manifesto commitments. Only a tiny minority of the electorate ever reads party manifestos; and as it is most unlikely that any voter will agree with every sentence of any manifesto, it is rarely possible to interpret a general election result as evidence of clear public support for any specific policy. In any event, manifestos are political documents, not legal texts, and proposed legislation

---

[7] Enunciated by the then Viscount Cranborne in 1945, but which built on an earlier version of the doctrine of the 'mandate' developed by his grandfather the Third Marquess of Salisbury in the late 19th century. See House of Lords, *The Salisbury Doctrine*. Library Notes. LLN 97/004. 1997.

[8] Lord Carrington, *Reflect on things past: the memoirs of Lord Carrington* (1988), page 77.

designed to implement political commitments will usually be far more detailed than, and therefore different from, what was in the manifesto. Thinking on any given issue inevitably develops or changes over time and legislation introduced in the third or fourth session of a Parliament may differ significantly from the relevant manifesto commitment. To deny such legislation constitutional protection, while providing additional safeguards for other proposed legislation simply because it happened to be truer to the original commitment, would be unreasonable. Also, issues that require legislation may arise during the course of a Parliament and could not therefore have been mentioned in the parties' manifestos.

4.24   There is no straightforward answer to these various difficulties. An updated version of the Salisbury Convention should express the new balance of political authority between the two Houses of Parliament and the Government; but it is unlikely to be possible to reduce it to a simple formula. The reformed second chamber will need to work out this new convention pragmatically. The House of Lords has been rather good at reaching generally satisfactory understandings about how business should be carried forward and we have every confidence that the reformed second chamber will be able to do the same.

> **Recommendation 7**: The principles underlying the 'Salisbury Convention' remain valid and should be maintained. A version of the 'mandate' doctrine should continue to be observed: where the electorate has chosen a party to form a Government, the elements of that party's general election manifesto should be respected by the second chamber. More generally, the second chamber should be cautious about challenging the clearly expressed views of the House of Commons on any public policy issue. It is not possible to reduce this to a simple formula, particularly one based on manifesto commitments. The second chamber should pragmatically work out a new convention reflecting these principles.

4.25   Our recommendations regarding the powers of the reformed second chamber in respect of secondary legislation are set out in Chapter 7.

Conciliation mechanism

4.26   If the above recommendations are accepted, it should be rare for the second chamber to mount a sustained challenge to proposed legislation which has the consistent support of the House of Commons. Equally, use of the House of Commons' power to override the settled opposition of the second chamber to a piece of proposed legislation should continue to be a major step which no Government would take lightly. The emphasis should be on resolving disagreements and, in practice, the House of Commons and the House of Lords have found ways of achieving this through a variety of informal procedures. We do not underestimate the capacity of such procedures to continue to achieve the mutually satisfactory resolution of any points of disagreement, but several of the written submissions suggested that they could usefully be supplemented by a more formal conciliation mechanism. Such a mechanism would be available to replace the current 'ping-pong' procedure. It could be brought into play at the request of either House once one had disagreed with amendments proposed by the other.

4.27 Were such a mechanism thought desirable it should, in our view, take the form of a Joint Committee. Joint Committees are already employed in the consideration of Statutory Instruments and Consolidation Bills and have been used to consider draft Bills. In each case, the Committee normally has an equal number of members from each chamber and reports to both chambers. Their work is notable for the constructive and non-partisan manner in which it is conducted. While the subjects currently covered are generally not of a party-political nature, whereas a disagreement between the two chambers over a public Bill probably would be, a Joint Committee procedure should offer a means for seeking a compromise acceptable to both chambers. This approach was recommended by the Bryce Conference in 1918.

4.28 Evidence from overseas suggests that such a Joint Committee would be most effective if the majority of its members were to be senior figures, appointed at the start of each session. Representatives from each chamber would reflect the party balance in that chamber, including any independents. In addition, it might be helpful to include a small number of individuals from each chamber with particular knowledge of the issues raised by the Bill in question, as recommended by Bryce. Since the aim would be to identify a workable compromise, rather than a final decision, the Committee's proposals should be open to further amendment and subject to approval by both chambers. However, the pressure on both chambers to accept what a Committee of leading figures had agreed would be considerable. It would also provide a convenient opportunity for either side to step back from an overt confrontation without having to admit defeat.

4.29 The practical details would require further consideration by both chambers, but the option of referring a contested Bill to a Joint Committee might provide both chambers with a useful breathing space. This need not be longer than a matter of days. It would also offer both Houses an opportunity for constructive and relatively private consideration of possible ways round any sources of disagreement.

> **Recommendation 8:** The two chambers should consider whether the current informal conciliation procedures could usefully be supplemented by the establishment of a Joint Committee designed to facilitate agreement between the two chambers over Bills.

Improving primary legislation

4.30 The rest of this chapter deals with the contribution which the reformed second chamber could make to the improvement of primary legislation. The volume and complexity of Bills have increased steadily throughout the century, yet Parliamentary procedures have not changed significantly, at least until recently. Most Bills still have to complete all their stages within the confines of a single session of Parliament.

4.31 Pressure on Parliamentary time has the effect of rationing the amount of new legislation that can be made. However, it also means in practice that Ministers and Departments tend to take the drafting of legislation seriously only when they have secured a slot in the legislative programme. By then it can often be too late to complete the policy development work, consultation, consideration of the operational implications and drafting to an acceptable standard; but the consequences of delay (losing the whole Bill) are so great that the Bill has to proceed anyway. Much legislation in recent years has also been driven by political imperatives which require legislation to reach the statute book within a particular timescale, whether or not there is sufficient time for adequate preparation; and by Ministers' natural desire to make their mark before being moved on to a different job.

4.32   Some of these problems have been tackled. Building on earlier initiatives, the first report of the House of Commons' Modernisation Committee:[9]

- encouraged greater use of draft Bills as a vehicle for pre-legislative scrutiny; and

- discussed the introduction of a 'carry over' procedure, so that a Bill which had not completed all its stages in one session could be reintroduced in the next session without having to start all over again.

4.33   Various options for scrutinising draft Bills have been experimented with. Two draft Bills – the draft Financial Services and Markets Bill and the draft Local Government (Organisation and Standards) Bill – have been considered by Joint Committees drawn from both Houses of Parliament. Evidence from the Clerk of Committees in the House of Lords suggests that these Committees were successful. The draft Freedom of Information Bill was considered by Lords and Commons Committees in parallel, which seems to have been a less effective way of deploying the complementary expertise of the two chambers. The House of Lords has traditionally been able to assemble committees of members with acknowledged expertise in relevant areas who have been well placed to take evidence from interested parties and conduct detailed scrutiny of legislative proposals. The less partisan atmosphere of the House of Lords has probably also facilitated such scrutiny. We intend that the reformed second chamber should also have these characteristics. It should therefore continue to be able to make a positive contribution to the consideration of draft Bills. More generally we warmly support the growing practice of pre-legislative scrutiny and would like to see it become an established feature of Parliamentary business. Apart from being more likely to produce better legislation, it should also reduce the chance of differences of view between the two chambers at a late stage in Parliamentary proceedings.

4.34   There is already a facility for the Lords to establish a Special Public Bill Committee which can take written and oral evidence on a Bill for up to 28 days before considering it clause by clause in the usual way. This option was introduced in the early 1990s following its successful use in the Commons. However, while praised by some witnesses (for example, the Law Society of Scotland), such committees have been appointed infrequently because there is a risk that their use would slow down the legislative process. Pre-legislative scrutiny may turn out to achieve the same results without the perceived disadvantages.

Recommendation 9: Pre-legislative scrutiny of draft Bills should become an established feature of Parliamentary business.

---

[9] Modernisation Committee First Report. *The Legislative Process*. Session 1997/98. July 1997. HC190.

The contribution of the second chamber

4.35 The present House of Lords is often referred to as a 'revising' chamber. It has been widely praised for its role in securing amendments to proposed legislation.

4.36 There are several reasons why the House of Lords appears to have been relatively successful at securing amendments to Bills.

4.37 **Bicameral system.** In a bicameral legislature there are two sets of opportunities for Government, the Opposition, interested parties and lobby groups to secure changes to a Bill once it has been introduced. The process which needs to be gone through if a Minister decides, or is persuaded, to seek to amend a Bill after introduction takes time. It usually requires a round of policy consideration, policy clearance, operational assessment and the preparation of possible amendments. These processes often cannot be finalised within the time it takes for a Bill to complete all its stages in one House. The net result is that, in whichever chamber a Bill starts, Ministers are frequently left in a position of saying the Government will 'reflect' on a point which has been raised and 'may/will return to it in the other place'. The point may then be dealt with by a Government amendment when the Bill reaches the other chamber. It is in any event essential that all the loose ends in any Bill are tidied up before it leaves the other chamber (whether that be the Lords or the Commons). By the time a Bill is approaching the end of its Parliamentary consideration the major policy questions have usually been settled but a plethora of technical or drafting points often remain to be sorted out. For these reasons, the chamber which considers a Bill second often makes the greater number of amendments. As most major Bills start in the Commons, the Lords are frequently credited with amendments which have their origins in or are consequential on points made in the Commons.

4.38 **House of Lords' timetable.** By convention, the House of Lords allows certain minimum intervals between stages of Bills. This, and the fact that amendments can be made right up to Third Reading, means that the process of taking a Bill through the Lords is more leisurely than taking it through the Commons. There is often adequate time for a Minister to respond to a point raised during an early stage in the Lords' consideration of a Bill by tabling a Government amendment before the Bill leaves the Lords. Commons Standing Committees often spend several weeks considering a Bill but subsequent stages are usually taken quite quickly. Points which arise early on in Standing Committee can therefore often be resolved in time for Report Stage, but it may be more difficult to achieve that in respect of points which arise towards the end of Committee Stage. Such points may therefore need to be attended to in the Lords.

4.39 **House of Lords' style.** Taking a Bill through the Lords is very different from taking it through the Commons. Debate in the Commons is often more confrontational and party political. The Minister in charge of the Bill is usually closely identified with the policy and challenges are perceived to be politically motivated. In most debates, especially in Committee, Ministers are seen as defending their policy proposals against Opposition criticism. In the Lords the consideration of Bills is at once less partisan and more unpredictable. Debate tends to focus on the merits of particular points, without a partisan edge, and Ministers cannot rely on uncritical support from their own party. The style of the debate – less party political and more courteous – makes it easier for Ministers to agree to reconsider points without appearing to 'lose'.

4.40   The composition and characteristics of the Lords. The blend of experience and expertise found among members of the House of Lords means that on any given issue there are usually a number of peers with relevant practical experience and knowledge or with long experience of grappling with the same policy issues. Such members usually have extensive contacts with the relevant interest groups. They can present their case forcefully and well. In the absence of strong party discipline and with a reasonable proportion of Cross Benchers, Ministers need to win the argument to be sure of winning the vote. In any event, the issues certainly get a thorough airing. A further factor is that the members of the House of Lords are equipped and prepared to take on the relatively unglamorous task of scrutinising the detailed wording of Bills and raising relatively minor, non-political and technical points.

4.41   House of Lords' procedure. The fact that members of the House of Lords are relatively free from procedural constraints also contributes to the House of Lords' effectiveness as a revising chamber. All stages of most Bills are taken on the floor of the House (or in a Grand Committee which any peer can attend). Any member can insist on an amendment being considered at virtually any stage and as there is no selection of amendments, all amendments can be debated. Groupings are more focused than in the Commons and members may in any event insist on their amendments being voted on individually. Above all, the Lords are more willing to devote time to discussion of detail and do not have any guillotine to cut off debate.

4.42   Lobbying. All the above factors make the Lords a more attractive and receptive target for lobbying than the House of Commons. A campaigning organisation or interested party can usually find a peer who supports their point of view or one with at least some knowledge and experience of the issue concerned who is ready to table and speak to amendments and press the Government to justify or change its position.

4.43   These points illustrate how a bicameral legislature with distinct characteristics can play a useful role in improving proposed legislation. We intend that these characteristics should be preserved in the reformed second chamber so that Parliament can continue to derive these benefits. We recognise, however, that these advantages could, in principle, be secured in other ways, even within a unicameral system. The primary constitutional importance of the second chamber's role in making law – as we argued in Chapter 3 – is not that it should carry out a 'revising' function but that it should provide a potential check on the ability of the Government of the day to bring about controversial or ill-conceived political and legislative changes without proper consideration.

4.44   It is important to note here the valuable work of the Delegated Powers and Deregulation Committee of the present House of Lords.[10] This Committee, initially established in 1992, has in effect been given the task of policing the boundary between primary and secondary legislation. It seeks information from sponsoring Departments and produces a Memorandum on every Bill introduced in the House of Lords. These Memorandums analyse the delegated powers (i.e. to make secondary legislation) which are being sought and comment on the extent to which they are proportionate and justified. They pay particular attention to 'Henry VIII' Clauses which make provision for primary legislation to be amended by secondary legislation. They draw attention to cases where the delegated powers sought seem excessive or where the degree of Parliamentary

---

[10] Described more fully in the Committee's Special Report. Session 1998/99. Twenty-Ninth Report. October 1999. HL112.

supervision of the exercise of those delegated powers might be considered insufficient. As a consequence, Ministers may be asked for assurances about the exercise of particular powers, or the degree of Parliamentary oversight may be increased. For example, this can be done by making the exercise of a particular power subject to the positive approval of both Houses of Parliament, rather than subject to annulment if either of them disagrees with it. The Committee has become influential. Its members have always commanded respect for their blend of legal expertise, administrative experience and pragmatism: its recommendations are usually accepted. Its legal adviser is frequently consulted informally by Departments when they are drawing up proposed legislation. The Committee's function is far from being eye-catching, but it plays a very important quasi-constitutional role in relation to primary legislation, which ensures the maintenance of an appropriate balance between the authority of Parliament and the powers of the executive in this area.

4.45   Our only comment on the existing role of the Committee is that its work tends to consist of resisting or restricting the grant of delegated powers. It may be that the Committee's role could evolve to include making recommendations that some provisions of Bills would be dealt with more appropriately in secondary legislation. It could also seek to build in greater flexibility for the future, for example by recommending that in exercising particular delegated powers Ministers might be given a choice between affirmative and negative procedure (as, for example, in Section 2 of the European Communities Act 1972). Alternatively, delegated powers might be granted on the understanding that when first exercised the Statutory Instrument concerned would be subject to affirmative resolution, with the option to make later instruments subject to negative procedure. (An approach on these lines was adopted when the student loans scheme was introduced.) Use of such options would give the Committee a broader role in helping to secure the benefit of less cluttered primary legislation and striking an appropriate balance between primary and secondary legislation.

> **Recommendation 10:** The Delegated Powers and Deregulation Committee's role could evolve to include making recommendations which would encourage greater flexibility in the use of delegated powers, making it easier to strike an appropriate balance between primary and secondary legislation.

Possible changes to legislative procedures

4.46   We received very few proposals for substantial changes to the way in which primary legislation is currently handled. Many of those which we did receive would have lost some of the technical benefits described above or undermined the second chamber's ability to play the important constitutional function we have outlined. We therefore have only a few minor observations to make in this area (in addition to the support we have already given to greater use of pre-legislative scrutiny).

4.47   The use of Grand Committees off the floor of the House to consider certain Bills has been widely regarded as a success. Any member of the House has been able to table amendments and participate in the debates. The level of scrutiny has therefore been as high as for Bills taken in a Committee of the whole House, but with a considerable saving of time on the floor of the House. Although no votes can be taken, the mood of the Grand Committee is usually clear and the issue can ultimately be determined at Report Stage. The Grand Committee's approach could provide a model for conventional Committee Stages. Votes at Committee Stage are relatively rare in any case and a practice of deferring votes until Report Stage might leave members freer to concentrate on the substantive issues.

> **Recommendation 11:** The reformed second chamber should consider whether the practice of deferring votes until Report Stage, which has been a feature of the use of Grand Committees off the floor of the House to consider certain Bills, should be extended to conventional Committee Stages.

4.48   We have received suggestions that the reformed second chamber should play a greater role in reviewing the quality of the statute book and keeping the law up to date. This is undoubtedly an important and desirable objective but we have some reservations about recommending that it should be a primary function of the second chamber. Much technical work in this area is already carried out by the Law Commissions and any more substantial review of the state of the law in particular areas would be bound to trespass into a consideration of policy issues. In our view, the initiative for such reviews should lie with the Government or with the Departmental Select Committees in the House of Commons. However, if any specific aspects of the law on a particular issue were identified – either in debate or by one of the Commons Select Committees – as meriting detailed consideration, it might well be appropriate for the second chamber to establish an *ad hoc* Committee for that purpose.

> **Recommendation 12:** Reviewing the quality of the statute book and keeping the law up to date should not be a primary function of the second chamber. However, if any specific aspects of the law on a particular issue were identified as meriting detailed consideration, it might well be appropriate for the second chamber to establish an *ad hoc* Committee for that purpose.

4.49   The House of Lords already plays a leading role in respect of Consolidation Bills, which are designed to tidy up and improve the statute book without creating any new law. Relevant Bills[11] are introduced into the House of Lords and referred after Second Reading to a Joint Committee, by convention chaired by one of the Lords of Appeal in Ordinary. Once the Committee reports, subsequent stages in both Houses are usually treated as a formality. We recommend that these arrangements should continue.

> **Recommendation 13:** The current arrangements for dealing with Consolidation Bills should continue.

4.50   The Chairman of the Law Commission for England and Wales, Mr Justice Carnwath, in his evidence to us, pointed out that there was a backlog of law reform proposals awaiting consideration. He and others have urged that a fast-track procedure, perhaps involving the second chamber in particular, should be developed to help reduce this backlog, especially for those Law Commission Bills dealing with 'non-controversial' matters. We agree in principle that this is something to which the reformed second chamber should give careful consideration. However, we have some reservations about

---

[11] Bills prepared pursuant to the Consolidation of Enactments (Procedure) Act 1949; Bills to consolidate enactments with amendments to give effect to Law Commission recommendations; Consolidation Bills, whether public or private; statute law revision Bills; and Bills prepared by one of the Law Commissions to repeal enactments which are no longer of any practical utility.

the suggestion that Law Commission Bills should automatically benefit from the adoption of a fast-track procedure. One person's tidying up of the law can be another's assault on fundamental values, and it is not always easy to tell which Law Commission proposals are controversial or how controversial they will turn out to be.

4.51   In its Report on the Government's proposals for amending the Deregulation and Contracting Out Act, the Delegated Powers and Deregulation Committee suggested that law reform proposals from the Law Commissions might be taken forward in a procedure analogous to that used for Deregulation Orders. This suggestion was taken up by the Government in its response.[12] The case for this is pragmatic. It would provide a means of tackling the backlog of law reform Bills through a process which has been shown to deliver real opportunities for proper consultation. However, it would result in law being made by Statutory Instrument in areas where primary legislation would often be more appropriate. A more formal process of pre-legislative consultation on the draft Bills enclosed with Law Commission law reform proposals might achieve the same objectives without running the same risk. Consideration might then be given to developing an accelerated procedure where those draft Bills were shown to be non-controversial.

Recommendation 14: The reformed second chamber should consider what steps might be taken to expedite the Parliamentary consideration of law reform Bills proposed by the Law Commissions.

4.52   Another category of legislation on which the second chamber might be invited to play a greater role is private legislation. As the House of Commons has waived its financial privilege which formerly limited the categories of private Bill on which the House of Lords could lead, those Private Bills which are received are divided evenly between the two Houses. Since the passage of the Transport and Works Act 1992 there have been fewer private Bills. It may be that the characteristics of the reformed second chamber will make it appropriate for a larger proportion of such Bills to be considered first by the second chamber. Those private Bills which apply to individuals – 'personal Bills' – are invariably considered first by the House of Lords.

Conclusion: The characteristics of the reformed second chamber may make it appropriate for a larger proportion of private Bills to be considered first by the second chamber.

4.53   Finally, several witnesses suggested to us that the second chamber should have some responsibility for post-legislative scrutiny – checking that legislation fulfils its intended purpose. We acknowledge the importance of such scrutiny but doubt whether there is a distinctive role for the second chamber. The Government or the Departmental Select Committees in the House of Commons may be better placed to take the lead.

Conclusion: There is no distinctive role for the second chamber in post-legislative scrutiny.

---

[12] Select Committee on Delegated Powers and Deregulation. Proposed extension of the Deregulation and Contracting Out Act 1994, Session 1998/99. Fourteenth Report. April 1999. HL55; and Proposed Amendments to the Deregulation and Contracting Out Act 1994 – Government response and Further Report. Session 1998/99, Twenty-Eighth Report. October 1999. HL111.

Chapter 5 – Protecting the constitution

5.1   The British constitution – "the collection of rules which establish and regulate or govern the government"[1] – has shown itself over centuries to be extraordinarily dynamic and flexible, with the capacity to evolve in the light of changes in circumstances and in society. There are many who would argue that it is this very flexibility which has allowed the United Kingdom to avoid the kind of upheavals which have forced other countries to return to the constitutional drawing board.

5.2   It is both a strength and a potential weakness of the British constitution that, almost uniquely for an advanced democracy, it is not all set down in writing. There can be little question that the raft of constitutional legislation introduced by the current Government in its first two years in office – including the Devolution Acts, the incorporation of the European Convention on Human Rights into British law and the registration of political parties – would have been impossible under the laborious systems required to amend the written constitutions of many other countries. The risk, however, is that a Government with a secure majority in the House of Commons, even if based on the votes of a minority of the electorate, could in principle bring about controversial and ill-considered changes to the constitution without the need to secure consensus support for them. It could force them through the second chamber by use of Parliament Act procedures if necessary. Similar concerns could arise in respect of legislation that might represent a breach of human or civil rights. As Professor Sir William Wade succinctly put it, "One safeguard conspicuous by its absence from the constitution is the entrenchment of fundamental rights".

5.3   While our terms of reference require us to take "particular account of the present nature of the constitutional settlement", we recognise that the open nature of our unwritten constitution relies on those in positions of authority operating within a web of understandings and conventions as to what is and is not permissible. As Gladstone wrote over a century ago, the British constitution "presumes, more boldly than any other, the good faith of those who work it".

5.4   Given those circumstances, one of the most important functions of the reformed second chamber should be to act as a 'constitutional long-stop', ensuring that changes are not made to the constitution without full and open debate and an awareness of the consequences. This is one of the classic functions of a second chamber and one the House of Lords has on occasion played in the past.

> **Recommendation 15:** One of the most important functions of the reformed second chamber should be to act as a 'constitutional long-stop', ensuring that changes are not made to the constitution without full and open debate and an awareness of the consequences.

[1] Sir Kenneth Wheare.

Powers in respect of constitutional matters

5.5   The House of Lords currently has an absolute veto over the dismissal of a number of key office holders, including senior judges, the Comptroller and Auditor General and the Data Protection Registrar. This helps to secure their independence from the executive. Similarly, the Parliament Act 1911 deliberately excluded from its scope any Bill to extend the life of a Parliament beyond five years. This preserves the House of Lords' absolute veto over any attempt by a Government with control over the House of Commons to legislate itself into extended existence. Finally, the House possesses a suspensory veto over all Bills (other than Money Bills). It therefore has the capacity to delay controversial legislation and force the Government to think again or justify its position once more to the House of Commons. On each of the five occasions since 1911 when Acts have been passed under Parliament Act procedures, they have dealt with what were arguably 'constitutional' matters.

The House of Lords voting on the Parliament Bill, 1911

5.6   A number of those who submitted evidence to us argued that the second chamber should be given significant additional powers over constitutional and human rights legislation. It was suggested either that the reformed second chamber should have an absolute veto in respect of such matters or that the extent of the suspensory veto should be extended to at least two years in such cases. We do not support any such proposals, both for practical reasons and also on principle.

Balance between the two chambers

5.7   Our fundamental concern about any such proposal is that it would alter the current balance of power between the two chambers and could be exploited to bring the two chambers into conflict. It would be inconsistent with the requirement in our terms of reference "to maintain the position of the House of Commons as the pre-eminent chamber of Parliament" and with our view of the overall role that the second chamber should play.

> **Conclusion:** Increasing the powers of the second chamber in respect of any particular category of legislation would be inconsistent with maintaining the position of the House of Commons as the pre-eminent chamber of Parliament.

Constitutional legislation

5.8   So far as 'constitutional' matters are concerned, it would in any event be virtually impossible in practice to define which legislation should be within the scope of such additional powers. With no written constitution there is no way of distinguishing between 'constitutional' enactments and others. As a matter of legislative form, the Parliament Act 1911 had exactly the same standing as the Poultry Act and the Telephone Transfer Act, which received Royal Assent on the same day. Any attempt to draw up a list of 'designated' legislation, which might include the three Devolution Acts, the Human Rights Act 1998 and the European Communities Act 1972, rapidly runs into problems. A short list would clearly be incomplete, while a fuller list would rapidly become unwieldy. Problems would arise over the fact that many quite inoffensive Bills would give rise to a need for consequential amendments to be made to Acts which would appear on many lists of 'constitutional' legislation – for example, the Representation of the People Acts or the Devolution Acts. It would be inappropriate for such minor amendments to attract the protection of any additional powers which the second chamber might have in respect of constitutional matters. In addition, such a list would rely for its effect on an assumption that changes to the constitution would require the amendment or repeal of existing constitutional legislation. Such a belief would be unfounded: the Human Rights Act 1998 involved no amendment to existing constitutional legislation, while the Scotland Act 1998 included only a minor amendment (which could probably have been avoided) to the European Communities Act 1972. Since major constitutional changes can be made without the need to amend existing constitutional legislation, the value of relying on a list of designated legislation would be very limited indeed.

The Rt Hon Lord Strathclyde, Leader of the Opposition in the House of Lords (on the right)

> **Recommendation 16:** The second chamber should not be given additional powers in respect of a list of designated constitutional legislation.

Constitutional issues

5.9   An alternative would be for any additional powers to apply in respect of a list of constitutional *issues*, rather than specific items of legislation. This would also be far from easy to achieve. Asquith demonstrated the difficulties involved when he showed that there was no coherent theme discernible in the 23 'constitutional' issues identified by various MPs during the debates on the 1911 Parliament Bill. Moreover, there would always be scope for argument as to whether a particular Bill raised a 'constitutional' matter or not. The various debates on the question of whether any particular Bill was of 'first class constitutional importance', and should therefore be referred to a Committee of the Whole House, have failed to produce any convincing definition or criteria which could be applied on a consistent basis. Drawing a line would be even more difficult if the definition were extended to include human rights.

5.10   Even a relatively short list of subject areas would be almost impossible to apply in practice without effective machinery to adjudicate in disputes over whether a particular piece of legislation was or was not covered. In other countries this function is performed by a special constitutional court, whose decisions are binding. These courts have a relatively defined task because they are working within the context of a written constitution. While the Devolution Acts have assigned a related role to the Judicial Committee of the Privy Council,[2] the absence of a written constitution for the United Kingdom as a whole and the difficulty of adequately defining what constitutes a 'constitutional' matter mean that the courts would be in no position to adjudicate satisfactorily. Giving the courts any role in assessing whether a provision was 'constitutional' or not would in any event sit uncomfortably with the doctrine of Parliamentary sovereignty. Above all, it would be bound to result in delay or uncertainty and incur some risk of retrospective judgements which could give rise to all kinds of complications, especially if major constitutional changes were involved. Such a system might also be exploited by those opposed to particular Bills, who would all too easily be able to mount a case that a constitutional issue of some kind was involved.

5.11   An alternative might be to develop a system by which the Speaker, or some other figure, could 'certify' constitutional Bills. This would be a development of the procedure under which the Speaker – guided by specific criteria set out in the Parliament Act 1911 – currently certifies Money Bills. In practice, this approach too would be difficult to operate without a clear statement of what makes up a 'constitutional' matter. It would impose an unduly onerous burden on the individual concerned.

> **Recommendation 17:** The second chamber should not be given additional powers in respect of constitutional *issues*. There is no satisfactory basis on which this could be done and no suitable machinery for adjudicating on whether a particular Bill raised constitutional issues.

5.12   In short, none of the various proposals by which the second chamber could be given additional powers over constitutional legislation is free of difficulty. Most of the practical objections set out above would apply equally to any attempt to give the second chamber additional powers in respect of human rights legislation in general. They would *not*, however, apply to the narrower proposal, put forward in some submissions, that the Human Rights Act itself should be specifically exempted from the scope of the Parliament Acts. This would give the second chamber an absolute veto over any attempt to amend that Act. However, this would run up against our deeper objection of principle to any suggestion that the reformed second chamber should have greater powers than at present in respect of defined pieces or categories of legislation.

> **Recommendation 18:** The second chamber should not be given additional powers over constitutional or human rights issues or legislation.

---

[2] This, coupled with the fact that much of the Scottish constitution is now set out in a single piece of legislation, allowed the Scotland Act 1998 to include a list of reserved matters pertaining to the constitution – Schedule 5, paras 1–5.

Changes to the Parliament Acts

5.13   The current balance between the two chambers has evolved over many decades and should not be changed lightly.[3] There is, however, one point which concerned us and which was drawn to our attention by a number of witnesses. It is a potential weakness of the Parliament Acts that they can themselves be amended using Parliament Act procedures, as was done in 1949. We recommend that this loophole should be closed, in order to protect the current balance of power between the two Houses of Parliament from being changed except with the agreement of both chambers.

5.14   The present position gives the second chamber power effectively to delay the enactment of any Commons Bill (except a Money Bill) by a few months, while requiring the House of Commons to reconsider it and to reaffirm its support for the legislation. It makes it possible for any Bill consistently supported by the Commons (except a Bill to extend the life of a Parliament) to be enacted within 13 months of Second Reading in the Commons, even in the face of objections from the House of Lords.

5.15   That seems to us to strike the right balance. Any change to the detriment of the second chamber would risk leaving it with insufficient powers to carry out its overall role effectively. We therefore recommend that the Parliament Acts should be amended to exclude the possibility of their being further amended by the use of Parliament Act procedures. This would, in effect, give the second chamber a veto over any attempt to constrain its existing formal powers in respect of primary legislation. On the basis of expert advice, we believe that this could be achieved by a simple and straightforward amendment, for example by inserting the words "to amend this Act or" after "provision" in Section 2(1) of the 1911 Act.[4] This would avoid opening up the whole of the Parliament Acts to debate and amendment.

Recommendation 19: The Parliament Acts should be amended to exclude the possibility of their being further amended by the use of Parliament Act procedures.

5.16   This recommendation would also secure the second chamber's veto over any Bill to extend the life of a Parliament, since that provision is written into the Parliament Act 1911. Our consultation exercise revealed overwhelming support, from all the main political parties and from the public, for the preservation of the House of Lords' existing veto over any such Bill.

Recommendation 20: The second chamber's veto over any Bill to extend the life of a Parliament should be reinforced. Our previous recommendation would achieve that.

---

[3] See the discussion in Chapter 4.

[4] S.2(1) would therefore apply to any public Bill "other than a Money Bill or a Bill containing any provision to amend this Act or to extend the maximum duration of Parliament beyond five years". The provisions which apply to Money Bills are set out in S.1 of the Parliament Act 1911.

A Constitutional Committee

5.17 If the second chamber is not to have additional *powers* in respect of constitutional or human rights matters, how should it discharge its role as a 'constitutional long-stop'? We propose that the second chamber should establish an authoritative Constitutional Committee to act as a focus for its interest in and concern for constitutional matters. In making this proposal, we are building on recommendations made from across the political spectrum, including the Labour Party and the Rt Hon John Major MP as well as the influential Delegated Powers and Deregulation Committee of the present House of Lords.

5.18 The Labour Party's evidence recommended that the second chamber should establish "a sessional committee devoted to constitutional affairs which would: scrutinise all Bills to consider their constitutional implications and in particular their implications for designated legislation; [and] keep under review the operation of the 'constitution', including the recent reform initiatives, as well as any which may be enacted in the future".[5]

5.19 Mr Major suggested in his speech on the Second Reading of the House of Lords Bill[6] that the second chamber should establish a 'Constitutional Committee'. He expanded on this suggestion in a meeting with our Chairman and in further written evidence to the Commission, arguing that it would be "highly desirable to have in place a respected Committee of distinguished people who understand how the British constitution works and who are under a duty to produce independent, dispassionate and authoritative reports on problem areas within the constitution and on proposals for changing it. … The general aim would be to limit the scope for ill considered constitutional change whilst also ensuring that simmering discontents are identified and dealt with in a flexible and evolutionary way. A Lords Committee would have the characteristics necessary to play an effective role in this area."

5.20 The Delegated Powers and Deregulation Committee in its evidence noted that, apart from its own specific activities, "there is no other forum in the House of Lords where issues of constitutional principle are discussed on a regular basis". It suggested that there were many occasions on which "the House of Lords could have been considerably assisted by advice from a Constitutional Committee whose members were well versed in such issues and – an important point – used to examining legislation from this view point on a regular basis".

Function of a Constitutional Committee

5.21 An authoritative Constitutional Committee could be expected to enhance the ability of Parliament as a whole to take full account of all the constitutional implications when considering proposed legislation and scrutinising the actions of the executive. Since its terms of reference would not be set out in legislation, there would be no need for a precise definition of 'the constitution'. Certain key items of legislation, however, might be designated as being of particular relevance. A Committee of the second chamber could be expected to have members with a keen awareness of the web of understandings and conventions that underpins the effective workings of the constitution. It would be sensitive to the constitutional implications of proposed legislation. It would also be

---

[5] Labour Party submission, paragraphs 4.9 and 4.10.
[6] Hansard (HC). 2 February 1999 (House of Lords Bill. Second Reading Debate).

in a strong position to identify and draw Parliament's attention to developments or legislative proposals with significant constitutional implications. These might otherwise be missed or raised at a late stage when lack of time might hinder proper consideration.

5.22   The details would be for the second chamber itself to resolve, but we envisage that the proposed Constitutional Committee would adopt a similar approach to that of the Delegated Powers and Deregulation Committee. It would consider all public Bills – other than those concerned with Supply or Consolidation – upon their arrival in the second chamber and prepare a comprehensive report on any constitutional implications. More generally, it should keep the operation of the constitution under review. Reports from the Constitutional Committee would draw the attention of Parliament, and also the media and the public, to points of concern. These points could then be taken fully into account as legislation was considered by Parliament, rather than emerging only later. In our judgement, the establishment of a Constitutional Committee would be both a more appropriate and a more effective way of protecting the constitution than giving additional formal powers to the reformed second chamber.

> **Recommendation 21**: The second chamber should establish an authoritative Constitutional Committee to act as a focus for its interest in and concern for constitutional matters.

Human rights

5.23   There is a fine line between constitutional matters and human rights issues, but the latter arise in a broader range of circumstances and therefore merit separate consideration. The picture is affected by the passage and imminent coming into effect of the Human Rights Act 1998, which our terms of reference require us to take into account when formulating our conclusions and recommendations.

5.24   There is a tradition of members of the House of Lords taking the lead in the promotion of human rights legislation and in drawing attention to the human rights implications of other proposed legislation.[7] Bills to achieve incorporation of the European Convention on Human Rights (ECHR) into United Kingdom law were introduced into the House of Lords on ten separate occasions prior to the Human Rights Act 1998. Six of these received a Third Reading and were passed to the Commons, where they fell for lack of time. Members of the House of Lords have also been responsible for attempting to initiate numerous other pieces of legislation to promote human rights, such as the Civil Liberties (Disability) Bill 1995. Most frequently the House of Lords has made amendments to Government legislation to protect fundamental freedoms, such as on telephone tapping in the Telecommunication Act 1984 and the authorisation of surveillance in the Police Bill 1997. Much of this activity has focused on the rule of law and due process rather than on human rights more generally, reflecting the significant legal expertise available to the House of Lords.

---

[7] A. Reidy. *Reforming the House of Lords: Its Role in a Human Rights Culture*. Constitution Unit, the original text of which can be found on the CD-ROM enclosed with this report.

5.25 The Parliamentary scrutiny of human rights issues is likely to be transformed by the passage of the Human Rights Act 1998. Parliament will wish to be confident that the legislation it passes is unlikely to give rise to a breach of the ECHR or at least that any such breach is deliberate and considered. Parliament's consideration of these questions will be assisted by the requirement under Section 19 of the Human Rights Act for Ministers sponsoring Bills to make a statement of compatibility with the ECHR.

European Court of Human Rights, Strasbourg

5.26 Parliament will also need to decide what to do about any declaration of incompatibility which may be made by the courts. A fast-track procedure for remedial Orders to put right any deficiencies in primary legislation is set out in Section 10 of the Act and arrangements will need to be made to scrutinise these in draft.

5.27 More widely, the developing 'human rights' culture which was reflected in the passage of the Human Rights Act may make it appropriate for Parliament to monitor the operation of the Human Rights Act, take an interest in the observation of the United Kingdom's other international human rights obligations and consider human rights issues more generally.

Joint Committee on Human Rights

5.28 The Government has already announced its intention to ask both Houses of Parliament to establish a Joint Committee on Human Rights. In making the announcement, the Rt Hon Margaret Beckett MP, President of the Council and Leader of the House of Commons, said:

> "We envisage that the Joint Committee's terms of reference will include the conduct of inquiries into general human rights issues in the United Kingdom, the scrutiny of remedial orders, the examination of draft legislation where there is a doubt about compatibility with the ECHR, and the issue of whether there is a need for a human rights commission to monitor the operation of the Human Rights Act."[8]

5.29 The proposed Joint Committee will play a valuable role in enhancing Parliament's ability to take full account of human rights issues in shaping legislation. Equally obviously, the second chamber will need to provide members for the Joint Committee. It would be natural for those members to provide a focus for the second chamber's own consideration of human rights issues where this goes beyond the remit of the proposed Joint Committee.

[8] Hansard (HC). 14 December 1998 (Human Rights Committee).

The second chamber's interest in human rights

5.30   There are a number of respects in which the second chamber's interest in human rights issues might indeed go beyond the terms of reference of the proposed Joint Committee. It has been suggested, for example, that the terms of reference of the Joint Committee will enable it to review the compatibility of Bills with the ECHR only where Ministers have been *unable* to make the necessary statement of compatibility under Section 19. In our view there should be a mechanism, at least in the second chamber, for looking behind Ministerial statements of compatibility and checking that all provisions of a Bill really *are* compatible with the ECHR. The experience of the Joint Committee on the draft Financial Services and Markets Bill[9] illustrates how human rights issues can emerge unexpectedly from the detailed consideration of proposed legislation on other matters. It is also possible that potential incompatibilities with the ECHR will arise in *secondary* as much as in primary legislation. Statutory Instruments may therefore need to be scrutinised from that perspective. This could be a very considerable task.

> **Recommendation 22:** There should be a mechanism, at least in the second chamber, for looking behind Ministerial statements of compatibility under Section 19 of the Human Rights Act 1998 and checking that all provisions of a Bill really are compatible with the ECHR.

5.31   This kind of technical scrutiny of Bills, draft Bills and Statutory Instruments for their human rights implications would fit very well with the role we envisage for the second chamber and with the kind of expertise and characteristics which its members should have. Irrespective of decisions about the precise role and terms of reference for the proposed Joint Committee, we therefore propose that a Committee of the second chamber should be given a wide ranging role in relation to human rights. That would give it scope to carry out technical scrutiny; to contribute effectively to the consideration of draft remedial Orders under Section 10 of the Human Rights Act; and to act as a general focus for the consideration of human rights issues by the second chamber.

> **Recommendation 23:** The second chamber should establish a Committee with a wide-ranging remit in relation to human rights.

5.32   The contribution which such a Committee could make to the effectiveness of Parliamentary scrutiny of the human rights implications of proposed legislation is of crucial importance. Once the Human Rights Act has been brought into effect, it is inevitable that the courts will be invited to play a larger part in determining the legality of public policy as expressed in both primary and secondary legislation. This should *not* relieve Parliament of its primary responsibility for human rights. The human rights aspects of legislation should be identified and resolved *before* the law is made. Parliament should be proactive in ensuring that law meets relevant human rights standards, rather than reacting only when the courts strike down a Statutory Instrument or declare a piece of primary legislation incompatible with the ECHR. An authoritative second chamber Committee of members with appropriate knowledge and expertise would be well placed

---

[9] Joint Committee on Financial Services and Markets. First Report. Draft Financial Services and Markets Bill. Session 1998/99. Volumes I and II. April 1999. HC328 I and II.

to draw attention to any human rights implications of proposed legislation. This would enable Parliament as a whole to reach a fully informed judgement before the die is cast.

A Human Rights Sub-committee

5.33   We considered whether this role could be carried out by the Constitutional Committee proposed above. We concluded, however, that while that Committee would probably be concerned with broad trends in human rights development, it might not provide a suitable vehicle for the continuing oversight of human rights issues – partly because of workload. On the other hand, there could be considerable overlap with the work of the Constitutional Committee in terms of the expertise of potential members, staff resources and the issues which might arise. Although this is a matter for the second chamber itself to decide, our suggestion is that the Constitutional Committee should establish a Human Rights Sub-committee, with an ability to co-opt other members,[10] to serve as the focus for the second chamber's interest in human rights. That Sub-committee might also provide the second chamber's members of the proposed Joint Committee on Human Rights.

Recommendation 24: The second chamber should consider whether the proposed Constitutional Committee should establish a Human Rights Sub-committee to serve as the focus for the second chamber's interest in human rights. That Sub-committee might also provide the second chamber's members of the proposed Joint Committee on Human Rights.

---

[10] Such a structure would mirror that of the House of Lords' European Union Committee.

Chapter 6 – Giving a voice to the nations and regions

6.1   Deciding what relationship the reformed second chamber should have with the devolved institutions has been one of the most interesting and important aspects of our work.

6.2   One widely canvassed possibility is that the devolved institutions should be directly represented in the reformed second chamber. This would provide a degree of indirect electoral authority for the second chamber. It might also enable the second chamber to become a unifying force within the United Kingdom at a time when devolution and pressures for greater decentralisation within England could create centrifugal tensions.

6.3   In its White Paper *Modernising Parliament: Reforming the House of Lords*, the Government posed the question "whether the second chamber should have some overt role as the representative of the regions, or of the regional bodies". It commented that, "Using the second chamber in this way would give it a role distinct from that of the House of Commons, where the local links will continue to be the much more immediate one of the MP and his or her constituents. The second chamber could provide a forum where diversity could find expression and dialogue, and where such an expression could work towards strengthening the Union".[1] Many respondents to our consultation paper agreed that regional representation as a feature of the reformed second chamber could act as a kind of 'constitutional glue'. The Rt Hon Lord Richard QC and Damien Welfare[2] echo the views set out in a number of submissions that "representation in the second chamber offers a route to a shared identity which is political but which does not directly affect the control of the government of the country… a reformed second chamber could be the missing piece of the constitutional jigsaw, serving as the pinnacle of the structure and a focus of unity".

6.4   Our terms of reference require us to take particular account of the present nature of the constitutional settlement, "including the newly devolved institutions". We felt it was right to interpret the point broadly and to take account of the imminent establishment of the Greater London Authority (and the new office of Mayor for London) and the emerging political identities of the English regions. We were also conscious that devolution is a very recent and novel development. We cannot be sure how it will work out in practice, what problems and tensions may arise and what the political consequences will be. It has been suggested that "devolution is a process, not an event".[3] It would certainly be rash to base decisions on an assumption that the nature or extent of devolved powers will not alter over time. Powers have so far only been devolved to Scotland, Wales and Northern Ireland and certain powers will be transferred to the Mayor for London and the Greater London Authority when they take up office in July 2000. There is, however, no clear view on how further decentralisation of power within England might be achieved. The emerging Regional Chambers could play a co-ordinating and advisory role and influence the Regional Development Agencies, but there is no consistent pressure for them to develop into elected Regional Assemblies. Such developments will

---

[1] Cm 4183, Chapter 7, paragraph 9.
[2] I. Richard and D. Welfare, *Unfinished Business – Reforming the House of Lords*. Vintage UK. 1999.
[3] The Rt Hon Ron Davies MP, MWA former Secretary of State for Wales.

probably occur, if at all, on an asymmetric basis and over a considerable period of time. Meanwhile, there are other pressures in favour of elected mayors for the major conurbations on the model of the Mayor for London. It is not clear how far any such developments would be compatible with any transfer of power to *regional* institutions.

6.5   The present situation is fluid and the future unclear. The reformed second chamber should therefore be so constructed that it could play a valuable role in relation to the nations and regions of the United Kingdom whatever pattern of devolution and decentralisation may emerge in future. An overseas lesson may be relevant here. The pace of devolution to the autonomous communities in Spain seems not to have been anticipated by those who designed the post-Franco constitution, with the result that the Spanish Senado is still struggling to find a means of expressing its 'regional' role.

> **Recommendation 25:** The reformed second chamber should be so constructed that it could play a valuable role in relation to the nations and regions of the United Kingdom whatever pattern of devolution and decentralisation may emerge in future.

Basis of representation

6.6   Many second chambers around the world (see Chapter 3), in unitary as well as in federal states, are constituted on a territorial principle, providing a voice for the distinct interests of different states or regions. This principle may provide a democratic basis for the second chamber which is less directly linked to population than that of the lower chamber, thus reducing any threat to the latter's political pre-eminence. In federations in particular, the second chamber is usually designed to represent the states, frequently on an equal or at least graduated basis, while the lower chamber is constituted on a population basis.

6.7   The United Kingdom, however, is not a federal state. The present arrangements have been described as "creating a form of asymmetric quasi-federalism".[4] The reality is that the contrasts between the different components of the United Kingdom are at present very significant. Scotland and Northern Ireland have extensive legislative devolution. The National Assembly for Wales is able to exercise discretion in respect of secondary legislation within the framework of primary legislation passed at Westminster. Legislation and policy for England are settled at Westminster and in Whitehall although the Government Offices for the Regions have begun to ensure that implementation reflects regional circumstances. The Mayor for London, the Greater London Authority and the various English regional structures may

---

[4] V. Bogdanor, *Devolution in the United Kingdom.* Oxford University Press. 1999.

exert an increasing influence. These differences may militate against certain forms of regional representation in the second chamber. The reformed second chamber, however, will be part of the national legislature. It is therefore self-evident that it should be, and be seen to be, a chamber which serves the interests of the whole of the United Kingdom.

> **Recommendation 26:** The reformed second chamber should be, and be seen to be, a chamber which serves the interests of the whole of the United Kingdom.

6.8   The second chamber must therefore contain people from all parts of the United Kingdom and at least a proportion of the members should provide a direct voice for the various nations and regions of the United Kingdom. Regional members[5] would:

The Scottish Parliament, Edinburgh

- underline the fact that, in broad terms, the second chamber should be representative of the whole of the United Kingdom;

- contribute to cohesion;

- help resolve concerns about the protection of Scottish interests in the second chamber arising from the removal of the Scottish hereditary peers;[6]

- provide a resource which might assist the second chamber to play a role in relation to the devolution settlement;

- build on the emerging political identity of the nations and regions of the United Kingdom; and

- leave options open for the future if the United Kingdom were to move to a more explicitly federal structure.

> **Recommendation 27:** At least a proportion of the members of the second chamber should provide a direct voice for the various nations and regions of the United Kingdom.

---

[5] Throughout this report, 'regional members' should be taken to refer to members from the nations and regions.
[6] Raised in particular by Lord Gray during the debates on the House of Lords Bill 1999.

Role and function

6.9 Before looking at *how* such regional members might best be secured, it is necessary to reflect on what *role* or *function* the second chamber might play in respect of the nations and regions of the United Kingdom.

Federal parliament

6.10 Several submissions argued that the House of Commons should become an 'English Parliament' and the reformed second chamber a kind of 'federal legislature', supporting a 'federal' government. Such a structure would represent a version of 'devolution all round' and potentially resolve the West Lothian question.[7] However, it would immediately run up against a whole range of fundamental difficulties, quite apart from being a radical departure from the present nature of the constitutional settlement and arguably outside our terms of reference. Among the fundamental difficulties we envisage are:

■ it would be even more difficult to disentangle 'reserved' from 'transferred' matters in respect of England than it was in respect of Scotland and Wales;

■ in practice, the House of Commons would be more appropriate than the second chamber to become the 'federal' chamber. The whole of the United Kingdom is already represented there directly, and the Government and MPs might prefer to retain the 'reserved' powers in their present location;

■ wherever the 'federal' chamber was located, it would still be necessary to have a second chamber; and

■ the 'English Parliament' and English members of the federal chamber would be so dominant as to make the system effectively unworkable.

All in all, such proposals raise more problems than they solve. There may well be a separate case for Parliament as a whole to reflect on how business which can be identified as exclusively 'English' should be handled in the future, but that is not a matter for this Commission.

> **Recommendation 28:** The second chamber should not become a 'federal legislature', supporting a 'federal' government.

Inter-governmental forum

6.11 An alternative potential function for the second chamber would be to provide a focus for *inter-governmental* contact and co-operation. This is the model suggested by the Bundesrat in Germany. The Bundesrat brings together delegations from the administrations in the German Länder. It ensures that their interests are brought to bear on the development of federal policy and legislation, particularly those aspects which the Länder will be responsible for implementing.

---

[7] The West Lothian question was posed in the 1970s by Tam Dalyell, MP for West Lothian. He asked why, after devolution to Scotland, it should be possible for Scottish MPs to vote on domestic matters, such as health and education, in England, when English MPs would no longer be able to vote on these matters in Scotland.

6.12   However, the whole structure of the German federal system is completely different from the political system in the United Kingdom. In the United Kingdom, as in Australia and Canada, executive liaison is more appropriately and effectively carried on outside Parliamentary institutions. Command Paper 4444[8] contains a Memorandum of Understanding and a series of concordats setting out the structure of Ministerial and official committees which will facilitate contact and co-operation between Whitehall Ministers, Scottish Ministers and the Cabinet of the National Assembly for Wales and describing the spirit in which they intend to work together. The Northern Ireland Executive Committee will be invited to enter into a similar set of understandings. Such contact and co-operation could not be facilitated further by giving Ministers from Scotland, Wales or Northern Ireland seats in the second chamber, especially as the territorial Secretaries of State, if they remain, would probably still be based in the House of Commons.

Recommendation 29: The reformed second chamber should not become a forum for inter-governmental liaison. Liaison between the Government and the executive authorities in Scotland, Wales and Northern Ireland is most appropriately and effectively carried on outside Parliamentary institutions.

Seats for the devolved institutions

6.13   There are other significant objections to giving seats in the second chamber to members of the devolved administrations, or to members of the Scottish Parliament and other devolved assemblies. These apply with even greater force to the idea that they might nominate representatives from outside their own ranks.

6.14   **Dual mandates.** People cannot be required to do two jobs at once. It was made abundantly clear to us while in Edinburgh and Cardiff that membership of the Scottish Parliament or National Assembly for Wales – still more membership of the Scottish and Welsh administrations – was a full-time job. It would leave no time for regular participation in the work of the second chamber (quite apart from the fact that having recently escaped from Westminster's 'apron strings' they have no desire to risk appearing to return). The same is no doubt true in Northern Ireland. We would not rule out some members of devolved legislatures having a place in the second chamber on a personal basis, as now; but it would be wrong to impose it as a requirement.

6.15   **The accountability gap.** It would be inappropriate to invite members of the Scottish Parliament (or the other devolved assemblies) to sit in a second chamber whose responsibilities cover everything *except* matters devolved to the Scottish Parliament (and the other devolved assemblies). It is not easy to see how, having been elected to do a job in the Scottish Parliament for example, they could reasonably be held accountable for their contribution in the second chamber. The line of accountability would be even more uncertain in the case of any representatives nominated by members of the devolved institutions.[9]

6.16   **An extreme form of the 'West Lothian question'.** English voters and MPs would be likely to react badly to a situation in which English MPs (and members of the second chamber) were unable to influence Scottish devolved matters while Scottish MPs could vote on equivalent English matters in the House of Commons *and* selected MSPs could vote on them in the second chamber. Such a position would be untenable.

---

[8] Published on 4 October 1999.
[9] See Richard and Welfare, *Unfinished Business*, pages 142–154.

6.17 Delegation rather than representation. Elected office holders are accountable to their electorate. MPs and local councillors traditionally operate on the basis that they are elected to represent their constituents' interests according to their own judgement. Where the electorate consists of a small group of politicians, there is a significant risk that the members of the second chamber selected in this way would be regarded as the delegates of the bodies that elected them, voting according to instructions rather than conscience. This would cut across the nature of Parliamentary representation as understood in this country.

6.18 The English regional issue. At least for the moment, inter-parliamentary representation could come only from Scotland, Wales and Northern Ireland. The English regions may or may not acquire elected Regional Assemblies in due course. It is not clear what status and powers these might have. Some alternative non-'inter-parliamentary' means of representing the English regions would need to be found.

6.19 While it would clearly be desirable to promote the development of links between the various legislatures across the United Kingdom, dual membership of the various devolved assemblies and the second chamber is not the right way to achieve it. It is for the members of the various Parliaments and Assemblies to decide what links they should establish, perhaps building on the experience of the British-Irish Inter-Parliamentary Body.

> **Recommendation 30:** While it would clearly be desirable to promote the development of links between the various legislatures across the United Kingdom, none of the members of the various devolved assemblies should be automatically entitled to sit in, or nominate others to join, the second chamber.

Speaking for the nations and regions

6.20 The role of the reformed second chamber in relation to the nations and regions of the United Kingdom should not be to provide a vehicle by which the devolved institutions themselves could be represented in Parliament. Rather, its primary role in this context should be to provide a voice in Parliament for all the nations and regions of the United Kingdom. All parts of the United Kingdom are already represented in the House of Commons, but the unit of representation there is the Parliamentary constituency. Although there are regional groupings of MPs, there is no member of either House of Parliament who can claim a mandate to speak in that House for the whole of any nation or region. In the circumstances of devolution and bearing in mind the possibility that the English regions may develop stronger institutions and political identities, it would be desirable to create a new category of people within Parliament who could speak for each of those units as a whole. The question of how such people might be selected is discussed in Chapters 11 and 12.

> **Recommendation 31:** The role of the reformed second chamber in relation to the nations and regions of the United Kingdom should not be to provide a vehicle by which the devolved institutions themselves could be represented in Parliament. Its primary role in this context should be to provide a voice in Parliament for all the nations and regions of the United Kingdom.

6.21   While such members' primary role should be to serve as a voice for the nations and regions of the United Kingdom in the national Parliament, they might bring other benefits. They should, for example, be well placed to make contacts and encourage dialogue across different levels of government. They would be speaking for units which have the same boundaries as European Parliament constituencies, the existing devolved institutions and the new structures being established in the English regions. They would share a regional perspective with MEPs, the members of the devolved institutions, those involved in the Regional Chambers and Regional Development Agencies and with the existing groupings of local authorities. That mutual interest might be exploited to encourage and facilitate greater contact across the different levels of government and a more effective regional voice, for example in Europe. It should also enable the people concerned to bring a valuable regional perspective to the deliberations of the second chamber, one which took full account of the inter-connections between those deliberations and the work of European, regional and local government institutions.

National Assembly for Wales, Cardiff

They would also be well placed to contribute to the consideration of any legislation which related specifically to their own regions. Currently, this last consideration is most likely to be relevant to Wales. There could well be circumstances in which the National Assembly for Wales would like to promote Westminster legislation on matters outside its competence. It might be helpful to have people in the second chamber who could speak in support of such a Bill.

A 'Devolution' Committee

6.22   This kind of regional perspective would enable the reformed second chamber to play a broader role in Parliament's consideration of the various issues raised by devolution. We do not, however, envisage the reformed second chamber playing a 'monitoring' role or acting as a 'second chamber for the devolved institutions'. Fears regarding such proposals were expressed to us in Edinburgh and Cardiff. We do not see any case for such a role.

6.23   Nevertheless, there are a number of important questions raised by devolution which have yet to be resolved. Others may well emerge. The wider implications of any trend to greater decentralisation within England could also be very significant. Some of these issues might be classified as 'constitutional' matters, of the sort we have recommended should be kept under review by a Constitutional Committee. (It is most probable, for example, that any list of designated legislation that might be incorporated in the terms of reference of any Constitutional Committee would include the three Devolution Acts.)

There may also be an important interface between the operation of the devolved arrangements and of the Human Rights Act 1998, particularly as measures passed by the Scottish Parliament, the Northern Ireland Assembly and the National Assembly for Wales could be struck down directly by the courts. Other issues that Parliament as a whole may need to grapple with include:

■ the implications and future handling of inter-regional transfers,[10] which are becoming more transparent;

■ the overall operation of the Memorandum of Understanding and Concordats published on 4 October 1999 and of the other bilateral concordats which are being drawn up; and

■ lessons that might be drawn from the actual operation of the devolution arrangements and how they might be adjusted to meet legitimate concerns.

6.24   Having access to members with a regional perspective, the reformed second chamber would be well placed to play an important role in reflecting and reporting on these issues. It might be in a better position than the House of Commons to consider the implications of any points of friction which may arise. Since the Government might be one of the parties to a dispute with the devolved institutions, the House of Commons would not necessarily be seen as impartial.

6.25   We recommend that the reformed second chamber should consider establishing a Committee to provide a focus for this work. Such a Committee could draw on the experiences and perspectives of those members of the second chamber who were providing a voice for the nations and regions but should not be composed exclusively of such members. Given the overlaps with the broader role we envisage for a Constitutional Committee and with the operation of the Humans Rights Act, such a Committee might be constituted most conveniently as a further Sub-committee of any Constitutional Committee.

Recommendation 32: The reformed second chamber should consider establishing a Committee to provide a focus for its consideration of the issues raised by devolution, possibly as a further Sub-committee of the proposed Constitutional Committee.

6.26   The work of such a Committee and the overall role of the second chamber in this area would become much more significant in future if there were a greater decentralisation of powers to the English regions. In those circumstances, the value of providing a regional perspective in the second chamber would become even more apparent. Our proposal is designed to provide the necessary flexibility to facilitate such developments but without pre-empting either their pace or their direction.

---

[10] It is becoming clearer, not only in relation to the devolved institutions, that some regions are net contributors to national finances while others are net beneficiaries.

A peripatetic house

6.27   A number of submissions argued that in the context of devolution and the emergence of new structures in the English regions, the second chamber should not only become a 'Chamber of the Regions' but should also meet outside London from time to time. We agree that the reformed second chamber should have a regional role but we do not believe that it should be an exclusively 'regional' chamber. That aspect of its role might well develop over time. Meanwhile, it would be difficult, in terms of logistics and cost, for the second chamber as a whole to meet outside London, even occasionally. However, it could be appropriate for Committees of the chamber, perhaps particularly any 'Devolution' Committee, to meet in the various regional centres from time to time. These issues will be matters for the second chamber itself to determine.

> **Recommendation 33:** The reformed second chamber as a whole should not meet outside London but it should consider whether Committees, perhaps particularly any 'Devolution' Committee, should meet in the various regional centres from time to time.

Overseas territories

6.28   In its recent report on Gibraltar,[11] the Foreign Affairs Committee of the House of Commons noted that a number of witnesses had suggested that "in the new variable geometry of the United Kingdom, with different levels of self-government for Scotland, Wales, Northern Ireland, London and the English regions, Gibraltar could form another part of this picture. It might be that Gibraltar would have to give up some of its present powers which would be repatriated to London." In its conclusions, the Committee recommended that the Royal Commission should consider whether Gibraltar should be represented in a reformed second chamber. In its response,[12] the Government noted that the issue had been referred to the Royal Commission for consideration.

6.29   Gibraltar is one of relatively few remaining British Overseas Territories.[13] Our proposals envisage the reformed second chamber continuing to be part of the national Parliament of the United Kingdom. Its members would be drawn from throughout the country and some would provide a direct voice for the nations and regions. All the Overseas Territories have their own governments: none is represented in the House of Commons. Although Gibraltar is a part of the EU, it is not a part of the United Kingdom: its citizens are United Kingdom nationals for EU purposes only. We therefore see no case at present for any of the Overseas Territories to be formally represented or given a voice in the second chamber.

---

[11] Foreign Affairs Committee. Fourth Report. Gibraltar. Session 1998/99. June 1999. HC3.

[12] Fourth Report from the Foreign Affairs Committee. Session 1998/99. Gibraltar: Response of the Secretary of State for Foreign and Commonwealth Affairs. 28 October 1999. Cm 4470.

[13] Apart from Gibraltar, these comprise Anguilla, Bermuda, the British Virgin Islands, the Cayman Islands, the Falkland Islands, Montserrat, the Pitcairn Islands, St Helena and its dependencies Ascension and Tristan da Cunha, and the Turks and Caicos Islands. Including Gibraltar, these have a combined population of slightly less than 190,000 people.

6.30   We note, however, that the Government has stated[14] that it intends to offer British citizenship – and so the right of abode – to those citizens of the Overseas Territories who do not already enjoy it, and who meet certain conditions. In the light of the closer ties between the Territories and the United Kingdom that this might encourage, there may be a case for individuals from the Territories to be offered membership of the second chamber on a personal basis.

Recommendation 34: The Overseas Territories should not be formally represented or given a voice in the second chamber; but individuals from the Territories might be offered membership on a personal basis in the light of the closer ties that may develop.

---

[14] *Partnership for Progress and Prosperity. Britain and the Overseas Territories.* March 1999. Cm 4264.

Chapter 7 – Scrutinising Statutory Instruments

7.1   We have already commented (in Chapter 4) on the role played by the Delegated Powers and Deregulation Committee of the present House of Lords in scrutinising the grant of delegated powers. Once granted, those powers are used by Ministers and a whole range of statutory authorities to make secondary legislation, in the form of Statutory Instruments, which affects virtually every aspect of society. During this century there has been a huge growth in the numbers of Statutory Instruments made each year, and an even larger growth in their volume and complexity.

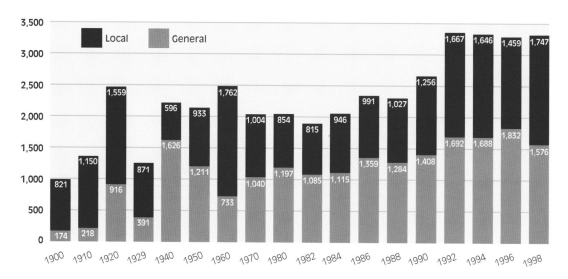

Growth in the number of Statutory Instruments since 1900

The figure for 1940 includes a large number of wartime regulations; those for 1920 and 1950 include many arising from the post-war situation.

Advantages of secondary legislation

7.2   Several of the written submissions expressed concern that the growth in the number of Statutory Instruments represented a substantial shift of legislative power away from Parliament and towards the executive. That concern was compounded by the perceived shortcomings of the arrangements for scrutinising Statutory Instruments. The Delegated Powers and Deregulation Committee, in its Memorandum of Evidence, commented that "the increased importance of secondary legislation in recent years means that parliamentary procedures which may have been satisfactory in the past are no longer adequate, and there is already a pressing need to change them". We concur with that view. The reformed second chamber can and should play a useful role in improving Parliamentary scrutiny of Statutory Instruments.

7.3   It is important to remember the advantages which Government, Parliament and society derive from the existence of delegated powers. Ministers and other statutory authorities are able to legislate on detailed points within the limits of the original delegated power. In consequence:

- Bills can be restricted to their essentials. There is a saving in Parliamentary time, Parliament can concentrate on the key principles underlying legislation, and Acts can be better understood by those who may be affected;

- there is no need to wait until the fine detail of every practical implication of a policy has been worked out before legislating. Such details can be filled in later;

- there is less need for corrective amendments to primary legislation. Secondary legislation can be amended or replaced much more easily than primary legislation;

- it allows for flexibility to adapt to changing circumstances over time, without the delay which would result from having to wait for a suitable Bill; and

- it is easier to tailor the legislative requirements in the parent Act to the different circumstances which may apply in particular cases.

7.4   Other pressures seem likely to tilt the balance between primary and secondary legislation even further towards the use of secondary legislation in future. There is growing pressure to simplify the drafting of primary legislation to produce clearer statements of the overall policy intention, leaving secondary legislation to fill in an even greater proportion of the detail. Welsh MPs and the National Assembly for Wales may also press for more 'skeleton' Bills. The National Assembly for Wales can only make secondary legislation but has the opportunity to debate and vote on amendments to such legislation. An increase in the use of 'skeleton' Bills would therefore give the National Assembly greater discretion to adapt the principles of 'England and Wales' Bills to the particular circumstances of Wales. Similar points might also arise in respect of legislation in the 'reserved' category: the Scottish Parliament and the Northern Ireland Assembly might reasonably ask that more should be left to delegated powers exercisable by Scottish or Northern Ireland authorities.

7.5   In addition, the operation of the Human Rights Act may well reveal that much potential incompatibility between the European Convention on Human Rights (ECHR) and United Kingdom law arises from secondary legislation. The Delegated Powers and Deregulation Committee Memorandum drew attention to this point. It argued that scrutiny of draft secondary legislation on 'compatibility' grounds would be highly desirable and "could be a very considerable task".

7.6   These factors reinforce the case for enhanced Parliamentary scrutiny of secondary legislation.

> **Recommendation 35:** There is a strong case for enhanced Parliamentary scrutiny of secondary legislation. The reformed second chamber should make a strong contribution in this area.

Current scrutiny arrangements

7.7   The current scrutiny arrangements depend on the distinctions drawn between different categories of delegated powers. These distinctions have been drawn on the basis of principles which are somewhat arbitrary and imprecise. More than half of the 3,000 Statutory Instruments made each year are subject to no Parliamentary procedure at all. Most of the rest (see chart) are subject to 'negative resolution': they could in theory be overturned by a negative vote in either House of Parliament. A minority – usually the most significant ones – require the positive approval of both Houses of Parliament before they can be made. Although the Delegated Powers and Deregulation Committee has ensured greater consistency of approach since 1992, before then it was often a matter of chance or political circumstances which determined whether particular delegated powers were made subject to affirmative or negative resolution procedure. The situation is further complicated by the range of different procedures that govern the exercise of existing delegated powers (some dating from the last century); and by the practical requirement for some powers to be exercisable, in an emergency, without prior Parliamentary approval.

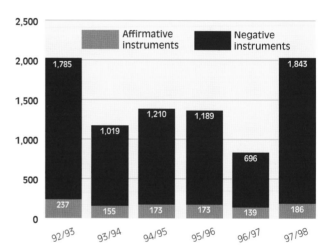

Split between numbers of negative and affirmative resolution instruments

7.8   When delegated powers are exercised, technical scrutiny of those Statutory Instruments which are subject to scrutiny by Parliament is carried out by the Joint Committee on Statutory Instruments (JCSI).[1] The JCSI reviews the *vires*, drafting and certain other technical aspects of Statutory Instruments, such as whether they are retrospective. It may draw attention to any 'unusual or unexpected' use of a delegated power, but is not allowed to consider the merits of any particular Statutory Instrument.

Obstacles to effective scrutiny

7.9   Parliament does have opportunities to consider the merits of those Statutory Instruments which are subject to affirmative or negative resolution procedure, but there remain a number of obstacles to effective scrutiny.

7.10   **Statutory Instruments cannot be amended.** Affirmative resolution instruments can only be approved or rejected. As they rarely raise major issues of principle, there is a natural reluctance to go to the length of rejecting the whole Instrument when most of it gives rise to no cause for concern.

---

[1] There is also a House of Commons Committee on Statutory Instruments, which scrutinises those few Statutory Instruments that deal with financial matters, which are subject to proceedings in the House of Commons alone.

7.11   There is no realistic prospect of a Statutory Instrument being defeated in the House of Commons. Although in 1994 the House of Lords (on a motion from Lord Simon of Glaisdale) asserted its "unfettered freedom to vote on any subordinate legislation",[2] in practice there has (so far) been no serious challenge since 1968[3] to the convention that the House of Lords does not reject Statutory Instruments. Nevertheless, members of the House of Lords have found various ways in which to indicate their concern about particular Statutory Instruments. These have occasionally resulted in Ministers adjusting their proposals.

7.12   Very little time is made available for debates on Statutory Instruments in the House of Commons. Affirmative resolution instruments are routinely referred to Standing Committees, rather than debated on the floor of the House. The Committees cannot consider amendments or debate substantive motions: They are required to report that they have 'considered' the Statutory Instrument, which is then moved formally in the House. Negative resolution instruments may be 'prayed against' within 40 sitting days but only a minority of those 'prayed against' are referred (by agreement between the Party Whips) to a Standing Committee, where in any case the same conditions apply. The pressure of time is less acute in the House of Lords. Affirmative resolution instruments and *all* 'prayers' against negative resolution instruments are debated, and all are taken on the floor of the House; but they have accounted for only about 5 per cent of the time of the House in recent years.

7.13   Negative resolution instruments usually come into effect about 40 days after being made and laid before Parliament. Members may therefore feel that there is little point in seeking to negate something which has already come into effect, especially given all the attendant practical and legal difficulties.

7.14   The sheer volume of Statutory Instruments and their level of detail. This makes it difficult for any individual MP or member of the second chamber to get to grips with the substantive issues.

Proposals for change

7.15   The report on Delegated Legislation by the House of Commons Procedure Committee, published in June 1996,[4] detailed concerns about the arrangements for scrutinising Statutory Instruments and offered some proposals for improvement. Its main recommendations were that:

■ **there should be a new category of 'super affirmative' instruments**, subject to scrutiny before they are formally laid in draft;

■ **a Sifting Committee should be established to make recommendations on the handling of particular Statutory Instruments** (for example, to refer them to the relevant Departmental Select Committee or recommend debate in a Standing Committee) and that the period for 'praying against' negative resolution instruments should be extended from 40 to 60 days; and

---

[2] Hansard (HL). 20 October 1994.

[3] When the House of Lords voted not to approve the Southern Rhodesia (United Nations Sanctions) Order 1968, precipitating the collapse of the inter-party talks on Lords reform. The House of Lords approved a virtually identical order some weeks later.

[4] Fourth Report. Session 1995/96. HC152.

■ **debates in Standing Committee should be on a substantive motion**, perhaps beginning with an opportunity for members to ask questions. The House should not consider a Statutory Instrument until after the JCSI had reported on it, and there should be at least a 1½ hour debate on any Statutory Instrument which was either not approved or recommended for annulment by the relevant Committee.

7.16 These recommendations from the Procedure Committee are of course matters for the House of Commons, but our proposals are very much in line with the spirit of the Procedure Committee's report. The two could be considered in parallel. Our proposals build on those strengths of the present House of Lords which we believe should be preserved in the reformed second chamber. They may provide another example of the way in which the two Houses could play complementary roles in bringing the Government to account more effectively.

7.17 There are a number of factors which should make it appropriate for the reformed second chamber to make an important contribution to the scrutiny of Statutory Instruments:

■ such scrutiny would be a natural development of the interest which the present House of Lords has taken in the granting and subsequent exercise of delegated powers;

■ the reformed second chamber will, we hope, continue to contain people with a range of skills suited to discharging a technical scrutiny function;

■ our proposals also envisage that members of the second chamber will often have direct knowledge of the areas affected by particular pieces of secondary legislation, and be able to speak authoritatively on their likely effect; and

■ such technical scrutiny is unlikely to attract public attention. As the Delegated Powers and Deregulation Committee put it when describing their existing tasks, "the largely invisible nature of a Committee which usually sits in private and whose work is ill-designed to grab headlines is particularly appropriate for a second chamber".

7.18 Our specific proposals in this area involve both 'procedural' changes and changes to the powers of the second chamber in relation to Statutory Instruments.

Pre-publication scrutiny

7.19 We strongly support the proposal that more proposed Statutory Instruments should be published in draft so that they can be subjected to detailed comment by interested parties and members of both Houses of Parliament before being formally laid before Parliament.

7.20 'Pre-legislative' scrutiny of proposed Statutory Instruments has a limited but respectable pedigree:

■ Deregulation Orders under the Deregulation and Contracting Out Act 1994 (which often arise from a process of external consultation) are subject to a statutory period of formal consultation and must be laid before Parliament in draft for a period of at least 60 days. They are referred for consideration to the Deregulation Committee in the House of Commons and the Delegated Powers and Deregulation Committee in the House of Lords. When the final draft Order is presented for approval it must be accompanied by a Memorandum setting out the points raised on the original draft and any changes made as a result;

■ a similar procedure to that covering Deregulation Orders has been established for remedial Orders under the Human Rights Act 1998 (following expressions of concern in the House of Lords); and

■ successive Governments have made an administrative practice of publishing 'Proposals' for draft Orders in Council under the Northern Ireland Act 1974, along with an Explanatory Memorandum, and allowing a six to ten week consultation period. This procedure has been put on a statutory basis in the Northern Ireland Act 1998. Now that the Act has come into effect the procedure will apply to legislation on certain 'reserved' matters.

7.21 All these examples relate to Statutory Instruments which amend (or, in the latter case, are, in effect) primary legislation and where a specific statutory requirement for formal consultation has been seen to be appropriate. In other instances, Departments, as an administrative practice, publish Statutory Instruments in draft as a basis for consultation with experts and interested parties. Additionally, the Delegated Powers and Deregulation Committee occasionally recommends that certain delegated powers should not be exercised without prior consultation. The potential advantages of consulting on Statutory Instruments by publishing them in draft are obvious. Interested parties welcome the consultation and

have an opportunity to influence and improve the drafting of the Statutory Instrument concerned. The overall result should be better legislation. The Delegated Powers and Deregulation Committee's view, arising from its experience, is that, "We consider the experiment of pre-legislative processes inherent in the deregulation procedure to have been a considerable success, and one which could be usefully built on by extending the exercise to selected public Bills and Statutory Instruments".

7.22 The Delegated Powers and Deregulation Committee is itself in a position to encourage such prior consultation. It could recommend a statutory requirement for prior consultation on the exercise of particular delegated powers or seek assurances from Ministers as the delegated power concerned is being debated that such consultation will be undertaken. We would also encourage Ministers and Departments to consider publishing particularly significant Statutory Instruments in draft wherever there seems to be benefit in doing so. We see no advantage in requiring prior consultation on defined categories of Statutory Instrument because the existing categories, especially in respect of delegated powers granted before 1992, do not necessarily reflect the significance of the substantive issue concerned.

> **Recommendation 36:** The Delegated Powers and Deregulation Committee should encourage the practice of publishing particularly significant Statutory Instruments in draft so that they can be subjected to detailed comment by interested parties and members of both Houses of Parliament before being formally laid before Parliament. Ministers and Departments should consider doing so wherever that would be beneficial.

A 'sifting' mechanism

7.23   We believe it would strengthen Parliamentary scrutiny of Statutory Instruments if a 'sifting' mechanism could be established. This would be designed to look at the significance of every Statutory Instrument subject to Parliamentary scrutiny; call for further information from Departments where necessary; and draw attention to those Statutory Instruments which are important and those which merit further debate or consideration. Such a mechanism, perhaps in the form of a Committee, could be established by either House, or jointly, as a procedural matter. Its value would lie in focusing Parliamentary attention on those few Statutory Instruments which were of real significance. Its judgement would depend on not only the intrinsic significance of the issue concerned, but also its current political salience (which might vary over time).

> **Recommendation 37**: A 'sifting' mechanism should be established to look at the significance of every Statutory Instrument subject to Parliamentary scrutiny; call for further information from Departments where necessary; and draw attention to those Statutory Instruments which are important and those which merit further debate or consideration.

7.24   Depending on what decisions are taken on the Procedure Committee report referred to above, the logical course could be to establish a Joint Sifting Committee. There could be some complications in practice, although these should not be insuperable. For example:

- as with the JCSI, there would need to be a Commons-only Committee to deal with Statutory Instruments on financial matters;

- only members of the relevant House would be able to decide which Committee of that House should be asked to scrutinise a particular Statutory Instrument; and

- only the members of the relevant House would be able to decide whether to recommend a particular Statutory Instrument for debate in that House.

7.25   Nevertheless, such an arrangement would ensure consistency of approach between the two Houses, avoid any potential for duplication of staff effort and build on the experience of the JCSI.

7.26   Alternatively, we recommend that the reformed second chamber should consider setting up some machinery to sift Statutory Instruments in the way proposed. This task would have a number of parallels with the work of the Delegated Powers and Deregulation Committee. It would involve making judgements about the significance of particular proposals to exercise delegated powers and categorising them accordingly. The existing Committee's role in scrutinising draft Deregulation Orders has given it experience of commenting on the exercise of delegated powers. This is a valuable addition to the Committee's experience in making recommendations about the basis on which delegated powers should be granted. The reformed second chamber might therefore wish to consider whether the Delegated Powers and Deregulation Committee could take on this task.

> **Recommendation 38:** A joint Committee should be established to sift Statutory Instruments. Alternatively, the second chamber should consider setting up machinery to sift Statutory Instruments, perhaps inviting the Delegated Powers and Deregulation Committee to take on the task.

7.27   Where any sifting mechanism identified a Statutory Instrument as being worthy of consideration and debate, it might be considered either by the whole second chamber or – in the absence of a structure of Departmentally-related Committees – by *ad hoc* Committees. Such Committees would provide opportunities for members to question Ministers about the proposals and for Ministers to explain and justify them. A Committee recommendation to oppose an affirmative resolution instrument or annul a negative resolution instrument would obviously need to be debated by the whole chamber. If no such recommendation were made, a convention might arise that the relevant instrument should be approved without debate.

Other procedural changes

7.28   As far as other procedural improvements are concerned, we endorse the view of the Procedure Committee that neither House should consider a Statutory Instrument until the JCSI has reported on it.[5] We also agree that the statutory 'praying time', in respect of negative resolution instruments, should be extended from 40 days to 60 days by amending the Statutory Instruments Act 1946.

> **Recommendation 39:** Neither chamber should consider a Statutory Instrument until the JCSI has reported on it. The Statutory Instruments Act 1946 should be amended to extend the statutory 'praying time' in respect of negative resolution instruments from 40 days to 60 days.

7.29   We see no case for making it possible to amend Statutory Instruments once they have been formally laid before Parliament. Any comprehensive system for considering detailed amendments to secondary legislation would negate the advantages of secondary legislation. On the other hand, any attempt to limit the scope for amendments in some arbitrary way (for example, by setting an upper limit on how many amendments could be debated) would be difficult to justify. Changes to proposed Statutory Instruments have occasionally been secured when Ministers have agreed to withdraw draft instruments or introduce replacement provisions. These options would remain open. The practice of consulting on proposed Statutory Instruments, which we hope to encourage, would reduce the number of occasions on which serious criticisms might be levelled at the drafting of Statutory Instruments.

> **Conclusion:** There is no case for making it possible to amend Statutory Instruments once they have been formally laid before Parliament.

---

[5] The House of Lords already observes such a rule in relation to affirmative resolution instruments.

7.30   More generally, we see scope for the second chamber to adopt an open-minded, flexible and innovative approach to the consideration of Statutory Instruments within the present procedural arrangements. The Delegated Powers and Deregulation Committee already interacts with Departments and any Sifting Committee could do likewise. Where Ministers can choose between affirmative or negative resolution procedures, the Committee might seek to influence that choice or it might request drafts of particular instruments on an informal basis, irrespective of the statutory requirements.

> **Recommendation 40**: The reformed second chamber should adopt an open-minded, flexible and innovative approach to the consideration of Statutory Instruments within the present procedural arrangements.

Powers in relation to secondary legislation

7.31   The powers of the present House of Lords in respect of Statutory Instruments are more absolute than those it has in respect of primary legislation. On the other hand, as we noted in paragraph 7.11, there has since 1968 been no serious challenge to the convention that the House of Lords does not reject Statutory Instruments. Its *influence* over secondary legislation is therefore paradoxically less than its influence over primary legislation.

7.32   This may all seem anomalous. The formal explanation is that the two kinds of legislation are not comparable. Primary legislation is the result of a Bill being passed by the two Houses of Parliament and receiving Royal Assent. Secondary legislation is made by Ministers under powers generally conferred by primary legislation. It is not itself the product of Parliament at all. But on a less theoretical level, the reality is that the Government is the prime mover in relation to nearly all legislation, both primary and secondary. If the second chamber is to have the role we envisage for it, it should have real influence over both kinds of legislation.

7.33   On the face of it the present arrangements give the second chamber some powerful weapons. It can refuse to approve draft instruments (under the affirmative procedure) or strike down instruments already made (under the negative procedure). These powers should enable the second chamber to bring irresistible pressure to bear on the Government. But they are too drastic. That is the reason why they are not in practice used now and we would not suggest that a reformed second chamber should be more willing than the present House of Lords to persist in blocking an instrument altogether.

7.34   One way forward might be to leave the powers as they are, but to develop a convention that they would be used in much the same way as a suspensory veto, so as to delay rather than block. This might be achieved by establishing a practice of adjourning the debate on a motion to approve a draft, or to annul an instrument, until the House of Commons and Ministers had had an opportunity to consider the objections raised. If a satisfactory solution could be agreed, a revised instrument or draft could be put forward. Otherwise the Government's proposals, supported by the House of Commons, could be allowed to prevail, the reservations of the second chamber having been considered.

7.35   In our view a system of broadly this kind is desirable, but it would not be satisfactory to rely on its developing informally. The second chamber should be given a tool which it can use to *force* the Government and the House of Commons to take its concerns seriously. There is, in our view, not much point in the second chamber having a theoretically greater power which it does not in reality exercise. It should have powers which it can actually exercise, and which would require the Government and the House of Commons to take some positive action either to meet its concerns or override its reservations.

7.36   We therefore recommend that changes be made by legislation, so that:

■   where the second chamber votes against a draft instrument, the draft should nevertheless be deemed to be approved if the House of Commons subsequently gives (or, as the case may be, reaffirms) its approval within three months; and

■   where the second chamber votes to annul an instrument, the annulment would not take effect for three months and could be overridden by a resolution of the House of Commons.

7.37   In both cases we envisage that the Minister concerned would be expected to publish an Explanatory Memorandum within a stated period. It would also be open to the Minister to withdraw a draft Statutory Instrument and substitute a replacement or, as appropriate, to make a new negative resolution instrument to supersede the previous one. In either case, the second chamber would have the opportunity to reconsider its position and, if appropriate, to lift its 'suspended sentence'. However, if it chose not to do so, the House of Commons should have the decisive voice and be able to determine on an affirmative vote that the Statutory Instrument should be approved or remain in force. In doing so, the members of the House of Commons would be fully aware of the second chamber's concerns, the Minister's response and any wider public and media reactions. The proposal is therefore entirely in line with our view of the second chamber's overall role. It would give it greater scope to challenge Government proposals for secondary legislation and draw the issues to the attention of the House of Commons, who would take the final decision.

> **Recommendation 41**: Where the second chamber votes against a draft instrument, the draft should nevertheless be deemed to be approved if the House of Commons subsequently gives (or, as the case may be, reaffirms) its approval within three months.

Recommendation 42: Where the second chamber votes to annul an instrument, the annulment should not take effect for three months and could be overridden by a resolution of the House of Commons.

Recommendation 43: In both cases the relevant Minister should publish an Explanatory Memorandum, giving the second chamber an opportunity to reconsider its position and ensuring that the House of Commons is fully aware of all the issues if it has to take the final decision.

7.38   A proposal on these lines would not require any recategorisation of Statutory Instruments to make it work. Nor would it require any amendment of the Parliament Acts. It could be achieved by amendments to the Statutory Instruments Act 1946, supplemented if neccessary by changes to Standing Orders. At the cost of weakening the formal power of the second chamber, in comparison with that of the present House of Lords, we believe it would actually strengthen its influence and its ability to cause the Government and the House of Commons to take its concerns seriously. It therefore strikes an appropriate balance between the power of the two Houses of Parliament in relation to Statutory Instruments. It illustrates a further way in which the functions of the reformed second chamber could complement those of the House of Commons. In the terminology of the Labour Party's written evidence, our proposal seeks to govern the operation of the second chamber's powers in respect of secondary legislation in a way which fairly reflects the House of Commons' pre-eminence.

Conclusion: Changing the nature of the second chamber's powers in relation to Statutory Instruments would actually strengthen its influence and its ability to cause the Government and the House of Commons to take its concerns seriously.

Retention of the current absolute veto

7.39   We did consider the option of retaining the second chamber's present absolute veto over Statutory Instruments, particularly in relation to specific delegated powers (for example, those in the Human Rights Act or others with constitutional implications). We concluded that this was less likely to achieve the desired result. In practice, the vetoing or annulment of a Statutory Instrument by the second chamber would not trigger a constitutional crisis. The Government would probably reintroduce an identical or similar instrument and secure the support of the House of Commons, and the second chamber would need to think very carefully about challenging the instrument for a second time. In theory, retaining an absolute veto might place the second chamber in a stronger position to enforce its opposition, but in practice we doubt that this would be the case. The absolute nature of the House of Lords' powers in relation to secondary legislation is more apparent than real. A contested item of secondary legislation could always be reintroduced in the form of a Bill and enacted, if necessary, under Parliament Act procedures. Moreover, it would be easy to misrepresent any use of the second chamber's current power to veto secondary legislation as a challenge to the democratically-elected Government, which should be resisted for that reason alone. Our proposal would provide a better context for enabling the two Houses to work together in scrutinising Statutory Instruments more effectively, guided by their considered views of the substance of the issues.

Chapter 8 – Holding the Government to account

8.1   One of Parliament's prime functions is to hold the Government to account. The more effectively this is done, the better for everyone. More accountable Government is better Government.

8.2   The House of Commons directly reflects the political views of the electorate and can sustain a Government in office or withdraw its confidence and force a change of Government. It is right that it should play the primary role in holding the Government to account. Our ambition for the reformed second chamber is that it should enhance the overall ability of Parliament as a whole to hold the Government to account. It should do this by using its particular strengths to develop arrangements which complement and reinforce those of the House of Commons. The achievement of that objective will require the reformed second chamber to have characteristics distinct from those of the House of Commons, a point to which we return in Chapter 10.

8.3   Chapter 4 discussed the role the reformed second chamber should play in scrutinising proposed primary legislation. Chapter 5 considered its role in protecting the constitution and scrutinising Government initiatives for compliance with relevant human rights standards. Chapter 7 examined the part the second chamber should perform in scrutinising the exercise of delegated powers. In this chapter we consider four other ways the second chamber should contribute to the task of holding the Government to account:

- scrutinising Ministers;

- scrutinising European Union business;

- general debate and specialist investigation; and

- scrutinising the exercise of prerogative powers.

Scrutinising Ministers

8.4   Perhaps the most direct way in which the Government can be held to account by Parliament is through the questioning of Ministers. The ability of the House of Lords to do this directly has declined over the past century as the majority of senior Ministers have come to sit in the Commons.[1] A number of submissions recommended that this trend should be drawn to its logical conclusion and that the practice of appointing Ministers from the second chamber should be discontinued. It was argued that this would deter the politically ambitious from seeking to become members of the second chamber purely for the purpose of achieving a Ministerial appointment. It might also allow the chamber to concentrate more effectively on its role of scrutinising the actions of the executive, in the absence of political pressure to support or oppose Government Ministers.

---

[1] The last Prime Minister to sit in the Lords was the third Marquess of Salisbury (1895—1902). Since 1964 only two peers by succession (Lord Carrington and Lord Gowrie), one hereditary peer of first creation (Lord Pakenham) and four life peers (Lord Shackleton, Lord Young of Graffham, Lord Cockfield and Lord Robertson of Port Ellen) have held Cabinet posts other than as Lord Chancellor or Leader of the House of Lords.

8.5   On the other hand, the ability of the second chamber to hold the Government to account would be significantly reduced if members were not able to present their case direct to Ministers. It has been argued that the limited practical influence of the Canadian Senate and Irish Seanad is underlined and perpetuated by the minimal Ministerial presence in those chambers. Ministerial accountability to the second chamber could, in theory, be provided by Ministers based in the Commons taking part in the second chamber's debates, as is the case in many other parliaments. We do not support this idea. For Ministers to be able to take full account of the views of the second chamber and to respond effectively to its concerns, they must have a full understanding of the ambience, conventions and style of that chamber. These characteristics are likely to continue to be significantly different from those of the Commons.

8.6   It is desirable that ongoing or protracted business (such as proceedings on particular Bills or the consideration of long-running issues) should be handled by Ministers who have a long-term relationship with the second chamber. Such a relationship would most conveniently derive from their being members of it. Ministerial membership of the second chamber would also maximise the opportunity for informal contact between Ministers and members. This can usefully supplement formal exchanges within the chamber. The continuous presence of Ministers who are directly accountable to the second chamber for important areas of Government responsibility is likely to encourage a higher quality of debate and scrutiny. Finally, having Ministers based in the second chamber has the effect of extending the 'pool' of people from among whom the Prime Minister of the day can select the Government. It thus retains the possibility that Ministers can be appointed from outside the ranks of professional politicians. It should therefore continue to be possible for Ministers to be drawn from and to be directly accountable to the second chamber. To what extent this is realised is clearly a matter for the Prime Minister of the day but we believe it would be desirable if the second chamber were to continue to furnish several Ministers of State and at least two members of the Cabinet.

Recommendation 44: It should continue to be possible for Ministers to be drawn from and be directly accountable to the second chamber.

8.7   The leading role in the scrutiny of the Government should clearly continue to lie with the Commons, where most Cabinet Ministers sit. However, one weakness of the present arrangements is that the wider perspectives and relevant expertise of members of the House of Lords cannot be brought to bear directly and regularly on those senior members of the Government with the lead responsibility for most major areas of public policy. It would enhance overall Parliamentary scrutiny of the executive if Ministerial accountability to the second chamber could be strengthened.

Recommendation 45: A mechanism should be developed which would require Commons Ministers to make statements to and deal with questions from members of the second chamber.

8.8   In making this proposal we would not wish to undermine the relationship between second chamber Ministers and other members. Nor do we believe it would be necessary to alter the long-standing Westminster convention that members of one chamber do not speak in the other. We want to maintain the principle that the role of the second chamber should be to complement, and not duplicate, the work of the House of Commons. The precise arrangements should be for the reformed second chamber itself to determine in consultation with the Government. One possibility would be for a Committee of the whole second chamber to meet regularly off the floor of the chamber to hear a statement from, and then question, a Commons Minister. The event should promote the exchange of views in a constructive atmosphere. To ensure topicality, there might be no fixed rota of Ministers nor advance notice of questions. The second chamber might invite Ministers responsible for current issues to appear before the Committee at a few days' notice, and give them the opportunity to explain their position. We would not expect such an arrangement to be used for the political equivalent of 'ambulance chasing'. Instead, we envisage that it would explore issues of longer-term or underlying significance.

Scrutinising European Union business

8.9   There is a vital role for Parliament in scrutinising European Union (EU) business. The reformed second chamber should build on the high quality work done by the present House of Lords. A new relationship might develop between United Kingdom Members of the European Parliament (MEPs) and the reformed second chamber. Both points are within our terms of reference which invite us to "take particular account of… developing relations with the European Union". We consider these issues in this chapter because the chief mechanism by which EU national parliaments can scrutinise and control developments in the EU is to bring national Ministers to account for the decisions to which they contribute in the Council of Ministers.

8.10   Recent developments have underlined the growing significance of the Council of Ministers among the EU institutions, and underlined the importance of the role of national parliaments in holding the Council of Ministers to account. Meetings of the Council, particularly at head of government level, are now far more significant events in the European political and institutional calendar than was originally envisaged. That trend has been accelerated by the formal incorporation of the Second and Third Pillars of the European Union,[2] which are the exclusive responsibility of the Council of Ministers. The extension of 'co-decision' in other areas has still left the Council of Ministers with a very considerable say over most EU directives. Neither the Council as a whole nor individual national Ministers are accountable to the European Parliament. The only way for European national parliaments to assert an influence on the Council of Ministers is through their own national Ministers.

8.11   The importance of this was acknowledged in the Maastricht Treaty, which proposed closer contacts between the European Parliament and national parliaments. The Governments of the Member States committed themselves to ensure "that national parliaments receive Commission proposals for legislation in good time for information or possible examination". The 1997 Treaty of Amsterdam included a protocol on the role of national parliaments in the EU, which laid down that all Commission consultation

---

[2] Common Foreign and Security Policy and Co-operation on Justice and Home Affairs.

documents and proposals for legislation should be made available to national parliaments in good time and that a six-week period should elapse between a proposal being made and its appearance on the agenda of the Council of Ministers.

Current scrutiny arrangements

8.12   The United Kingdom Parliament already has one of the most highly developed systems in the EU for considering proposed European legislation and other proposals and for ensuring that Ministers are aware of the balance of opinion within Parliament before they commit the United Kingdom to any significant new position. The systems currently in place[3] provide a good example of the two Houses taking complementary and mutually reinforcing approaches.

8.13   The House of Commons' European Scrutiny Committee provides a mechanism for rapidly sifting *all* proposals under consideration in the Council of Ministers (some 400 per year), including business under the two inter-governmental Pillars of the European Union. The Committee seeks further information from the relevant Department, flags up proposals of particular significance or political relevance and recommends those which should be subject to debate or consideration in one of the European Standing Committees. Those Standing Committees question the relevant Minister about the background and the Government's approach before debating the issues. The European Scrutiny Committee may also seek opinions from Departmentally-related Select Committees within specified timescales and hold joint meetings to help establish a common position. The scrutiny arrangements also allow a regular dialogue with Departments over the business coming before the Council of Ministers. This includes the option of calling Ministers and/or officials to give evidence to the Committee before and after Council meetings.[4]

8.14   The House of Lords' European Union Committee[5] identifies 30 or 40 items of EU business each year for in-depth study and analysis by one of its six sub-committees. These sub-committees between them draw on the services of some 70 members of the House of Lords, many with long experience of the issues concerned. The proposals considered by these sub-committees will typically raise major issues of principle or policy. Their reports are widely regarded, throughout Europe, as being of extremely high quality[6] and are capable of having a significant influence on policy development.

8.15   These scrutiny arrangements are supplemented by the European Scrutiny Reserve, a requirement imposed by a House of Commons resolution that (other than in exceptional circumstances) Ministers should not enter into any new commitments in the Council of Ministers until the Commons scrutiny process in relation to the proposal concerned has been completed. A virtually identical resolution now applies to the House of Lords' scrutiny process, replacing a previous informal understanding to the same effect.

---

[3] Helpfully described in *The European Scrutiny System in the House of Commons.* House of Commons. November 1998.

[4] The Committee's remit was expanded in November 1998 when the House of Commons approved the principal recommendations of the Modernisation Committee's report, *The Scrutiny of European Business*, June 1998.

[5] A number of changes to procedure, including a formal scrutiny reserve, and a change in the name from the European Communities Committee to the European Union Committee, recommended in the Fifth Report of the House of Lords' Select Committee on Procedure (November 1999. HL116), were adopted on 10 November 1999.

[6] Comments to this effect have been made by the Institute of European Environmental Policy, The Law Society, The British Bankers' Association and the Confederation of British Industry. Select Committee on the Committee Work of the House. Session 1991/92. February 1992. HL35.

8.16   The combination of rapid assessment of all proposals by the Commons and in-depth analysis of a few particularly significant ones by the Lords has considerable value. It minimises the risk of overlap between the work of the two Houses and plays to their respective strengths. The system works well and should be maintained. The reformed second chamber should, if possible, maintain the contribution currently made by the House of Lords' European Union Committee. That work should also be properly resourced. We return to the general issue of resourcing in Chapter 17, and the question of how resources should be distributed must ultimately be a matter for the second chamber itself. Our assessment, however, is that the excellent work of the European Union Committee could be further developed. We recommend that the reformed second chamber should consider making additional staff and other resources available to the European Union Committee.

> **Recommendation 46:** The current complementary system of scrutiny of European Union business by the two Houses of Parliament should be maintained and improved.

> **Recommendation 47:** The reformed second chamber should consider making additional staff and other resources available to the European Union Committee.

MEPs and the second chamber

8.17   One of the questions we have had to consider is whether the second chamber's contribution to the scrutiny of European Union business would be strengthened by developing formal links with the United Kingdom MEPs. We have also attempted to assess what other advantages might be gained from such links. The White Paper, *Modernising Parliament: Reforming the House of Lords*, makes the point that "MEPs in the future will be elected on a regional basis, so a role for them in relation to the second chamber would therefore reinforce its regional links as well as improving links between Westminster and Strasbourg". It also makes the point that "a specific role for MEPs in the second chamber might yield particular benefits, so that each Chamber could take advantage of the particular expertise of members of the other, and thereby maximising the effectiveness of the United Kingdom's input".

8.18   The case might also be made (although no one put it to us in quite these terms) that by giving membership of the second chamber to some United Kingdom MEPs, who have themselves been elected, the second chamber would gain a degree of indirect electoral authority. There was little positive support for this proposal and what there was tended to rely on the practical advantages. As Graham Mather MEP put it in his written evidence, "MEPs could provide the Chamber with a highly focused and attuned set of eyes and ears in the European institutions". He drew attention to the fact that "MEPs frequently, and especially under co-decision, will have an inside track and appreciation of useful options and approaches which would be difficult to find elsewhere".

8.19   As we argued in Chapter 6, we see difficulties of principle with indirect election. MEPs are elected with a specific mandate to represent the United Kingdom in the European Parliament. For MEPs to serve as members of the second chamber would require a significant change in the basis on which they were elected and give rise to a lack of clarity about their accountability to the electorate for their actions. MEPs who were members of the second chamber would be in an unusual position: they would be expected to engage in a double layer of scrutiny. There would also be some risk that any MEPs selected by their fellows to be members of the second chamber would see themselves as delegates, rather than as independent-minded members. A selection procedure would also need to be created, which might not be straightforward. In any event, we would be concerned about giving seats in the United Kingdom Parliament to people who had chosen to stand as MEPs and who might have wider political ambitions, including ambitions for the House of Commons. Finally, there could be a difficulty over length of tenure. We discuss the general point in Chapter 11, but in principle we believe the reformed second chamber will be more cohesive if all its members serve for the same length of time, and MEPs would only be able to serve during their term of office.

8.20   There are also practical obstacles to MEPs serving in the second chamber. Membership of the European Parliament is a demanding full-time job, involving heavy travel commitments. It leaves little time for additional activities. Those members of Parliament who have secured such a dual mandate in the past have struggled to fulfil both posts adequately. We therefore agree with those who argued that membership of the second chamber would be too onerous a task to combine with the increasingly exacting task of being an MEP. We note that the European Parliament is itself opposed to the idea that any of its members should have a dual mandate. For our part, we have no objection in principle to individuals seeking a dual mandate, but it would be wrong to make it a requirement. The workload pressures on MEPs would also count against the alternative suggestion that some United Kingdom MEPs might be co-opted to serve as members of the European Union Committee. We see little additional benefit in MEPs becoming members of committees without also becoming members of the second chamber. For all these reasons, we do not think that anyone should become a member of the second chamber by virtue of being a United Kingdom MEP.

> **Recommendation 48:** No one should become a member of the second chamber by virtue of being a United Kingdom MEP.

8.21   While we see no formal role for United Kingdom MEPs in the second chamber, the absence of such a role should not prevent closer links being established between them and the second chamber. MEPs could, for example, be invited more frequently to give evidence to the European Union Committee. More generally, we gained a sense that MEPs did not feel welcome at Westminster. If true, this is in our view unfortunate and represents a missed opportunity to develop and maintain a coherent and consistent set of policies on EU issues *and* maximise the United Kingdom's impact on the institutions of the EU. We recommend that the reformed second chamber should consider what steps it could take to make United Kingdom MEPs feel more welcome and provide greater opportunities for them to contribute to the development of Parliament's understanding of and approach to EU issues.

> **Recommendation 49:** The reformed second chamber should consider what steps it could take to make United Kingdom MEPs feel more welcome at Westminster. It should also consider how it might provide greater opportunities for United Kingdom MEPs to contribute to the development of Parliament's understanding of and approach to EU issues.

8.22   The present scrutiny arrangements regarding EU business could be reinforced by taking advantage of the arrangements we propose for inviting Commons Ministers to make statements to and take questions from a second chamber committee. Regardless of whatever arrangements may be made in the House of Commons, it should become regular practice for Commons Ministers to appear before the proposed Committee prior to and/or on their return from meetings of the Council. This practice would supplement the pre- and post-Council scrutiny arrangements already operated by the Commons European Scrutiny Committee.

Other proposals

8.23   We agree that the Parliamentary scrutiny of European Union proposals should embrace a careful assessment of the extent to which they comply with the principle of subsidiarity. Although the House of Commons European Scrutiny Committee is best placed to take the lead, we would encourage the European Union Committee to co-operate fully in this task.

> **Recommendation 50:** The House of Commons European Scrutiny Committee is best placed to assess the extent to which European Union proposals comply with the principle of subsidiarity, but the European Union Committee should co-operate fully in that task.

8.24   The second chamber's interest in EU matters could be given wider expression through the institution of a regular opportunity for dealing with Questions for Oral Answer on EU matters. While this would be a departure from the traditions of the House of Lords under which any member can raise any issue on any day, we believe it would reinforce the effectiveness of the chamber's interest in EU matters and provide a forum in which the detailed knowledge built up by members of the European Union Committee could be brought to bear.

> **Recommendation 51:** The reformed second chamber should set aside a regular time for dealing with Questions for Oral Answer on EU matters.

8.25   We do not support the idea that there should be joint European Sub-committees, possibly structured on Departmental lines and with members drawn from both Houses. Such an arrangement would run counter to the essentially complementary approaches currently taken by the two Houses which we believe should continue. The existing informal arrangements for liaison between the committee structures in the two Houses seem to work well: overlaps are avoided and each House can benefit from the views of the other.

8.26   We support the suggestion that the second chamber should continue to play its part in developing inter-parliamentary contact and co-operation within the EU, with both the European Parliament and the other national parliaments of Member States. The regular meetings of Speakers and Presidents, six-monthly gatherings of the Conference of European Affairs Committees (COSAC)[7] and the other contacts which take place between various committees and *rapporteurs* all help to enhance Parliament's understanding of EU matters and to advance the United Kingdom's interests in Europe.

> **Recommendation 52:** The second chamber should continue to play its part in developing inter-parliamentary contact and co-operation within the EU, both with the European Parliament and with the national parliaments of EU Member States.

General debate and specialist investigation

8.27   One of the most important roles of the House of Lords is that it provides a forum for the general debate of major public issues "in an atmosphere less pressurised than the House of Commons by party political issues".[8] Several submissions noted that the quality of debate in the House of Lords is often high and that the able and distinguished members from diverse backgrounds who contribute to this work play a significant role in maintaining the effectiveness of the chamber's role in holding Government to account. Others commented that the less 'party political' nature of the present House of Lords produces an environment which encourages rational analysis and objectivity. A vital factor in this approach to debate is the presence of the Cross Benchers, since the political parties need to gain their support to win a vote. There was unanimous support among those submitting evidence for the reformed second chamber to continue to provide a distinctive forum for national debate.

> **Recommendation 53:** The reformed second chamber should continue to provide a distinctive forum for national debate.

8.28   An increasing aspect of the House of Lords' work in recent years has been specialist investigations by Committees such as the Science and Technology Select Committee. Recent inquiries have considered the management of nuclear waste[9] and the scientific and medical evidence concerning cannabis.[10] The resulting reports are highly regarded and add considerable authority to Parliament at home and abroad. The quality of reports is due to a considerable extent to the expertise available to the House of Lords when Committee members are selected. For example, current members of the Science and Technology Committee include a gynaecologist, a civil engineer, a chemist and a biophysicist.

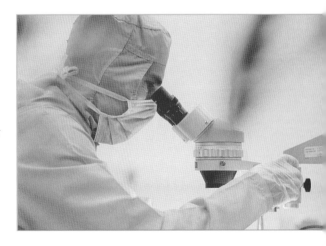

---

7 Conférence des Organes Spécialisés dans les Affaires Communautaires et Européennes de l'Union Européenne.

8 *Modernising Parliament.* Cm 4183, Chapter 7, paragraph 14.

9 Management of Nuclear Waste. Session 1998/99. Third Report. March 1999. HL41.

10 Cannabis: The Scientific and Medical Evidence. Session 1997/98. Ninth Report. November 1998. HL151.

8.29 Specialist committee work of this nature adds significantly to the overall ability of Parliament to contribute to the development of public opinion on major issues. It should continue to be an important function of the reformed second chamber. In Chapter 10 we argue that membership of the second chamber should continue to be, for many, a part-time occupation. This will ensure that Committees can call on members with a range of current expertise. In determining which subjects should be investigated, priority should be given to those which complement the scrutiny undertaken by the Departmental Select Committees in the Commons and those which cross Departmental boundaries and might otherwise be overlooked by Parliament. In particular, the second chamber's atmosphere should enable it to deal with politically highly charged issues which the House of Commons may find difficult to tackle objectively.

> **Recommendation 54**: Specialist committee work should continue to be an important function of the reformed second chamber.

Scrutinising the exercise of prerogative powers

8.30 A consequence of the continuity in British political and legal structures is that the Crown still retains significant powers under common law, which are not subject to direct Parliamentary control. In practice, these 'prerogative powers' are now exercised by Ministers and their officials.

8.31 The executive action authorised by the Royal Prerogative at common law includes some of the most basic and important tasks of Government, including the power to declare war, conduct international relations and appoint people to public office. Reliance on the 'prerogative powers' allows the Government to respond rapidly in fast-moving situations and take decisive action when required. The controversial feature of these powers is that the Government may use them to adopt major policies and decisions without the need for any formal approval by either House of Parliament. For example, the significant restructuring of the civil service through the Next Steps programme, which led to the establishment of over 140 Executive Agencies employing almost 80 per cent of civil servants, was undertaken without any formal reference to Parliament. Indeed, such powers may be exercised entirely without Parliamentary scrutiny or discussion.

8.32 A number of members of both Houses of Parliament, most notably The Rt Hon Tony Benn MP, have campaigned for many years for aspects of the Royal Prerogative to be placed on a statutory footing and subjected to formal Parliamentary control. Although few of the submissions received in response to our consultation exercise referred to this question, those that did were generally supportive of such proposals.

8.33 The two aspects of the prerogative that are of most relevance to the governance of this country are those concerning public appointments and the making of treaties.

Scrutiny of public appointments

8.34 Scrutinising public appointments is a relatively common function of parliaments overseas. For example, the United States Senate holds confirmatory hearings during which the political and social attitudes and history of Presidential nominees may be subject to detailed scrutiny. By contrast, the Westminster Parliament has no such formal role.

8.35 The selection process for public appointments has become significantly more open and transparent in recent years, largely as a consequence of the present and previous Governments' acceptance of the recommendations of the Committee on Standards in Public Life – the 'Nolan principles'. These new arrangements have so far proved effective in ensuring that appointments are made on merit to individuals with relevant experience and expertise, but the system is still developing. We consider that Parliament should continue to exercise a strong scrutiny of the Government's general conduct in making appointments.

8.36 We see considerable disadvantages arising, however, should major public appointments be subject to any kind of formal 'confirmation' hearings by Committees of Parliament. There would be a considerable risk that good candidates would decline to be considered for appointment for fear of being subjected to intrusive and perhaps partisan questioning. It would also not be right for a Parliamentary Committee to seek to substitute its judgement for that of the responsible Ministers in their choice of whom to appoint. It may be that a satisfactory balance can be found which would enable an appropriate Committee to contribute in some way to the appointments process but we see no distinctive role for the second chamber in this area.

> **Recommendation 55:** Parliament should continue to scrutinise the Government's general conduct in making public appointments, but there is no distinctive role for the second chamber in this area.

Scrutiny of treaty obligations

8.37 The power to make treaties is vested in the Crown as part of the Royal Prerogative, but treaties are not self-executing. They have no effect within the United Kingdom unless they are enacted by Statute into domestic law, in which case they are subject to full Parliamentary scrutiny under the normal procedures. The Crown is thus disabled from using its treaty-making powers as a device for legislating without the consent of Parliament. By contrast, much EU legislation – including secondary legislation adopted under the European Community treaties and international agreements concluded with third States by the Communities – *does* have effect in the domestic law of the United Kingdom. This legislation is therefore subject to the system of Parliamentary scrutiny described earlier. Legally binding instruments adopted under the EU's Second and Third Pillars are now also subject to the same level of scrutiny, even though they do not have the power to alter domestic law directly and are not part of European Union law. There is therefore a rigorous system in place to prevent the treaty-making prerogative being used to effect change in domestic law without scrutiny by and the consent of Parliament.

8.38   The negotiation of treaties inevitably requires a degree of flexibility over some issues, which it may not be possible to set out in advance. There might be dangers in any arrangements for enhanced Parliamentary scrutiny which could constrain Ministers' abilities to make judgements in the course of fast-moving negotiations. We therefore agree with the conclusion in the comprehensive memorandum we received from the Foreign and Commonwealth Office (FCO) that "the huge variety of treaties and of political and diplomatic circumstances in which they are negotiated would preclude a general commitment [to compulsory pre-conclusion scrutiny]". We nevertheless welcome the FCO's suggestion that Parliament should be consulted in advance on some treaties, perhaps off the floor of the two chambers. As a first step in this direction, the Government, virtually alone amongst its major allies, set out its intended policy approach to the main issues on the establishment of an International Criminal Court. This allowed the approach to be debated in Parliament before the June/July 1998 UN conference on the subject.

The United Nations building

8.39   Once a treaty has been negotiated, Parliament has no formal role in approving the assumption of treaty obligations by the Government, except where this is expressly required by the treaty. However, as the FCO memorandum explains, successive Governments have invited consideration of treaties under the 'Ponsonby Rule'. Under this procedure, treaties requiring ratification are published and laid before Parliament for a period of 21 sitting days prior to ratification, with a commitment that time will be found to debate any such treaty should there be a demand. In January 1998, the Ponsonby procedure was extended. It now also covers treaties subject simply to mutual notification of the completion of constitutional or other internal procedures.

8.40   While the existing system incorporates safeguards over the use of the Royal Prerogative, there may be scope for Parliament's involvement to be enhanced. We believe that there should be a mechanism for scrutinising the 25–40 treaties laid before Parliament each year under the Ponsonby Rule, to establish whether they raise issues which merit debate or reconsideration before they are ratified.

8.41   In February 1999, Lord Lester of Herne Hill QC and a number of colleagues put to the House of Lords' Liaison Committee a detailed proposal recommending the establishment of a Select Committee to scrutinise international treaties into which the Government proposed to enter. The Liaison Committee noted the proposal,[11] but decided to postpone consideration of the question until after we had reported.

[11] Liaison Committee. Session 1998/99. First Report. March 1999. HL49.

8.42   The proposed Committee would provide exactly the mechanism we believe is required to carry out the technical scrutiny of such treaties. Such a mechanism could draw the attention of members of both Houses to any significant implications in time for those to be debated before the end of the 21 day period provided for under the Ponsonby Rule. We therefore recommend that the Liaison Committee should consider how the proposal might best be carried forward in the reformed second chamber.

Recommendation 56: The Liaison Committee should consider the establishment of a Select Committee to scrutinise international treaties into which the Government proposed to enter.

Chapter 9 – The Law Lords and the judicial functions of the second chamber

The appellate function

9.1   We received an impressive range of evidence on the question of whether the reformed second chamber should continue to exercise the judicial functions of the present House of Lords.[1] In practice, the House acts on the advice of its Appellate and Appeal Committees, composed of the Lords of Appeal in Ordinary[2] and other holders or former holders of high judicial office.[3] A number of weighty and well argued submissions, exemplified by the report of a distinguished Working Group established by JUSTICE and chaired by Lord Alexander of Weedon QC, contended that these functions should no longer be exercised by the second chamber and should instead be transferred to a separate Supreme Court for the United Kingdom.

9.2   Other interested parties and commentators argued that the issue of whether there should be a separate United Kingdom Supreme Court, and what its jurisdiction should be, is not a matter which should be settled as a by-product of reforming the House of Lords. It was further argued that any such move would need to be carefully considered by a Royal Commission or other appropriate inquiry specifically appointed for that task. That was the line taken by the Lords of Appeal in Ordinary in their written evidence to us.

9.3   We recognise that the question of how the superior courts of the United Kingdom should be structured raises a number of complex technical issues. Dealing with this question would involve a consideration of the appellate functions of the Judicial Committee of the Privy Council[4] as well as those of the House of Lords. Moreover, any proposal to adjust the arrangements for taking appeals from the Court of Session in Scotland would raise issues under the Act of Union and would appear to involve changes in a matter for which the Scottish Parliament is now responsible. Any such changes would therefore need to be taken forward in consultation with the Scottish Executive and require the consent of the Scottish Parliament.[5] These issues are outside our terms of reference, but we cannot simply leave them to one side.

9.4   For a start, much depends on the method or combination of methods which will be used to constitute the reformed second chamber. It might, for example, be thought anomalous for appointed Law Lords to sit as members of an otherwise wholly elected second chamber. More generally, we are required to consider what the role and functions of the reformed chamber should be. Another Commission would need to be established

---

[1] The House of Lords is the highest court of appeal for civil and criminal cases in England, Wales and Northern Ireland and for civil cases in Scotland.

[2] The 12 Lords of Appeal in Ordinary are salaried members of the House of Lords, appointed as life peers under the Appellate Jurisdiction Act 1876 from among senior judges and practising barristers to assist the House of Lords in hearing and determining appeals.

[3] Other members of the House of Lords who are entitled to sit on the Appellate and Appeal Committees include former Lords of Appeal in Ordinary, current and former Lord Chancellors and other holders or former holders of high judicial office, most of whom would be members of the House by virtue of being made a life peer under the Life Peerages Act 1958. No one can sit judicially after they have reached the age of 75.

[4] This has jurisdiction to decide disqualifications from the House of Commons, appeals from some Commonwealth countries, and determining appeals, a number of professional disciplinary tribunals and certain ecclesiastical matters. It also hears cases raising 'devolution issues' under the Devolution Acts.

[5] See the written and oral evidence received from The Rt Hon Lord Hope of Craighead.

to decide how the superior courts of the United Kingdom should be organised if the second chamber ceased to exercise judicial functions. But it is part of our responsibility to reach a view on whether there is anything to prevent the second chamber from continuing to exercise those functions. The separate question whether the Law Lords – especially the Lords of Appeal in Ordinary but also other holders and former holders of high judicial office – should continue to sit as legislators in the new chamber also touches on our responsibility to consider how the second chamber should be constituted. We are also required to take particular account of the impact of the Human Rights Act 1998, which may have a bearing on the position of the Law Lords. For these reasons, we took the view that we should at least consider the issues to the extent of deciding whether the current arrangements should remain in place pending any future dedicated inquiry into the arrangements for a separate Supreme Court for the United Kingdom.

9.5   One of the arguments for change is that it is wrong in principle for members of a legislature to exercise judicial functions. The 'separation of powers' doctrine, however, has never strictly applied in the United Kingdom. In practice there is, by convention, an absolute separation between the judicial and other work of the House of Lords. As the well known passage in Bagehot puts it, "[The judicial function] is a function which no theorist would assign to a second chamber in a new Constitution, and which is a matter of accident in ours…. No one indeed would venture *really* to place the judicial function in the chance majorities of a fluctuating assembly: it is so by a sleepy theory; it is not so in living fact".[6] The fact that those exercising judicial functions would also be members of the legislature is not, of itself, an argument against the second chamber continuing to exercise the judicial functions of the present House of Lords.

> **Conclusion:** There is no reason why the second chamber should not continue to exercise the judicial functions of the present House of Lords.

The Law Lords

9.6   The Law Lords make a positive contribution to the work of the House of Lords. They chair or serve on Committees. By convention, Law Lords chair the Joint Committee on Consolidation Bills, the Ecclesiastical Committee and Sub-Committee E (Law and Institutions) of the European Union Committee. They also give decisive opinions on the Privileges Committee. The Law Lords contribute to general debates and to the consideration of proposed legislation, giving the benefit of their extensive judicial experience. Even when they cannot offer personal views they can usefully clarify legal points or help to identify issues which require decision. They can often bring to bear their understanding of how law works in practice. Finally, the Law Lords can draw on their commitment to the rule of law and due process to identify proposed legislation or other developments which could threaten either of those concepts.

---

[6] Walter Bagehot. *The English Constitution* (1867), Chapter 3. The situation he described was reinforced by the Appellate Jurisdiction Act 1876.

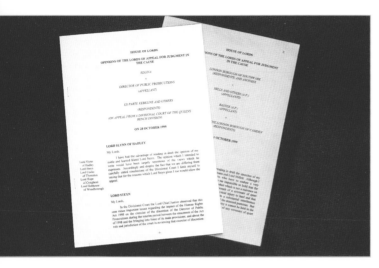

A judgment of the House of Lords

9.7　We accept that similar contributions could be, and indeed are, made by other members of the second chamber with legal expertise or experience. We would be reluctant, however, to see the Law Lords' contribution to the second chamber removed, unless that was judged to be essential. There is also a powerful argument that in the exercise of their judicial functions the Law Lords – and the judicial system generally – benefit from their membership of the second chamber. Their involvement in the second chamber raises their own awareness of the broader political context in which legislation and policies are formulated. Now that the European Convention on Human Rights has been enshrined in British law, it is even more vital that the members of the senior judiciary are alert to the wider political context of their work. We therefore conclude, subject to clarification of the conventions about their role, that it would, on balance, be beneficial to Parliament for the Lords of Appeal in Ordinary to continue to be *ex officio* members of the reformed second chamber and to carry out its judicial functions. Given the effective separation between the appellate work and the other functions of the second chamber we do not consider that the continuation of the present arrangements would undermine the independence of the judiciary or public confidence in the judiciary. We consider the arrangements for appointing holders of other high judicial offices to the second chamber in Chapter 13.

> **Recommendation 57**: The Lords of Appeal in Ordinary should continue to be *ex officio* members of the reformed second chamber and carry out its judicial functions.

9.8　In view of our later recommendations about the length of members' terms of service in the second chamber, the terms for which Lords of Appeal in Ordinary can be appointed to the second chamber under the Appellate Jurisdiction Act 1876 should be amended to bring them into line with those of other members of the second chamber. To avoid any suggestion that their tenure could be affected by subjective considerations, they should automatically be reappointed if necessary for as long as they are entitled to sit on the Appellate or Appeal Committees.[7]

> **Recommendation 58**: The terms for which Lords of Appeal in Ordinary can be appointed to the second chamber under the Appellate Jurisdiction Act 1876 should be amended to bring them into line with those of other members of the second chamber, subject to automatic reappointment for as long as they are entitled to sit on the Appellate or Appeal Committees.

9.9　It is important that those exercising judicial functions should be, and be seen to be, open-minded and impartial in dealing with cases. Some mischief or inconvenience could arise if a Law Lord's participation in a debate or vote in the second chamber subsequently limited his or her ability to hear a related case. There is an argument that since the passage of the Human Rights Act and the Devolution Acts such risks have increased because

[7] i.e. until they reach the age of 75.

legislation on which members of the second chamber have commented or voted is more likely to be justiciable in the future. However, we consider that any problems can be dealt with by the judges exercising good sense and observing some basic conventions. The Rt Hon Lord Slynn of Hadley and The Rt Hon Lord Nicholls of Birkenhead explained when they came to see us that serving Law Lords would think seriously before expressing a view on a contentious issue and, if they did so, would then exclude themselves from considering any related case in the future.

9.10   We appreciate that these conventions have been under some pressure in recent months. It would be helpful, in our view, if they could be set out in writing so that there was a clear framework of principles within which Law Lords could decide what course of action they should take and against which those decisions could if necessary be measured.[8] Any such statement should clarify the line between the Law Lords' judicial functions and their role in the legislature and deal with the concerns referred to above.

> **Recommendation 59**: The Lords of Appeal should set out in writing and publish a statement of the principles which they intend to observe when participating in debates and votes in the second chamber and when considering their eligibility to sit on related cases.

The Lord Chancellor

9.11   It may be convenient at this point to respond to the proposals which have been put to us regarding the role of the Lord Chancellor. The fact that the Lord Chancellor is head of the judiciary in England and Wales and may sit on the Appellate Committee of the House of Lords is outside our terms of reference. The Lord Chancellor's role as a senior Cabinet Minister and head of an increasingly powerful executive Department is a matter for the Prime Minister. As we have said, we see advantage in maintaining the position that at least two Cabinet Ministers should be members of the second chamber and it could be seen as appropriate that major 'legal' Bills for which the Lord Chancellor is responsible should be introduced in the second chamber. The pending judgment of the European Court of Human Rights in the *McGonnell* v *the United Kingdom* case may require the position to be reviewed, but we do not consider that the present situation is incompatible with the public interest in an effective second chamber.

9.12   The Lord Chancellor's role as Speaker of the second chamber carries with it no powers and so has no implications for the post holder's other functions. We consider the point further in Chapter 16 in the context of discussing the role of the Speaker in the reformed second chamber.

The Lord Chancellor

---

[8] The Court of Appeal judgment in the *Lockabail* etc case, issued on 6 November 1999, deals with many of the issues which such a statement would need to cover.

Chapter 10 – Characteristics of the reformed second chamber

10.1 We have considered and made recommendations on the role and functions of the second chamber. Under our terms of reference our task now is "to make recommendations on the method or methods of composition required to constitute a second chamber fit for that role and those functions".

10.2 We decided that there was a necessary interim step. We considered what characteristics the second chamber's members, individually and collectively, should possess before deciding how those might best be secured.

Characteristics

10.3 Our consultation paper asked what characteristics the members of the second chamber should possess and what steps might be taken to secure them. We have been influenced by the suggestions we received and by the conclusions we reached about the second chamber's overall roles and functions. Our overriding concern has been to develop a vision of a reformed second chamber which has the necessary authority to do an effective job and is consistent with the principles underlying Parliamentary democracy. We conclude that the reformed second chamber should be:

- authoritative;

- confident; and

- broadly representative.

It should incorporate:

- breadth of expertise and a broad range of experience;

- particular knowledge and skills relevant to constitutional matters and human rights;

- an ability to bring philosophical, moral or spiritual perspectives to bear;

- personal distinction;

- freedom from party domination;

- a non-polemical style; and

- the ability to take a long-term view.

Authoritative

10.4 The reformed second chamber should be authoritative. It can and should play a vital role in scrutinising the executive, holding the Government to account and shaping legislation. It should therefore have the authority to ensure that its views and concerns are taken seriously. We have proposed that it should retain the power to hold up the enactment of primary legislation and have power to delay the implementation of secondary legislation. It should have the authority to wield those powers.

10.5 It is essential that the second chamber's authority should not be such as to challenge the ultimate authority of the House of Commons which derives directly from the electorate, through popular elections. It does not follow that there can be no role for the electorate in choosing members of the second chamber and we discuss possible options further in Chapters 11 and 12. But the greater the 'democratic legitimacy' of the second chamber, the greater the risk of damaging constitutional conflicts arising between the two Houses of Parliament.

10.6 It is, however, an error to suppose that the second chamber's authority can only stem from democratic election. Other potential sources of authority include:

- the extent to which the second chamber's members are broadly representative of the changing society which it seeks to serve;

- the breadth of experience and range of expertise which they possess;

- their individual personal distinction;

- the quality of the arguments they can bring to bear; and

- their ability to exercise an unfettered judgement, relatively free from partisan political control.

10.7 In our view, the members of the reformed second chamber, both collectively and individually, should possess all these characteristics in any case. But their presence will, in addition, contribute substantially to its overall authority and to its ability to make itself heard. A second chamber drawing on such a wide range of sources of authority would be well placed to carry out effectively the roles and functions we have recommended.

> **Recommendation 60:** The reformed second chamber should be authoritative. That authority could be derived from a number of sources, but should not be such as to challenge the ultimate democratic authority of the House of Commons.

Confident

10.8 The reformed second chamber should also be sufficiently confident to use its powers in what it judges to be the most effective and appropriate manner. Throughout the 20th century the House of Lords was inhibited both by its lack of authority and its lack of confidence. The reformed second chamber must be free of such debilitating inhibitions.

10.9   The second chamber should be cohesive. In determining how it should be composed and in considering its working practices, it will be important to ensure that members should be able to work well together, without being troubled by any sense or suggestion that some have a higher authority than others. Without such cohesion it would be difficult to generate the necessary confidence on the part of the second chamber as a whole.

> **Recommendation 61**: The reformed second chamber should be sufficiently confident and cohesive to use its powers effectively and appropriately.

Broadly representative

10.10 The reformed second chamber should be broadly representative of British society as a whole. The House of Commons is obviously representative in that MPs represent their individual geographic constituencies and reflect the electorate's basic political choices. Nevertheless, there is a gap to be filled. It is not possible for voters to reflect all aspects of their personality and experience through a single vote in a general election. The second chamber could gain significant strength and authority from being seen to be representative of British society in all its dimensions. However, it cannot and should not be a mere statistical microcosm of British society. The long-term aim should be for all sectors of society to feel they have a voice in the second chamber, expressed by a person or persons with whom they can identify. This might be achieved through a combination of:

- regional representation;

- gender balance;

- representation for ethnic and other minorities;

- vocational representation; and

- appropriate representation for voluntary, cultural, sporting and other organisations.

10.11 We discuss how such a breadth of representation might be achieved in later chapters of this report. The key point to register here is that a more broadly representative membership could provide a vigorous alternative source of authority for the second chamber without threatening the democratic authority of the House of Commons. It could also play an important role in reconnecting ordinary people with the political process.

10.12 For the reasons set out in Chapter 6, the reformed second chamber should provide a voice for the nations and regions of the United Kingdom. The people of all parts of the United Kingdom should know that their interests are being spoken for in the second chamber by people with whom they can identify. The level of direct regional representation should be sufficient to enable the second chamber to contribute effectively to the discussion of devolution and regional matters. It might well be raised if developments in the process of devolution or decentralisation make that appropriate.

10.13 The House of Lords has for far too long contained an excessive proportion of white males. Even the present life peerage, although it includes a higher proportion of women and members of minority ethnic groups than the former House of Lords, is far from being representative of British society in either respect. The reformed second chamber should be different. There should be steady progress towards gender balance and a more substantial representation of minority ethnic groups.

> **Recommendation 62:** The reformed second chamber should be broadly representative of British society as a whole.

Breadth of experience and range of expertise

10.14 One of the characteristics of the present House of Lords which was widely applauded during our consultation exercise was that it contains a substantial proportion of people who are not professional politicians, who have experience in a number of different walks of life and who can bring a considerable range of expertise to bear on issues of public concern. The support for this was reflected in the substantial number of proposals we received that members of the reformed second chamber should be drawn in some way from professional bodies, vocational groups and other organisations representative of specific sectors of society.

10.15 We discuss this concept and its practicalities further in Chapter 11, but it seems to us desirable that the reformed second chamber should continue to have members with a wide variety of experience in different walks of life. This would contribute to the goal of extending the range of perspectives from which issues are viewed by Parliament. It would be consistent with our desire to see a second chamber which was broadly representative of British society as a whole. It would reinforce the authority of the second chamber. Above all, the ability to call on at least some people with practical experience or relevant expertise in particular areas would reinforce the scrutinising role of the second chamber by helping it to assess the workability of proposals.

10.16 Having members with a range of relevant experience in the second chamber should not be seen as a substitute for consulting interested parties or taking evidence from relevant experts. Nevertheless, we see advantage in having people present in the second chamber who are familiar with the broad issues in a given area, who know what questions to ask and how to interpret the answers. People who have acquired relevant experience and expertise outside Parliament should be in a position to contribute actively to debates. Expert advisers, brought in from outside, however persuasive, could not have the same impact.

10.17 The present House of Lords has benefited from many of its members continuing their careers outside Parliament or maintaining contact with their former professions or occupations. Arrangements for constituting the reformed second chamber should allow this tradition to be maintained, so that at least some members can spend a proportion of their time actively engaged in work outside Parliament. Part-time membership of the second chamber should continue to be facilitated and even encouraged. There should be no minimum attendance requirement.

10.18 The range of expertise expected of members of the second chamber need not be prescribed in detail or remain constant over time. It should cover a broad spread of fields. Some particular types of expertise, likely to be of continuing relevance to the work of the second chamber, should always be represented in sufficient strength. The second chamber should contain people with a good grasp of the political and constitutional context within which the chamber will operate. It should contain people with an expert understanding of legal concepts and terminology and with practical experience of making and operating the law or developing public policies in a range of areas. There should be people with broad experience in public affairs and good analytical, influencing and debating skills. It should also contain people with broad experience of international, including European, affairs.

> **Recommendation 63:** The reformed second chamber should contain a substantial proportion of people who are not professional politicians, who have continuing experience in a range of different walks of life and who can bring a broad range of expertise to bear on issues of public concern. Accordingly, part-time membership of the second chamber should continue to be facilitated and even encouraged. There should be no minimum attendance requirement.

Particular knowledge and skills relevant to constitutional matters and human rights

10.19 In view of what we say in Chapter 5 about the second chamber's roles in relation to constitutional matters and human rights, its membership obviously needs to include people with knowledge and expertise in these areas.

10.20 In other countries, the consideration of constitutional matters and human rights issues is carried out by people of acknowledged independence with extensive legal and judicial experience. In this country, a strong contingent of experienced lawyers should be present in the reformed second chamber to help with this work. As currently, serving Law Lords would need to avoid committing themselves on particular issues which they might subsequently have to rule on. But retired Lords of Appeal in Ordinary or former holders of high judicial office would be free to contribute more fully. However, the consideration of constitutional and human rights matters is not a task which need, or should, be left exclusively to people with judicial experience or to lawyers. People with experience or expert knowledge of human rights issues and international human rights instruments would be required. Many of those members with the kind of qualities mentioned in paragraph 10.18, or others with a stock of accumulated wisdom, would be well placed to contribute to this work.

> **Recommendation 64:** The reformed second chamber should include members with the knowledge and skills necessary to enable it to discharge effectively its roles in relation to constitutional matters and human rights issues.

Philosophical, moral or spiritual perspectives

10.21 The House of Lords, uniquely among second chambers, provides seats in the legislature for representatives of an established religious body: the Church of England. We discuss the implications of this arrangement and whether it should continue in Chapter 15. But whatever the arguments for and against the representation of the Church of England, it is widely acknowledged that philosophical, moral or spiritual considerations should consistently be brought to bear on the discussion of public policy issues. The present House of Lords has benefited from having distinguished philosophers and leading members of other Christian denominations and other faiths – as well as Church of England bishops – among its members. There is a case for continuing to recognise the value and relevance of philosophical, moral and spiritual considerations in the constitution of a reformed second chamber. This could be accommodated in a range of ways, involving secular philosophers as well as religious leaders.

> **Recommendation 65:** The reformed second chamber should continue to include people who can help it to maintain a philosophical, moral or spiritual perspective on public policy issues.

Personal distinction

10.22 The second chamber should contain people of considerable personal distinction with established reputations in a variety of walks of life. Views and concerns expressed by such people are likely to be taken seriously. They can be expected to follow their conscience if it conflicts with the advice of their party whip and so will reinforce the second chamber's disposition to make independent judgements based on the merits of the issues concerned. Also, people who have already achieved a certain eminence may be better able to devote time to contributing to the work of the second chamber.

10.23 We see no tension between the desire to secure members of considerable personal distinction and the more general aim of constructing a truly representative second chamber. There should be opportunities for people from every sector of society to become members of the second chamber, whether or not they have achieved a recognised eminence. One important consideration will be the future of the current link between the award of a peerage and membership of the second chamber, which we discuss further in Chapter 18. Our view is that the link should be broken and that membership should be based on an evaluation of the contribution a person could make rather than being a reward for past services.

> **Recommendation 66:** The reformed second chamber should contain people of considerable personal distinction who have established reputations in various walks of life and can make a positive contribution to its work.

Freedom from party domination

10.24 As we observed in Chapter 3, it would be unrealistic to think that the second chamber could somehow be insulated from party politics or that it could function effectively without the involvement of political parties. As long as the second chamber retains a role in the determination of public policy and legislation, the political parties will demand access to it and find ways of securing a role for themselves.

10.25 It is nevertheless crucial that no one political party should be able to dominate the second chamber. If it were to be controlled by the party of Government it might become nothing more than a rubber stamp. If the main Opposition party were to gain control, it could be used to produce legislative deadlock and so trigger a series of constitutional conflicts. There should be a fair balance between the main political parties in the second chamber and no one party should ever be able to secure a majority. We accept, however, that the party of Government should have significant representation in the chamber so that it has a substantial pool of supporters to call on. The Government needs people who can serve as Ministers, explain and defend Government policies and provide some assurance that Government business will get through without undue delay or disruption.

10.26 We see advantages in preserving a strong independent element such as that represented in the present House of Lords by the Cross Benchers – members who are not affiliated to any political party. The existence of such an independent element would of course be consistent with our desire to see a second chamber which was more broadly representative of British society. People in all walks of life have political views, but the net should be cast sufficiently wide to ensure that a proportion of those selected to be members of the second chamber are not formally affiliated to any particular party and will sit on the Cross Benches. If the proportion of Cross Benchers were large enough, it would provide an absolute guarantee that no one political party could ever come to control the second chamber. The fact that the Cross Benchers might hold the 'balance of power' would encourage the parties' spokespersons to seek to win any arguments on their merits rather than by appealing to party loyalty or partisan interests. The authority of the second chamber would be reinforced if decisions were taken at least to some extent on the basis of an independent judgement of the merits of each case.

10.27 It would be wrong, however, to place the onus for ensuring independent-mindedness solely on Cross Benchers. During the consultation exercise our attention was repeatedly drawn – with approval – to examples of members of the House of Lords who were affiliated to a party but had not voted invariably in accordance with their party whip. We share the view that even those members of the second chamber who are affiliated to a party should be prepared to deal with issues on their merits and should exercise a certain independence of judgement.

10.28 More generally, members of the second chamber should not be beholden to or capable of being mandated by any other person or organisation. They should be 'representatives' in the Burkean tradition, not delegates. They should think and speak for themselves.

> **Recommendation 67:** The reformed second chamber should not be capable of being dominated by any one political party and its members should be encouraged and enabled to deal with issues on their merits.

A non-polemical style

10.29 The second chamber would benefit from preserving the relatively non-polemical style of the present House of Lords. This feature of the present House of Lords was widely supported by respondents to our consultation exercise. A non-polemical style would be a natural corollary of ensuring that no one political party could control the second chamber and that it contained a significant proportion of independents. Such a style would be consistent with the second chamber's general function of providing dispassionate, well-informed scrutiny of proposed legislation and of the actions of the executive.

Committee room in the House of Lords

10.30 Membership of the second chamber should not be seen as a stepping stone to membership of the House of Commons. If this were the case, it could lead to the development of a more partisan style within the chamber which could undermine attempts to deliver some of the other characteristics of the second chamber we have identified as being desirable.

> **Recommendation 68:** The reformed second chamber should preserve the relatively non-polemical style of the present House of Lords.

Longer-term perspective

10.31 One of the strengths of the present House of Lords is that its members often have a relatively long-term perspective – perhaps because they serve for life and do not need to seek reelection or reappointment. So far as possible, this feature should be perpetuated in the reformed second chamber. A long-term view makes for better legislation. The interests of future generations are more likely to be taken into account in shaping legislation and scrutinising Government proposals.

10.32 We would hope to see the chamber accumulating wisdom and experience and maintaining a broadly consistent overall approach. A reasonable degree of continuity of membership from one period to another would help to facilitate this.

> **Conclusion:** Members of the reformed second chamber should have a long-term perspective and the chamber should have a reasonable degree of continuity of membership from one period to another.

Chapter 11 – Principles of composition

11.1   In determining the method or methods to be adopted for constituting the second chamber, it is essential to bear in mind the characteristics (summarised in Chapter 10) which those methods will need to produce. In this chapter we set out and explain the broad conclusions we have reached on the composition of the second chamber. Chapters 12 and 13 discuss specific proposals and practical questions arising from those conclusions.

11.2   We begin by reviewing the likely performance of various proposed methods of composition in terms of their ability to deliver the characteristics we think the second chamber should possess.

Direct election

11.3   In a democracy there is a natural presumption in favour of election as the appropriate way of constituting the second chamber. There was considerable support for direct election among respondents to our consultation exercise. Election implies direct accountability to the electorate. It was also argued that, if the second chamber were to retain the power to veto, or at least delay, legislation passed by the House of Commons and to act as a check on the executive, it should have some electoral authority to justify the exercise of such power and to give it the confidence to use that power. A second chamber with at least a significant proportion of directly elected members would have the necessary political weight to carry out the responsibilities we propose it should have and its decisions would be more widely seen as politically legitimate. There is a danger that, without a directly elected element, the reformed second chamber might decline into an assemblage of respected but politically ineffective dignitaries. Directly elected members could provide an essential element in a body which would derive its authority from a number of sources.

11.4   These points led us to the view that the second chamber should contain at least some members who would be chosen on a basis which directly reflects the balance of political opinion within each nation and region of the United Kingdom; but, in reaching that view, we were conscious of the arguments against direct election. A review of those arguments, in the light of the characteristics summarised in Chapter 10, reveals the strength of the case against having a wholly – or even a largely – directly elected second chamber.

11.5   A second chamber which was wholly or largely directly elected would certainly be authoritative and confident, but the source of its authority could bring it into direct conflict with the House of Commons. There would be a risk that the second chamber would have a different political complexion from the House of Commons. Such a divergence would, whatever the formal distinctions between the chambers in terms of their powers and pre-eminence, be bound to give rise to constitutional conflicts. A different risk would arise if the second chamber had the same political complexion as the House of Commons because that could cause it to act as a compliant rubber stamp for whatever any future Government might want to do.

11.6 Regardless of its political complexion, the central objection to a directly elected second chamber is that it would, by its very nature, represent a challenge to the pre-eminence of the House of Commons and make it difficult to strike the balance between the powers of the two Houses that our terms of reference require and that we have recommended. There would, in particular, be no justification for a continuation of the Salisbury Convention (see Chapter 4). If a directly elected second chamber were to be opposed to a Bill, it would not be easy to argue that it should, save in exceptional circumstances, defer to the views of the other directly elected chamber. We would be strongly opposed to a situation in which the two Houses of Parliament had equivalent electoral legitimacy. It would represent a substantial change in the present constitutional settlement in the United Kingdom and would almost certainly be a recipe for damaging conflict.

11.7 Various ways of avoiding this problem of competing mandates were suggested to us, but none seems to us to be free of difficulty.

■ Any attempt to solve the problem by **limiting the formal powers** of an elected second chamber would be likely to fail because members of such a chamber would not regard the limits as justified.

■ The use of a **proportional electoral system** for the second chamber would distinguish it from the more decisive political contest for the House of Commons. This would reduce, if not eliminate, the risk of the second chamber being dominated by either the Government or the Opposition. But it could exacerbate the problem of competing mandates by enabling the second chamber to claim that it was *more* representative of public opinion than the House of Commons.

■ The use of **staggered terms** would tend to smooth out fluctuations in political opinion. It would mean that the second chamber could never claim an electoral mandate which was as contemporary as that of the House of Commons. But this would not eliminate the risks mentioned above.

■ Awarding an **equal number of seats in the second chamber to each national or regional unit** in the United Kingdom, rather than sharing them out on a population basis, might also tend to reduce the risk that the second chamber could claim a competing electoral mandate. However, the great disparity between the sizes of the different nations and regions of the United Kingdom means that an equal distribution of seats would be inappropriate (especially as, unlike the United States, which provides equal representation for each state in the Senate, the United Kingdom is not a federal entity). A more graduated distribution of seats broadly linked to population might still result in a second chamber with a mandate perceived to be capable of challenging that of the House of Commons.

■ Incorporating a small proportion of **non-elected members** in a largely elected second chamber might reduce the overall 'democratic legitimacy' of the second chamber. However, this particular blend of membership would maximise the risk of tensions developing between the two different components. There would be a tendency for observers to attribute greater political weight to the views and votes of the elected members than to those of non-elected members.

11.8   A wholly directly elected second chamber could not be broadly representative of the complex strands of British society. The fact is that elections can only be fought effectively by organised political parties which can attract large blocks of voters and who have the resources to organise television broadcasts, publicity, canvassing, public meetings and the like. While most major political parties are broad churches whose members and supporters are generally representative of British society, it is inevitable that in choosing electoral candidates they will select people who will epitomise the party's distinct ethos and who have demonstrated both their long-term loyalty to the party and their effectiveness in advancing its interests. Successful candidates for any direct elections to the second chamber would almost certainly come from a narrow class of people who are politically aware and highly partisan and who have to a very considerable degree already committed their lives to political activity. Putting it bluntly but accurately, a wholly elected second chamber would in practice mean that British public life was dominated even more than it is already by professional politicians.

11.9   By the same token, total reliance on direct election would in practice be incompatible with securing membership for people with relevant experience of and expertise in other walks of life. Such people would generally be reluctant to commit themselves to a party platform or engage in electioneering and would therefore be unlikely to put themselves forward as candidates for election. They would also be unlikely to be successful if they did so. While they might be well known in their field, such people rarely achieve widespread popular recognition or support. They lack the skills necessary to fight an electoral battle. Direct election would therefore be unlikely to produce members with the ability to speak directly for the voluntary sector, the professions, cultural and sporting interests and a whole range of other important aspects of British society.

11.10 In addition, most systems of direct election deliver results which may be geographically representative but which are seldom gender-balanced or provide appropriate representation for ethnic, religious or other minorities.

11.11 Direct elections are also not well suited to securing membership of the second chamber for those with specific expertise and authority in constitutional matters and the protection of human rights. Indeed, it could be counter-productive to base the selection of people with such characteristics on a popular election. There would be some risk that successful candidates would find it difficult to maintain the necessary detached and quasi-judicial approach to their responsibilities. Nor is it easy to see how direct election could reliably produce members of the second chamber who could make a specialist contribution to the discussion of philosophical, moral or spiritual issues.

11.12 Another fundamental criticism of any proposal that the membership should be wholly or largely elected is that it would significantly reduce the prospects for securing a second chamber which was relatively independent of the influence of political parties. Very few independents, if any, would secure election, even using a highly proportional system such as Single Transferable Vote (STV). Successful candidates for election would nearly all be closely associated with political parties and essentially dependent on those parties. Under the current system for appointing life peers to the House of Lords, the parties have been good at nominating at least some people who are not professional politicians, who are personally distinguished in their own right and who sometimes take a relatively independent line. But if the parties were nominating candidates for election, their criteria would be likely to change. The emphasis would be on selecting people with the political commitment and campaigning skills likely to bring out the vote and win the election. Moreover, such elections would be fought on manifestos or programmes which would bind those who were elected and reinforce the extent to which they would be creatures of party rather than relatively dispassionate individuals, albeit with party allegiances.

11.13 Another real obstacle to the use of direct election is the risk that the introduction of yet another round of elections, possibly involving yet another electoral system, would contribute to what has become known as 'voter fatigue'. A very low turnout for any election to the second chamber could serve to undermine its authority. Voters are currently expected to vote in local government elections, Westminster elections, European Parliament elections and, where relevant, for the Scottish Parliament and the Welsh or Northern Ireland Assemblies. Shortly, some of them will be voting for the London Assembly and the Mayor for London. The only two pairs of elections in that list which use the same electoral system are local government (in Great Britain) and Westminster elections and those for the Scottish Parliament and the National Assembly for Wales.[1] There is also a growing practice of inviting the electorate to express its views in referendums. Any increase in the number or variety of elections would be a recipe for voter alienation as well as confusion. In the light of US experience, which has seen the extension of opportunities to vote accompanied by a steady decline in turnout, we would be reluctant to propose an additional electoral contest, especially one using yet another electoral system.

11.14 There is, however, one point arising from our consideration of the option of direct election for at least some members of the second chamber that is worth noting at this stage. During the course of our work we commissioned two papers from the Public Policy Group at the London School of Economics[2] that discussed what principles might be applicable to elections to the second chamber and what options might be explored. They used general and European election data going back to 1974 to model the outcomes that might be expected from the use of different electoral systems to select members of the second chamber. One of the points to emerge most clearly was that if the overall political balance of the second chamber had been determined by reference to the parties' shares of the vote at national or regional level in any general or European election since the mid-1970s, it would always have produced a chamber in which every party had a proportional share of the seats, the Government party was normally the largest but no single party ever had a majority. This observation holds true for every general election since 1901, except for the two in the 1930s in which governing coalitions won more than 50 per cent of the popular vote. As we want to achieve a second chamber with exactly those characteristics, this finding seemed highly relevant to our work.

Indirect election

11.15 We discussed the pros and cons of indirect election from the devolved institutions in Chapter 6 and from among United Kingdom MEPs in Chapter 8. For the reasons given in these chapters, we do not support any system of representation in, or indirect

---

[1] In Northern Ireland the STV electoral system is used for European Parliament, Assembly and local government elections.
[2] P. Dunleavy and H. Margetts. *Electing Members of the Lords (or Senate)*. LSE Public Policy Group (consolidated and revised November 1999). Full paper available on the enclosed CD-ROM.

election to, the second chamber from these sources.[3] Similar objections apply to any proposal that members of the second chamber should be indirectly elected by local government electoral colleges.

11.16 Additionally, we see no reason to believe that indirectly elected members of the second chamber would be broadly representative of British society, be likely to have the requisite range of expertise and experience or possess the other specific characteristics which members of the second chamber should have. In any event, at least under present circumstances, indirect election would really only be relevant in respect of those regions which already have devolved institutions, i.e. Scotland, Wales, Northern Ireland and perhaps London. It could therefore only make a partial contribution to the composition of the second chamber and would be unfair to most of England. Further difficulties would probably arise from the fact that indirectly elected members would only be able to serve for the term of their sponsoring Parliament or Assembly.

Vocational/interest group representation

11.17 The consultation exercise showed that there was considerable interest in finding a way for various specified vocational or other interest groups to be represented in the second chamber. A number of ingenious schemes were presented to us.

11.18 We are sympathetic to the aims behind such proposals. In principle, any system which reliably identified leading figures from among the professions, the Chartered Institutes and a range of other vocational or interest groups should produce independent-minded people of some personal distinction. These people could be expected to have a range of expertise and experience from outside the world of politics and be broadly representative of British society in its various manifestations. Whether such people were appointed to the second chamber on an *ex officio* basis or elected through a variety of electoral colleges, they could reasonably claim a considerable degree of democratic legitimacy and authority.

11.19 However, further examination reveals serious practical obstacles to all such proposals.

11.20 Several proposals envisaged *ex officio* appointment to the second chamber of specified post holders in a range of organisations. One problem with this is illustrated by the fact that, of the dozens of lists of organisations put to us in evidence, no two were the same. It would probably be impossible to reach agreement on which sectors of society should be represented in the second chamber in this way, on the balance between the different sectors and on which organisations best represented them. Keeping abreast of changes in society and in the significance of particular organisations within the various sectors could also pose a problem. Any mechanism which required such assessments to be made would generate continued argument within and among professional, vocational and other interest groups as to which of them was most 'representative' of their sector of society. Several people suggested that a commission of some kind should be established to keep

---

[3] In essence, we do not favour dual mandates; there would be a total mismatch between the responsibilities which the people concerned were elected to discharge and their role in the second chamber, which would open up a significant gap in accountability; it would exacerbate, rather than resolve, the West Lothian Question; and there would be a risk that members chosen in this way would act as delegates from those who appointed them to the second chamber rather than as representatives in the wider sense. These difficulties would arise in an even more acute form if members of the second chamber were elected or appointed by, rather than drawn from, the institutions concerned.

under review the representative mix and the allocation of seats to particular organisations; but if required to reach judgements about the balances to be struck between organisations (as distinct from individuals), its members would have a difficult and unenviable task.

11.21 A further difficulty is that it might not be appropriate to appoint particular office holders to the second chamber. Some offices rotate on an annual basis, which would give holders insufficient time to make any mark in the second chamber. Some offices might be honorary while others might be full-time executive posts, leaving the holders little time to devote to the work of the second chamber. In any case, the qualities which bring recognition within a profession or organisation might not necessarily be relevant to membership of the second chamber. A more fundamental concern is that such posts might often be in the gift of a small and unrepresentative clique within the organisation concerned. One way round that, which was put to us in evidence, would be to require the organisations in question to observe minimum standards of democracy in the appointment of their office holders. We felt this would be an unacceptable intrusion into the internal affairs of those organisations, quite apart from being impossible to police effectively. There would also be a risk of drawing the second chamber into disputes over the constitution of relevant organisations, for example in respect of how accessible they are to women or members of minority ethnic groups.

11.22 Other proposals in this general area envisaged the establishment of a series of electoral colleges where people from a particular profession would be able, on presenting some appropriate accreditation, to vote for someone to represent that profession in the second chamber. In some versions of this idea, a whole series of different sets of candidates might be available for electors to choose from: a person might choose to exercise her vote as a woman, selecting a candidate representing women's interests; as a member of an ethnic or religious minority; or as a member of a particular profession. These proposals suffer from two main problems. First, it would be virtually impossible to ensure that the initial selection of candidates to go on the various lists was carried out on a fair and open basis. It would be easy for small groups within particular professions or sectors of society to dominate and control the nomination process. Second, and more significantly, it would be difficult for individual voters to develop the ability to exercise a sensible choice. Apart from the members of a few small and tightly organised professions, most voters in any such system would be presented with choices between candidates they did not know anything about and with no way of assessing their positions on major public policy issues. Some of the proposals put to us would also be liable to confuse and overawe voters by giving them such a range of choice that there would be no realistic prospect of them being able to exercise a meaningful judgement.

11.23 A further serious objection to most of the proposals in this category is that they would risk disenfranchising those people, often the relatively disadvantaged, who do not belong to a recognised professional or vocational group.

11.24 An even more fundamental objection to all of the various proposals for vocational and interest group representation is that they assume that human beings are to be regarded as being merely the sum of their 'interests', usually defined in terms of their occupational, professional or other economic interests. But of course that is not so – and indeed might be regarded as embodying a demeaning view of human nature and the human condition. Lorry drivers are not merely lorry drivers. Nurses are not merely nurses. They are also mothers, fathers, sons, daughters, football fans, DIY enthusiasts, gardeners, travellers and charity workers – and any one of these identities may well be more important to them than their identity as a lorry driver or nurse. No system of vocational or interest group representation is able to accommodate this fundamental fact.

11.25 All these points lead us to conclude that any formal system of vocational or interest group representation used to constitute the second chamber would run into insuperable practical obstacles as well as difficulties of principle. The objectives of those favouring this kind of approach could be more reliably delivered through the establishment of an appointments system which had a clear remit to secure the appointment of people broadly representative of British society in a variety of dimensions.

Random selection

11.26 A system of random selection might produce a microcosm of British society and thus achieve the target of a broadly representative second chamber which was gender-balanced and gave fair representation to all kinds of vocational, cultural, ethnic and other interests. However, even if the practical difficulties of enabling and persuading randomly selected individuals to take on the task of membership of the second chamber could be overcome, it would not deliver sufficient people with the specific personal qualities and expertise which would be desirable. Giving people the opportunity to put themselves forward for selection (as if entering a lottery) would undermine the whole concept of random selection without providing any significant additional reassurance that the people concerned would have the necessary qualities. Random selection would also be unlikely to secure members with sufficient individual or collective authority to challenge the Government and persuade the House of Commons to take the second chamber's concerns seriously.

Co-option

11.27 It was suggested by some, including the Democratic Audit, that the benefits of breadth of experience could be secured within a primarily elected second chamber by giving elected members authority to co-opt relevant experts to contribute to the work of the second chamber, either generally or in respect of particular Bills. This seems to us to represent the worst of both worlds. The directly elected element would bring all the disadvantages noted above; and, if the elected members and the political parties they represented were to control the co-option process, the nominated element could not claim to have been chosen on an independent and impartial basis. With two distinct categories of member, the chamber would be far from cohesive, with the views of the elected members likely to be overwhelmingly dominant. The proposal does not seem to us to offer any advantage over the current practice of appointing expert advisers to support the committee work of the present House of Lords.

An independent appointments system

11.28 We discuss the practical issues relating to the establishment and operation of an independent Appointments Commission in Chapter 13. At this stage we focus on the principle of an independent appointments system for the second chamber.

11.29 A genuinely independent appointments system, with appropriate terms of reference, ought to be able to ensure that the members of a reformed second chamber were broadly representative of British society. It would be an effective way to secure gender balance and an appropriate representation for ethnic, religious and other minorities. It could also ensure that different facets of life – cultural, sporting, the voluntary sector and so on – had a voice in the second chamber. Mechanisms could be established to ensure that any such system developed a good understanding of the whole range of professional and vocational organisations and interest groups and was in a position to identify people with appropriate experience and expertise who were likely to be able to make an effective contribution to the second chamber's work. An appointments system would be able, for example, to identify people who could support the functions of the second chamber in relation to constitutional matters and human rights. A continuation of the practice of appointing Law Lords to the second chamber would sit more easily alongside an appointments system, as would our proposals regarding the representation of religious faiths (see Chapter 15).

11.30 Above all, an appointments system independent of any political control would limit the influence of the political parties on the second chamber and provide the only sure way of securing a reasonable proportion of independent members to sit on the Cross Benches.

11.31 There are three possible disadvantages of an independent appointments system. First, it would have very substantial power which would need to be subject to appropriate safeguards and scrutiny. Second, there would be no voice for the electorate in the choice of members of the second chamber. Third, a centralised appointments system would not necessarily be good at identifying people to provide a regional voice in the second chamber. As we were told at our public hearing in Newcastle, people in the regions would not regard someone selected *for* their region by a London-based Appointments Commission as being an adequate substitute for someone selected *by* their region. (A possible way round this would be for an appointments system to establish regional panels, but that could give rise to concern that the circle of people in any one region who might be appointed to the panel or selected for appointment to the second chamber would become incestuous.) In any event, it would be necessary to find a way of determining the political balance in the second chamber. Without guidance, an independent appointments system would not be equipped to make the important political judgements which would be required.

Current arrangements for making appointments

11.32 Up to now the arrangements for appointing life peers have been somewhat haphazard. There is no system of inviting widespread nominations and assessing candidates through a hierarchy of expert assessment groups as there is for the honours system. In respect of 'working peers' the Government reaches an understanding with the other main parties in the House of Commons as to the number of nominations each is to make. The parties do not appear to have any systematic machinery for identifying appropriate candidates. Ministers, the Cabinet Secretary and other senior public servants may draw the Prime Minister's attention to deserving candidates. All nominations for life peerages are passed to the Political Honours Scrutiny Committee[4] which receives information from the parties' Chief Whips about the individuals' political donations and may also have access to checks run by the Inland Revenue, the Security Service, the police and relevant

---

[4] A Committee of Privy Counsellors set up in the 1920s following concern about the sale of honours.

Departments. The Committee may withhold its approval to a particular nomination on the grounds of propriety, but in practice only about 1 per cent of nominations are challenged (although the very existence of the Committee does presumably serve to inhibit potential abuse). The Prime Minister forwards the resulting list of nominations to the Queen.

11.33 In the White Paper *Modernising Parliament. Reforming the House of Lords*, the Government has set out its proposals for the handling of appointments to the interim House of Lords. These involve the establishment of an independent but non-statutory Appointments Commission which will be responsible for identifying suitable Cross Bench nominees and for vetting all party nominations (taking over the role of the Political Honours Scrutiny Committee). The Prime Minister will continue to be responsible for determining the numbers of nominations which each political party can make but he has committed himself to aiming for no more than parity of numbers as between Labour and the main Opposition party. He has also made clear that, save in wholly exceptional circumstances, he will not seek to exercise any influence over any nominations other than those from his own party. As to Cross Bench nominations, the White Paper says that the Appointments Commission "will operate an open and transparent nomination system for Cross Bench peers, both actively inviting public nominations and encouraging suitable bodies to make nominations. The general qualities being sought and the type of information required to support a nomination will be made public. It will seek to cast its net wider than the present system to achieve successful nominations". These interim arrangements will clearly be an improvement over the previous arrangements for appointing life peers, but in our view they would be unsatisfactory as a long-term basis for securing appointments to the second chamber.

Cross Benchers

11.34 As we have noted before, there is widespread support for the preservation of a strong cadre of independent members in the second chamber. Chapter 10 explains why we agree that this is essential. In the present House of Lords the proportion of Cross Benchers (excluding the Lords of Appeal in Ordinary) is just under 20 per cent of the total membership.[5] While in the past the attendance rate of Cross Benchers has been lower than that of party-affiliated members, Cross Benchers have regularly provided at least 10 per cent of the members present on a typical day. It is too early to say what pattern will develop in the interim House of Lords, but in our view at least 20 per cent of the members of the reformed second chamber[6] should not be affiliated to any of the main political parties. This would be a large enough proportion to ensure that no single party could achieve a working majority in the second chamber. It would also be sufficient to encourage the political parties to present their cases in a relatively dispassionate way, designed to attract the Cross Benchers' support.

Overall conclusions on principles of composition

11.35 Our recommendations on composition take account not only of all the points mentioned in this chapter and Chapter 10 but also of a number of the practical considerations which are dealt with in Chapter 12. We set out below our broad overall conclusions.

---

[5] In addition the 26 Church of England bishops do not take a party whip.

[6] Excluding the Lords of Appeal in Ordinary and any representatives of Christian denominations, but including members of smaller (e.g. regional) parties.

11.36 Our primary judgements are that we could *not* recommend:

- a wholly or largely directly elected second chamber;

- indirect election from the devolved institutions (or local government electoral colleges) or from among British MEPs;

- random selection; or

- co-option.

We were attracted by the principle of vocational or interest group representation but concluded that its objectives could more reliably be delivered through an independent appointments system. Overall, a genuinely independent appointments system seemed most likely to create a second chamber with most of the characteristics we were looking for; but by itself it would suffer from the disadvantages mentioned in paragraph 11.31. Our proposal for resolving these dilemmas is that an independent appointments system should be supplemented by an arrangement which would give the regional electorates a voice in the selection of members of the second chamber; these members would for the first time provide a voice in Parliament for the nations and regions of the United Kingdom. We also propose that the overall political balance in the second chamber should be determined by a simple formula. This would require the independent appointments system to ensure that the political balance within the reformed second chamber matches the overall balance of political opinion in the country as expressed in votes cast at the most recent general election.

> **Conclusion:** We cannot recommend:
>
> - a wholly or largely directly elected second chamber;
>
> - indirect election from the devolved institutions (or local government electoral colleges) or from among British MEPs;
>
> - random selection; or
>
> - co-option.

> **Recommendation 69:** Our broad overall recommendations on composition are that an independent appointments system should be supplemented by an arrangement which would give the regional electorate a voice in the selection of regional members and that the political balance in the reformed second chamber should match that of the country as expressed in votes cast at the most recent general election.

11.37 We acknowledge the importance of ensuring that all members of the new second chamber have equal status, whatever the basis of their membership of the chamber. We discuss the point further in Chapter 12.

11.38 In favouring an independent appointments system, we are building on the direction set by the Government in establishing an independent Appointments Commission to be responsible for appointments to the interim House of Lords. However, we consider that leaving the Prime Minister with the power to determine the political balance in the second chamber by deciding the number of nominations each party should make would be inconsistent with the need to establish the reformed second chamber's independence and its freedom from undue political influence. We also see no reason why an Appointments Commission should be limited to the task of identifying suitable Cross Bench members of the second chamber. In our view, an Appointments Commission should have a far wider remit. It should be geared towards constructing a second chamber which would be broadly representative of British society as a whole and should be empowered to appoint members who happen to be affiliated to a political party but who have characteristics which justify their appointment on wider grounds.

11.39 Arising from that brief summary of the broad factors which influenced our conclusions, it may be helpful if we summarise our overall recommendations at this point.

Recommendation 70:

- An Appointments Commission, independent of the Prime Minister, Government and the political parties, should be responsible for all appointments to the second chamber.

- A significant minority of the members of the second chamber should be 'regional members'[7] selected on a basis which directly reflects the balance of political opinion within the regional electorates, to provide a voice for the nations and regions of the United Kingdom.

- The Appointments Commission should ensure that at least 20 per cent of the members of the second chamber[8] are not affiliated to one of the major parties.

- The Appointments Commission should exercise its own judgement in selecting appointees who are affiliated to political parties. It should of course have regard to nominations made by the political parties, which it would also vet for propriety.

- In making appointments, the Appointments Commission should be required to ensure that members of the second chamber are broadly representative of British society on a range of stated dimensions. They should possess a variety of expertise and experience and various specific qualities appropriate to the role and functions of the reformed second chamber.

- It should be under a statutory duty to ensure that a minimum of 30 per cent of new members of the second chamber should be women, and a minimum of 30 per cent men, with the aim of making steady progress towards gender balance in the chamber as a whole over time. It should also be required to use its best endeavours to ensure a level of representation for members of minority ethnic groups which is at least proportionate to their presence in the population as a whole. It should also play a role in ensuring appropriate representation for religious faiths (see Chapter 15).

- One of the tasks of the Appointments Commission in making appointments to the second chamber should be to achieve or maintain an overall balance among all those members affiliated to political parties (both regional members and directly appointed members) which matches the distribution of votes between the parties at the most recent general election.

[7] From here on we use the term 'regional member' to include members drawn from Scotland, Wales and Northern Ireland as well as those drawn from the English regions.

[8] Excluding the Lords of Appeal in Ordinary and any representatives of Christian denominations, but including members of smaller (e.g. regional) parties.

11.40 The last recommendation should be subject to a quota. It should only apply to parties which secure more than, say, 2 per cent of the total votes cast in a general election. The quota should be high enough to prevent a proliferation of minor parties staking a claim to membership of the second chamber on the basis that about 0.2 per cent of the vote should give them one seat in the second chamber. On the other hand, it should be low enough to ensure representation for political parties whose support is thinly spread. Parties which are strong in particular regions could well secure a 'regional' seat in the second chamber, but the quota should otherwise operate to secure fair representation for them.

11.41 The overall result should be a second chamber that is more democratic and more representative than the present House of Lords. It will be *more democratic* because the membership as a whole (excluding the Cross Benchers) will reflect the balance of political opinion within the country as expressed at the most recent general election and because the 'regional' members will be proportionally representative of political opinion within their respective regions. It will be *more representative*, because it will contain members from all parts of the country and from all walks of life, broadly equal numbers of men and women and representatives of all the country's main ethnic and religious communities.

11.42 Chapter 12 makes further proposals and discusses a number of practical issues arising from these broad conclusions and Chapter 13 sets out our recommendations regarding the establishment and operation of an independent Appointments Commission.

Chapter 12 – Composition: specific proposals and practicalities

12.1 Several practical considerations significantly influenced the broad conclusions on the composition of the new second chamber we have set out in Chapter 11. In this chapter we explain our thinking on these points, in part to offer a rationale for those conclusions and also because it leads to some specific recommendations on the detailed implementation of our proposals.

12.2 The practical considerations can be grouped under three headings:

- mixed membership;

- terms of membership; and

- the selection of regional members.

12.3 We discuss the overall size of the reformed second chamber in Chapter 13. We do not believe it is necessary for the second chamber to have a fixed number of members or for there to be an upper limit on the number of its members. But, for the reasons given in Chapter 13, we would expect the new chamber to have in the region of 550 members overall, including many who would participate on a part-time basis. The specific recommendations made in the rest of this chapter are based on a membership in the region of 550.

Mixed membership

12.4 We referred in Chapter 10 to the importance we attach to ensuring that the reformed second chamber is a cohesive body, with none of its members regarded as having greater legitimacy or authority than any others. If some members were seen to have greater legitimacy than others, perhaps because they had been directly elected, any vote carried against the wishes of those members could, and probably would, be called into question.

12.5 Creating a cohesive second chamber is an important requirement. Once members have arrived in the chamber, by whatever route, they should so far as possible serve the same terms, benefit from the same allowances and facilities and be treated in all respects identically. If our proposals for the composition of the reformed second chamber are accepted, the rationale which underlies them should ensure that all the members enjoy parity of esteem.

12.6 There are, however, more practical reasons for believing that a second chamber composed along the lines we recommend will not encounter serious 'mixed membership' problems. First, the number of regional members we propose is not so large as to dominate the chamber or undermine its cohesiveness. Second, whereas the great majority of the votes cast by hereditary peers in the old House of Lords supported one political party, the regional members, like the directly appointed members in the reformed second chamber, will be politically balanced. Accordingly, the votes of regional members will only rarely be decisive in determining the outcome. Finally, and significantly, the political status of regional members, however they are chosen, will be on a par with that of the party-affiliated appointed members because the party balance of the second chamber as a whole will be determined by the outcome of the preceding general election.

> **Recommendation 71**: All members of the second chamber should so far as possible serve the same terms, benefit from the same allowances and facilities and be treated in all respects identically, in order to minimise the risk of 'mixed membership' problems. There are also more practical reasons for believing that our specific proposals would not give rise to 'mixed membership' problems.

Terms of membership

12.7   Apart from the Church of England bishops, all members of the present House of Lords – the Lords of Appeal in Ordinary, the life peers and the remaining hereditary peers – are members for life. Life membership, or something which amounted to nearly the same thing, would bring distinct benefits to the reformed second chamber. It would:

- encourage members to be independent-minded and take a long-term view;

- discourage the politically ambitious from seeking a place in the second chamber;

- contribute to a less partisan style of debate;

- allow members time to absorb the distinctive ethos of the second chamber and to learn how to contribute most effectively to its proceedings; and

- be consistent with part-time membership. If members were appointed for short terms, they might feel obliged to commit themselves to the work of the chamber full-time.

12.8   However, the continuation of life membership for the reformed second chamber would also have disadvantages.

12.9   Life membership for the new second chamber would result in an elderly chamber. The average age at death of members of the House of Lords in recent years has been 81.5. The departure of most of the hereditary peers has already led to an increase in the average age of the present House of Lords to 69. Given current trends in life expectancy, life membership in the second chamber would inevitably produce a continual rise in the average age of members. Younger members could, of course, be appointed to reduce the average age. But the constant compensation required for ageing life members would result in a consistent and ultimately enormous increase in the size of the second chamber. Introducing an option to retire would yield some reduction in the average age of members but probably not a large one: several life peers remain active members of the present House of Lords even though they are well into their nineties. Such an elderly chamber would not be representative of British society as a whole.

12.10 Life membership would also significantly reduce the number of new members entering the second chamber. If, on the basis of life membership, members served for an average of 30 years (roughly the average for current life peers) instead of, say, 15 years, it would halve the number of new members who could be introduced in an average year. The Appointments Commission would find it exceedingly difficult to achieve or maintain a properly balanced chamber.

12.11 Life membership would also be difficult to combine with any system of election, as distinct from appointment, to the reformed second chamber. Election for life is not a concept likely to find favour at the beginning of the 21st century.

12.12 Perhaps most fundamentally, life membership could easily lead over time, as the White Paper noted, to the emergence of awkward imbalances among the parties. To illustrate this point, the following chart shows the age profiles of the existing life peers by party. Assuming average mortality rates, the consequence of these profiles is that the party balance among the existing life peers over the next 15 years will change significantly. The Appointments Commission could in theory correct party imbalances whenever they began to appear; but that might not prove at all easy in practice, especially if the rate at which new members were introduced was low. Also, a 'see-saw effect' could develop. New members of one party would soon have to be balanced by new members of another party, who in turn would have to be balanced by more members of the first party. The whole cycle might continue indefinitely.

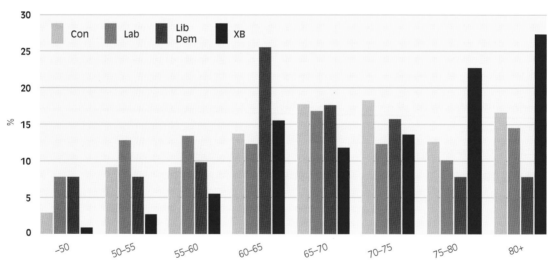

Age profile of existing life peers by party

12.13 A related consideration, already alluded to in paragraph 12.5, is that, in the interests of producing a cohesive second chamber, its members should serve for terms of similar length, however they are chosen. Taking all these considerations together, we recommend that all members of the second chamber should serve for the equivalent of three electoral cycles.

12.14 For reasons set out below, we envisage that regional members would be selected on either general election days or European Parliament election days. Whichever option is chosen, we recommend that regional members serve for three terms. Working on the basis of post-war experience and ignoring general elections which occurred within two years of the previous election,[1] if regional members were chosen on general election days, three terms would mean a minimum of 10 years and a maximum of 14, with the average being 12.6 years. To achieve approximate equivalence, appointed members might therefore serve for either 12 or 15 years. If regional members were chosen on the day of European

---

[1] Obviously, if there were a succession of short Parliaments, it would be necessary to count from the previous election which was not ignored.

Parliament elections, they would, in effect, serve a fixed term of 15 years. Other members could also be appointed for 15 years.

12.15 We did consider whether terms based on two electoral cycles, rather than three, would be long enough to secure our desired objectives. Working on the same principles as in paragraph 12.14, we calculated that, using a general election cycle, regional members would serve for between 6 and 10 years. An equivalent term for appointed members would perhaps be 9 years. Using the European Parliament electoral cycle would result in terms of 10 years for both regional and appointed members. However, having considered this option, we concluded that terms of this length would be too short for the purposes of creating the kind of second chamber which we envisage.

> **Recommendation 72**: Regional members, whatever the precise means of their selection, should serve for the equivalent of three electoral cycles and appointed members should serve for fixed terms of 15 years.

12.16 One possible criticism is that terms of this length would make it hard for regional electorates or anyone else to hold members of the reformed second chamber to account. But that is precisely the point. One of our central aims is to recommend the creation of a second chamber whose members can speak and vote with a substantial degree of independence and who are in a position to take a long-term view. We want the regional members, in particular, to act as a voice for their regions. We do *not* want them to be constantly looking over their shoulders at either their electorates or their regional party organisations. Electoral accountability should, in our view, be the province of the House of Commons and be the justification for that House's supremacy.

A minimum age

12.17 As we want the members of the second chamber to be relatively independent of both the electorate and the political parties and we want many of them to have had extensive experience of the world outside politics before entering the chamber, we considered whether a minimum age should be set for becoming a member. A minimum age requirement higher than that set for the lower house is a common feature of second chambers overseas, especially in Latin American countries and the Caribbean, but also in the United States, Canada, Italy, France and India. We concluded, however, that a requirement of this kind would be inconsistent with our desire to achieve a broadly representative second chamber and that it should be left to the Appointments Commission to ensure that the second chamber contained sufficient members with the requisite non-political experience and expertise.

> **Recommendation 73**: There should be no minimum age for members of the reformed second chamber.

Eligibility for reselection or reappointment

12.18 We also considered whether members of the reformed second chamber, having served for the equivalent of three electoral cycles, should be required to stand down or whether they could be eligible for reappointment or reselection. Given the relatively long terms we envisage, it may be that a large proportion of the members will, in practice, not want to serve for more than one full term. However, we imagine that some will feel able and will wish to continue. Indeed, some potential members might be reluctant to be considered for membership if they believed that, however well they performed, their membership would be limited to a single term. It would also be a pity, in our view, if the second chamber were arbitrarily to lose the services of members who were still able and willing to make a contribution. We therefore recommend that all members of the second chamber should, at the end of their term of service, be eligible for reappointment by the Appointments Commission for a further term. In the interests of flexibility, we recommend that the Appointments Commission be empowered to make such reappointments either for 15 years or for shorter periods of up to 15 years.

12.19 We want the regional members, as well as the appointed members, to be able to act as independently as possible, without having to worry about securing renomination or reselection. We therefore recommend that regional members should not be eligible for reselection on a regional basis but should, like all other members, be eligible for reappointment by the Appointments Commission.

> **Recommendation 74:** Both regional and directly appointed members should be eligible for reappointment, at the discretion of the Appointments Commission, for further periods of up to 15 years. Regional members should not be eligible for reselection on a regional basis.

Eligibility to retire

12.20 An assessment of the alternatives to life membership raises the question of whether members of the reformed second chamber, unlike the existing life peers, should be able to resign. Because of ill health or other reasons, members might conclude that they were no longer able to make a sufficient contribution to the chamber's work to justify continued membership. We recommend that members should be able to retire. Retirement should, in our view, be irrevocable; members should not be allowed to absent themselves but then decide they want to return at some later stage. In making this particular recommendation, we do not wish to imply that we are in favour of any particular minimum level of attendance or contribution. On the contrary, we wish to promote arrangements which will facilitate part-time membership, with a substantial proportion of members of the reformed second chamber continuing to be active in other walks of life.

> **Recommendation 75:** Members of the reformed second chamber should be able to retire.

Eligibility for election to the House of Commons

12.21 One question which arises from this recommendation is whether a person who stands down from the reformed second chamber should be eligible for election to the House of Commons. Given the kind of membership we wish the second chamber to attract, and given the role we believe it should play in the new constitutional order, we believe that the movement of individual members from the second chamber to the House of Commons should be discouraged. Would-be career politicians should not be encouraged to see membership of the second chamber as a springboard to membership of the Commons. We recommend, therefore, that members of the second chamber should not be eligible for election to the House of Commons for ten years following the expiry of their term of membership of the second chamber, whether or not they have served the whole of that term. We have taken legal advice on the compatibility of such a provision with Article 3 of Protocol 1 to the European Convention on Human Rights and with Article 25 of the United Nations International Covenant on Civil and Political Rights, and we believe that what we propose represents a reasonable and proportionate way of achieving the important objectives it is designed to secure.

> **Recommendation 76:** Members of the reformed second chamber should not be eligible for election to the House of Commons until ten years after their term of membership ends, whether or not they serve out their full term.

The selection of regional members

12.22 The method of selecting the members who are to give a voice to the nations and regions in the reformed second chamber constitutes a key part of our report. The choice that is made between the various available options could determine the extent to which all our other recommendations on the roles, powers and functions of the second chamber achieve their goals. The wrong choice could undermine the authority and the cohesion of the second chamber. It could also lead to a degree of tension between the members of the two Houses of Parliament which would damage the prospects of achieving a constructive and complementary relationship between the two.

12.23 For the reasons set out in Chapters 6 and 11, we recommend not only that a proportion of the members of the reformed second chamber should provide a voice for the nations and regions but also that they should be selected on a basis which accurately reflects the party balance among the regional electorates. The questions which therefore arise are:

- what method of selection should be used;

- which of the two electoral cycles mentioned above – general election or European Parliament election – should it be associated with; and

- how many regional members should there be, and what proportion of the new second chamber should they constitute?

All these questions are interrelated and all are affected by the other considerations discussed in this chapter.

Method of selection

12.24 We present three possible models for the selection of regional members. Each model has the support of different members of the Commission. Model B has the support of a substantial majority of the Commission.

12.25 The three models we propose have a number of important features in common and are all based on the assumption that:

- the selection of regional members will take place, as it were, in the 'margins' of other electoral contests. Candidates for the second chamber will not be required to engage in extensive personal electioneering;

- for the purpose of selecting the new regional members, the nations and the English regions will be taken to be coterminous with the large constituencies already used in connection with elections to the European Parliament. No new constituencies or electoral districts will be required;

- the electorate's votes, as cast directly at elections in these large constituencies, will by one means or another determine the party balance among the regional members of the second chamber;

- the number of members selected in each of these large constituencies will accurately reflect the balance of voting for the various parties in those constituencies. That is, the selection system used, whatever its other characteristics, will be a proportional one, not one based on first-past-the-post; and

- there will be no new round of elections. However regional members of the reformed second chamber are selected, the choice will be made on the same day as the election of members to either the House of Commons or the European Parliament.

In considering what follows, these common assumptions need constantly to be borne in mind.

Model A

12.26 Under this model, which we have dubbed 'complementary voting', voters would go to the polls, as usual, on general election day. They would cast their ballot for the person they wished to be their member of the House of Commons in the normal way. They would not be voting, directly, for anyone else. Up to this point, nothing, so far as the voters were concerned, would have changed.

12.27 However, under the complementary voting system, the political parties, prior to election day, would have drawn up and published their lists of nominees for the new second chamber. These lists could be posted at the voting stations.

12.28 When the voters had cast their ballots for members of the House of Commons, their votes would then be totalled on a party basis within each region. Each party would be awarded regional members of the second chamber in direct proportion to the share of the votes it had received in each region in the elections for the House of Commons.

Regional constituencies currently used for European Parliament elections

12.29 Under this model, there would be 65 regional members, the smallest number consistent with the use of a proportional system in the United Kingdom.[2] As it happens, this is also the number of MEPs to which the United Kingdom will be entitled if the European Union is enlarged along the lines currently envisaged.

12.30 The 65 regional members would be selected on a staggered basis. The complementary voting system would be applied at each general election in one-third of the United Kingdom's 12 nations and regions.

12.31 The perceived advantages of Model A are that the individual voter would not have to do anything more than he or she does at present. Although the choice of regional members would take place on general election day, there would be no ambiguity about the voters' verdict, and there could be no question of the members of a second chamber selected on this basis setting themselves up as challengers to the authority of the directly elected House of Commons. Turnout would be guaranteed to be high.

12.32 Possible criticisms of Model A are that voters would not be given the option of voting for the candidates of one party for the House of Commons while voting for the candidates of another party for the second chamber. Their choice would be constrained in that sense. That constraint might lead voters to modify their preference between candidates for the House of Commons, in order to affect the choice of candidates for the second chamber. In addition, as the parties would draw up their own lists of candidates for the second chamber, and as these lists would be closed under the terms of Model A, the voter would have no opportunity to vote for the individual candidate of his or her choice.

---

[2] In practical terms, the number of regional members selected in this way could be larger than 65, but those who support this model would not favour that.

More generally, voters would find themselves casting votes to elect candidates to one chamber of Parliament, only then to find that these same votes were being used to select the members of the other chamber. In any event, individual voters would only be able to influence the choice of regional members of the second chamber once every 10–14 years.

Model B

12.33 Under this model, there would not be an additional election day, but voters would nevertheless participate in an additional and separate election: that for regional members of the second chamber. The election would take place, not on general election day, as under Model A, but on the day of the quinquennial elections for the European Parliament. On that day, voters would be presented with two ballot papers instead of the present one: the first for the election of their regional MEPs and the second for the election of their regional members to the second chamber. Voters would be under no compulsion to vote for the same parties in both elections.

12.34 In our view, and because we do not want to see the number of electoral systems already in use in this country unnecessarily enlarged, if Model B were to be adopted we would wish the same electoral system to be used for elections to both the European Parliament and the reformed second chamber. It would be up to the Government and Parliament to decide which system to adopt. If Model B was accepted but the Government were then to consider altering the electoral system used in the European Parliament elections, we recommend that they should consider adopting a system which would also be appropriate for the election of regional members of the second chamber. Subject to that, a majority of those supporting this option would prefer the election of regional members to be conducted by a 'partially open' list system rather than the closed party-list system which was used in the 1999 European Parliament elections. The 'partially open' list system enables voters to vote for a party list *or* for an individual candidate on one of the party lists.[3] In the polling booth, the procedure is simple: each voter marks one X on the ballot paper; but (in contrast to the closed-list system) voters can, if they choose, exercise a preference for a particular candidate rather than simply endorse a party list. 'Partially open' list PR elections for the second chamber could therefore be held alongside any other 'X'-voting electoral system without too much risk of confusing the voters; but the risk of confusion would be eliminated if identical systems were in use.

12.35 Those who support this model believe there should be 87 regional members. This is the same as the number of United Kingdom members of the European Parliament. The same distribution of members between regions could be used.[4] But there is no necessary link between the number of regional members in the second chamber and the number of United Kingdom MEPs.

---

[3] Under a partially open list system, the candidates from each party are listed in an order determined by the parties themselves. Electors may vote either for an individual candidate *or* for the party list as presented. The votes for the individual candidates are totalled and the votes for the party list as a whole are added, to give the total for the party. This total is used to determine the number of seats won, using the d'Hondt formula. The total number of votes secured by the party is then divided by the number of seats won and compared to the votes secured by the individual candidates. Any who secured more than the quota are elected. If seats remain to be allocated, votes for the party list are added to those secured by individuals in order to achieve the quota, moving down the list in the order determined by the party. If a seat remains to be allocated when there are no longer enough votes left to bring any candidate up to the quota, the remaining candidate with the most personal votes, plus any remaining party votes, is elected.

[4] Again, in practical terms, the number of regional members elected under Model B could be higher or lower than 87, but those who support Model B believe that 87 regional members would provide the right balance in the second chamber.

12.36 As in the case of Model A, the regional members would be elected on a staggered basis, with elections taking place at each round of European Parliament elections in one-third of the United Kingdom's 12 nations and regions.

12.37 The perceived advantages of Model B as compared with Model A are that it would not complicate proceedings on the day of the main domestic electoral contest and would give more freedom to the individual voter. He or she could vote for different parties in the second chamber and European Parliament elections and also vote for a party different from the one he or she had supported at the general election. If a partially open list system of election is used, he or she could exercise a preference for an individual candidate. In addition, the elections to the second chamber under Model B would be free-standing elections, giving the members of the second chamber a separate and distinct electoral mandate. It would also be possible for smaller parties, or even independents, to secure election to the second chamber. For all these reasons, elections held under Model B would be 'proper elections'. As in the case of Model A, however, the proportion of directly elected members in the second chamber would be relatively small (87 compared with Model A's 65). An additional advantage of Model B is that, as members elected under this model would serve for fixed terms of 15 years, the appointed members of the second chamber could serve for fixed 15-year terms – that is, for terms of identical length.

12.38 One possible criticism of Model B is that, as happens in Germany and the United States, for example, holding separate elections for a second chamber could threaten to undermine the authority of the serving Government as voters use the opportunity to cast a protest vote. However, our recommendation that the overall political balance among the politically-affiliated members of the second chamber should reflect the most recent general election result is designed to answer the concern that the second chamber should not be out of step with the balance of political opinion as expressed at general elections, and would do so even if the choice of regional members was made on a day other than general election day.

This safeguard (coupled with the relatively small numbers involved) should allay fears that the selection of regional members on a day other than general election day would create the risk of a 'mid-term backlash' effect. A general criticism of Model B is that individual voters would only be able to vote for members of the second chamber at 15-year intervals. It might also be the case that second chamber elections held on the day of European Parliament elections would have a low – possibly an embarrassingly low – turnout of voters, although it is possible that interest in selecting members for the second chamber could increase turnout for the European Parliament elections. A further possible criticism of Model B is that, in principle, the issues relevant to the election of members of the second chamber of the United Kingdom Parliament are different from those which are relevant to the election of members of the European Parliament, which has a different set of responsibilities. However, in practice, such distinctions are unlikely to be drawn and there are other similarities between elections to the second chamber and elections to the European Parliament: both are essentially scrutinising and deliberative bodies.

Model C

12.39 This model in some respects resembles Model B. It also envisages direct and separate elections to the second chamber, which would nevertheless coincide with the quinquennial European Parliament elections.

12.40 However, in two important respects Model C differs from Model B. First, in Model C, the directly elected component of the second chamber would be considerably larger than in Model B. If Model B were adopted, there would be only 87 directly elected members of the second chamber, with each of the nations and regions voting only once every 15 years. Model C proposes, instead, that 65 members of the second chamber should be elected on the occasion of each European Parliament election, with all the nations and regions voting every time. The result would be a directly elected component of the reformed second chamber which would eventually, after three rounds of elections, amount to a total of 195. Second, under Model C, voters would use 'partially open' list proportional representation to elect the regional members of the second chamber, regardless of the system used for the European Parliament elections.[5]

12.41 The perceived advantages of Model C are identical to those of Model B except that, because there would be more regional members and elections to the second chamber would take place throughout the country every five years, the role of the electorate would be larger, so the second chamber would have a better claim to speak with democratic authority. Model C also reflects the widespread sense among the general public that the second chamber should have a more substantial directly elected component.

12.42 The possible criticisms of Model C are identical to those of Model B except that many of the disadvantages outlined in paragraph 12.38 would be accentuated under Model C. Because a significant number of regional members would be elected at the time of each European Parliament election there would be a greater risk of those members claiming a more up-to-date mandate than the House of Commons. The potential threat to the Government's authority would be correspondingly greater, as would the potential for tension between the two Houses of Parliament. And, because the political parties would control the drawing up of their lists of candidates, their influence on determining the composition of a second chamber with 195 directly elected regional members would inevitably be stronger than in the case of a second chamber, as on Model B, with only 87 such members. Finally, as with Model B, but more so, the cohesion of the second chamber in Model C might be weakened by a feeling that some of its members had a direct electoral mandate while others did not, with the former being seen as somehow more 'legitimate' than the latter.

---

[5] Northern Ireland might continue to use STV.

We present three possible models for the selection of regional members. Each model has the support of different members of the Commission. Model B has the support of a substantial majority of the Commission.

Model A

The regional members should be selected on the same day as a general election, using a system which we have called 'complementary' voting. Under this system the votes cast for the parties' general election candidates would be accumulated at regional level and the parties would secure a number of regional members for each region proportional to their share of the vote in that region.

There would be 65 regional members who would be selected on a 'staggered' basis, with the 'complementary' voting system being applied in one-third of the twelve nations and regions at each general election.

Model B

There should be a total of 87 regional members, elected by thirds at the same time as each European Parliamentary election (with one-third of the nations and regions voting for regional members at each European election). The system of election should be the same as that used for electing United Kingdom MEPs,[6] although a majority of those supporting this model would prefer the 'partially open' list system of proportional representation (PR).

Model C

The regional members should be directly elected on a regional basis, using a form of 'partially open' list PR.[7] Sixty-five regional members would be elected at the same time as each European Parliament election and serve for three terms, giving a total of 195 regional members in the reformed second chamber.

12.43 There are a number of other matters affecting all three possible methods of selection which need to be considered.

12.44 One concerns the quality of the parties' lists under all three models and whether the parties could be counted upon to select nominees whose personal qualities were in keeping with the kind of second chamber we are recommending. Ultimately, the choice of candidates would be up to the parties, but our view is that they should be required to bear in mind the sorts of qualities we have been outlining. In particular, they should be required to conform to the gender and minority ethnic targets set for the Appointments Commission. The media – and the other political parties – can almost certainly be relied upon to scrutinise closely the qualities, and the quality, of the parties' nominees. Parties with strong regional lists will have an electoral advantage.

[6] Currently 'closed list' PR in Great Britain and STV in Northern Ireland (which would continue to use STV under this model).
[7] Or STV in Northern Ireland.

12.45 A related issue concerns whether candidates under any of our three models should be vetted – as nominees for life peerages are now vetted – on grounds of personal probity and propriety. The strongest case for such vetting can be made in connection with Model A under which voters are required, in effect, to cast a second chamber vote for the same party for which they cast their first chamber vote. But our general view is that, just as there is no prior vetting of members of the House of Commons, so there should be no prior vetting of regional members of the reformed second chamber. If, however, there is to be no such vetting, then the second chamber, like the House of Commons, needs to have some procedure whereby, under a very restricted set of circumstances, a sitting member can be expelled.

Recommendation 77: The reformed second chamber should establish a procedure for expelling members whose continued presence would otherwise bring the chamber into disrepute.

12.46 The reformed second chamber, like the House of Commons, will need to have a procedure for filling vacancies among regional members. The procedure in the case of the House of Commons is the holding of by-elections. We do not favour such a procedure in the case of the second chamber: by-elections for the second chamber would further multiply the already large number of elections in this country and might attract derisory turnouts. By-elections would in any event be inappropriate as a means of filling vacancies among members selected on a proportional basis; and it would be a waste of public funds to hold a region-wide election to select a single member for the second chamber. We therefore recommend that vacancies arising within the first electoral cycle should be filled by the next available nominee on the relevant party's list. Thereafter, because it is not realistic to expect that lower-placed candidates would continue to be available to fill vacancies more than five years ahead, consideration should be given to introducing a system of co-option.

Recommendation 78: Vacancies among the regional members arising within the first electoral cycle after they join the second chamber should be filled by offering the vacant place to the next person on the relevant party list. Under Models A and B, consideration should be given to introducing a system of co-option where a vacancy arises some time after the original selection.

12.47 We see each of the three models as constituting, possibly, the first stage of a gradual evolution. For example, Model B envisages a total of only 87 regional members. If, however, the political parties consistently put forward high-quality nominees, and the second chamber seems to profit from the presence of a proportion of regional members, then it would be open to the Government and Parliament to consider, at some future time, whether the number of such members should be increased. Although the numbers of regional members vary from model to model, the proponents of each model believe that the number envisaged in each case is right for now. But we all believe that, whatever model is selected, the arrangements for selecting regional members should be kept under review, in the light of experience and also in the light of the evolution of the other elements of the United Kingdom's constitutional settlement.

Recommendation 79: The arrangements for selecting regional members should be kept under review, in the light of experience and taking account of any changes which flow from devolution or from the emergence of new structures in the English regions.

Chapter 13 – The Appointments Commission

13.1   The arrangements for appointing life peers which the Government has proposed should apply during the interim stage of House of Lords reform (see Chapter 11) will leave considerable control with the Prime Minister of the day. He or she will be able to control the size and party balance in the interim House by virtue of having the power to set the number of nominations made by each party and the number of Cross Benchers selected by the proposed Appointments Commission. He or she will also retain an ultimate veto over all nominations, through being responsible for putting the final list to the Queen. The present Prime Minister has committed himself to seeking no more than parity between Labour and Conservative members of the interim House of Lords and has undertaken not to challenge other parties' nominations (save in wholly exceptional circumstances). It would, however, be unsatisfactory to base appointment to the reformed second chamber on these or equivalent assurances. The Prime Minister should no longer play a role in appointing members of the second chamber.

Role

13.2   Members of the present House of Lords have to be peers and are appointed by the Queen. The Monarch acts only on advice so all recommendations for appointment must be made by the Prime Minister. We are adamant that the link between the peerage and membership of the second chamber should be broken (Chapter 18) and that the Prime Minister should not have any role in the appointment of members of the second chamber. The current system of appointment cannot be retained. We therefore recommend that the Appointments Commission should be charged by the Crown with a general duty to appoint members to the second chamber and empowered to appoint individual members on its own authority. This approach would have parallels with the system used for the House of Commons, under which the Crown issues a writ to the returning officer to hold an election but plays no part in the choice of members.

13.3   Precluding any scope for political patronage is a basic element of our scheme for the composition of the second chamber. The abolition of such patronage is essential if the chamber is to have the legitimacy and confidence required.

> **Recommendation 80:** The Appointments Commission should be charged by the Crown with a general duty to appoint members to the second chamber and empowered to appoint individual members on its own authority.

13.4   The role of the Appointments Commission for the reformed second chamber will therefore be much greater than that envisaged during the interim stage of Lords reform. The independent Appointments Commission should be the only avenue into the second chamber, whether individuals reach this point through selection as a regional member, through selection by the Commission or through appointment as a Lord of Appeal in Ordinary or representative of the Church of England. In this way, the differences between members of the second chamber would be minimised and the ability of the chamber to act as a cohesive body enhanced.

> **Recommendation 81**: The independent Appointments Commission should be the only route into the second chamber, whether individuals reach this point through selection as a regional member, through selection by the Commission, or through appointment as a Lord of Appeal in Ordinary or representative of the Church of England.

13.5   Although the Appointments Commission should be the sole mechanism for appointing members to the second chamber, there are three classes of member over whose appointment the Commission should actually have no discretion:

■ regional members;

■ Lords of Appeal in Ordinary;[1] and

■ any representatives of the Church of England.

13.6   In each of these cases, individuals will have been chosen through a specific process of selection and their legitimacy will rest on the established independence of this process. It would not, therefore, be appropriate for the Appointments Commission to intervene in the selection process and seek to substitute its own judgement. It should formally appoint those whose names emerge from these separate processes.

> **Recommendation 82**: The Appointments Commission should have no discretion over the appointment to the second chamber of regional members, Lords of Appeal in Ordinary, or any representatives of the Church of England.

13.7   The remainder of this chapter considers the means by which the independence of the Appointments Commission should be ensured and the arrangements for appointing individual members to the second chamber.

Ensuring independence

13.8   The Appointments Commission should not only be independent of the political parties in practice, but should also be seen to be so. A number of safeguards should therefore be set in place to ensure the independence of the Appointments Commission. These relate to its legal status, the means by which its members are appointed and their security of tenure, the procedures by which members of the second chamber are appointed and the reporting arrangements set in place.

13.9   While the Appointments Commission would be without any direct parallel either in the United Kingdom or abroad, it would by no means represent an entirely new approach in the British constitution. The constitution already includes several bodies responsible for a number of very sensitive elements in the relationship between the Government and Parliament. These provide useful examples on which our proposals draw.

---

[1] It has been the practice for other holders of high judicial office to be appointed to the House of Lords as life peers under the Life Peerages Act 1958. Once appointed, they can serve as members of the Appellate and Appeal Committees alongside the Lords of Appeal in Ordinary. In future, any such appointments would need to be made by the Appointments Commission, and for 15-year terms. No doubt the Commission would pay due regard to nominations made for this purpose by the Lord Chancellor.

13.10 The longest standing of the existing bodies is the National Audit Office (NAO), which audits the accounts of almost all Central Government bodies and undertakes some 50 value-for-money studies each year. The NAO, under the Comptroller and Auditor General, is not part of Government, but reports to the Commons Public Accounts Committee, by convention chaired by a senior Opposition MP. The Parliamentary Commissioner for Standards and the Commissioner for Public Appointments fall into the same broad category of organisations which play a vital role in ensuring the smooth running of the Parliamentary system. Finally, the Government has recently accepted the recommendation of the Committee on Standards in Public Life that there should be an Electoral Commission, which will have a number of functions relating to the conduct of elections and the funding of political parties. Since the Electoral Commission will be controlling the process by which individuals enter the House of Commons, it will occupy a broadly comparable position in respect of that House as will the Appointments Commission with regard to the second chamber.[2]

Legal status

13.11 The Appointments Commission could be grounded in statute, rely on a Royal Charter, or be entirely non-statutory, as will be the case for the Appointments Commission proposed by the Government for the interim House of Lords. A number of approaches have been adopted for other constitutional bodies. The NAO was established by statute and the Government proposes to do the same for the Electoral Commission. The posts of Parliamentary Commissioner for Standards and Commissioner for Public Appointments, by contrast, were both established through an Order in Council. This was done in the interests of speed and does not rule out the option of creating a firmer legislative basis for them in the future.

13.12 Establishment of the Appointments Commission on a non-statutory basis would mean that its internal operation could be altered or it could even be abolished without reference to Parliament. Establishment on the basis of a Royal Charter, as is the case with the BBC, might give greater independence and permanence, but it could not guarantee its immunity from Government interference. While establishment on a non-statutory basis may be appropriate for wholly advisory non-departmental public bodies (NDPBs), which merely provide an input to Departmental policy development, it would not offer the level of independence and entrenchment required for the Appointments Commission. Most executive NDPBs, such as the Environment Agency, are founded through primary legislation.[3]

13.13 We recommend therefore that the Appointments Commission should be established by primary legislation. Amendment of the legislation would require open debate in Parliament and the approval of the second chamber itself. Such amending legislation would also come under close scrutiny from the proposed Constitutional Committee of the second chamber. We doubt that any Government would risk the embarrassment of attempting to use the Parliament Acts to force through such legislation against the will

---

[2] Other similar constitutional bodies include the Parliamentary Commissioner for Administration (the Parliamentary Ombudsman), the Health Service Commissioner (the NHS Ombudsman) and the Data Protection Registrar.

[3] The Environment Agency was created by the Environment Act 1995.

of a second chamber. Establishing the Appointments Commission through primary legislation would therefore offer considerable entrenchment. Since a number of our other recommendations would involve legislation, it would be relatively straightforward to include clauses and a schedule relating to the Appointments Commission.

> **Recommendation 83:** The Appointments Commission should be established by primary legislation.

Number of Appointments Commissioners

13.14 The interim Appointments Commission will include representatives of the three main political parties and a number of independents. The latter will form a majority among the Commissioners and will provide the chairman, implying a total of at least seven Commissioners. Experience from other public bodies working in politically controversial areas, such as the Committee on Standards in Public Life, suggests that there would be significant merit in including nominees from each of the main political parties. While they would be expected not to behave in a partisan manner, their understanding of how Parliament and the political parties work and think would be of considerable benefit to the Appointments Commission. We therefore recommend that three of the Appointments Commissioners should be nominees from the main political parties. A Commissioner nominated by the convenor of the Cross Benchers would be a logical corollary. These four members should be balanced by four independent members, of whom one should be the chairman. The resulting total of eight[4] should allow scope for representation from Scotland, Wales or Northern Ireland, thereby ensuring that the Appointments Commission was not a solely English body.

> **Recommendation 84:** There should be eight Appointments Commissioners. Three should be nominees from the main political parties, one a nominee of the Convenor of the Cross Benchers and four should be independents, of whom one should be the chairman.

Selection of Appointments Commissioners

13.15 Since the first report of the Nolan Committee in 1995, both Conservative and Labour Governments have committed themselves to filling the majority of public appointments according to what have become known as the 'Nolan principles', notably that appointments should be made strictly on merit and should be free of the taint of favouritism or bias. The appointments made on the basis of the Nolan principles include a number of key constitutional posts, such as the Commissioner for Public Appointments. The Government has committed itself to applying the Nolan principles in selecting the independent members of the Appointments Commission which will operate during the interim stage of House of Lords reform. The Home Office has taken the same view with regard to the membership of the new Electoral Commission. We recommend that this approach should also be adopted in connection with the independent members of the Appointments Commission. Such an approach does not, of course, preclude 'head hunting' and the taking of private soundings.

> **Recommendation 85:** The independent members of the Appointments Commission should be selected according to the Nolan principles.

---

[4] An odd number of Appointments Commissioners would not be required, since the Appointments Commission should proceed by consensus rather than majority voting.

13.16 One question that might arise is whether it should be permissible for Appointments Commissioners to be themselves members of either chamber of Parliament. On the one hand, none of the members of the other constitutional bodies is permitted to be a member of either chamber of Parliament. This rule is set in order to avoid any possible conflict of interest or the appearance of conflict. Conversely, a sound knowledge of the workings of the second chamber would be a very substantial asset when selecting new members for that chamber. The current members of the Political Honours Scrutiny Committee, for example, are all peers. On balance, we believe that it would be inappropriate for any Appointments Commissioner to be a member of the Commons: members of one chamber should not be involved in the selection of members for the other chamber.[5] However, there would be significant benefits if a number of Appointments Commissioners, though not a majority, were at the same time members of the second chamber.

Recommendation 86: A number of Appointments Commissioners, though not a majority, should be members of the second chamber. None should be an MP.

Appointment of Commissioners

13.17 For most public appointments, the decision will be taken by the responsible Minister. Such direct Ministerial control would be unacceptable in the case of the Appointments Commission for the second chamber. The most common approach for appointments of a constitutional nature is for them to be made by the Queen, on the advice of the Prime Minister. The process is subject to certain controls, designed to ensure that the Prime Minister's advice has cross-party support.

13.18 The draft Bill to establish the Electoral Commission proposes placing a duty upon the Prime Minister to consult the leaders of all parties with more than two MPs and the chairman of the independent Speaker's Committee. This must be done before he or she moves a motion to present an Address to the Queen inviting her to appoint the proposed members of the Electoral Commission. Such safeguards are necessary in the Commons, because the governing party will normally enjoy an absolute majority and so could, in theory, impose its own nominees. By contrast, since no single party will ever have a majority in the second chamber, any such motion in respect of the Appointments Commission would by definition have to secure cross-party support. There is also a strong convention that the business of the present House of Lords proceeds by consensus and that procedural suggestions from the Leader of the House reflect prior consultation with the other party groupings. There is therefore no need for a second chamber equivalent of the Speaker's Committee. Since the Appointments Commission will operate in respect of the second chamber, it would be most appropriate for it to be that chamber whose approval is required, on a motion moved by the Leader of the House, following the normal consultation with the leaders of the other party groupings and the Convenor of the Cross Benchers.

Recommendation 87: Appointments Commissioners should be appointed by the Queen following an Address, on a motion moved by the Leader of the second chamber following the normal consultation with the leaders of the other party groupings and the Convenor of the Cross Benchers.

---

[5] Other than in their capacity as members of the public, for example voting in elections.

Length and security of tenure

13.19 All Appointments Commissioners, including party nominees, should have a long period in office with security of tenure in order to protect them against undue influence and encourage them to bring a long-term perspective to bear on their work. The Commissioner for Public Appointments has recommended that no one should hold a public office for more than ten years. The Government proposes to write such a limit into the legislation for the Electoral Commission. We recommend that the same limit should apply to Appointments Commissioners.

> **Recommendation 88:** Appointments Commissioners should hold office for no more than ten years.

13.20 While members should have security of tenure during their period in office, there should be a procedure for removing an individual whose behaviour has become inappropriate. Corrupt activity on the part of individual members would already be covered by the criminal law. The Government proposes that Electoral Commissioners should be removable only on a resolution of the House of Commons. Since the Appointments Commission will to some extent stand in the same position with regard to the second chamber, removal of an Appointments Commissioner should require a resolution of the second chamber.

> **Recommendation 89:** Removal of an Appointments Commissioner should require a resolution of the second chamber.

Scrutiny of reports

13.21 An important aspect of the Appointments Commission's work will be the information given in its annual report. This report will act as the vehicle by which the Appointments Commission will set out the characteristics required of members of the second chamber and its strategy for ensuring that there is an appropriate balance of members from all parts of society and among the political parties. This strategy might include setting out the types of nomination that would be particularly welcome over the coming year. The report should also provide a detailed breakdown of the composition of the chamber, in terms of party, gender, ethnicity, age and region and the extent to which the chamber's membership as a whole reflects the characteristics set out in the Appointments Commission's published specification. An important element of this information would be to report on changes in the political and other balances which the Appointments Commission will be required to strike, arising from the departure of members at the end of their term of office, the characteristics of the regional members and the results of each general election.

13.22 The report would provide the main means by which the Appointments Commission could be held to account. Such scrutiny should consider three aspects of the Commission's operation:

- whether the specification of the characteristics required of members of the second chamber was appropriate and whether the estimate of the number of members required was correct;

- whether the selection process was effective in identifying individuals with the required characteristics and whether the resulting composition of the second chamber, including the regional members, achieved the appropriate balances; and

- whether the Appointments Commission was using public funds efficiently and the expenditure involved had been made properly.

13.23 Since the Appointments Commission would be a statutory body, its reports should be presented to Parliament. It should not be possible to enquire into individual cases, but it would be right for the Appointments Commission to be held to account on its fulfilment of its statutory duties.

> **Recommendation 90:** The Appointments Commission should make an annual report to Parliament. This report should set out the characteristics required of members of the second chamber and the Commission's strategy for ensuring that there is an appropriate balance of members from all parts of society and between the political parties. The report should also provide a detailed breakdown of the composition of the chamber, in terms of party, gender, ethnicity, age and region and the extent to which the chamber's membership as a whole reflects the characteristics set out in the Appointments Commission's published specification.

Size and balance of the second chamber

Size of the chamber

13.24 There has never been a limit on the total number of members of the House of Lords and the size of the chamber has therefore varied over the years. It has always been open to the Prime Minister of the day to recommend to the Monarch that additional peers be created in order to change the political balance and so secure the Government's legislation. Queen Anne created 12 new hereditary peers to ensure approval of the Treaty of Utrecht in 1712, and George V agreed to create up to 500 new peers if necessary to secure passage of the Parliament Act in 1911. In theory, any Government could create additional peers to secure a majority in the second chamber. The power to determine the overall size of the second chamber is therefore of considerable political importance. We have earlier set out our reasons for recommending that no one political party should ever be able to control the second chamber. To protect this vitally important feature of the reformed second chamber, we recommend that the power to determine the overall size and political balance of the second chamber should no longer lie with the Prime Minister of the day.

13.25 It would be inappropriate to suggest a particular target size for the reformed second chamber in the longer term. Such a suggestion would, we believe, pre-empt careful consideration of the implications of our recommendations. Our proposals include the establishment of a Constitutional Committee with a number of Sub-Committees, a Treaty Committee and an enhanced procedure for the scrutiny of Statutory Instruments. These all seem likely to lead to an increase in the chamber's workload. At this stage, however, it is not possible to judge accurately how many members the reformed second chamber will need in order to meet these demands. The total number will also be affected by the average rates of attendance among members; our proposals are designed to encourage 'part-time' membership, with members able to remain active in other spheres of life.

On the other hand, it is possible that the introduction of fixed terms and the opportunity to retire will lead to a significant reduction in the average age of members and to an increase in their average rate of attendance. In the light of these factors, we conclude that it would not be appropriate to fix the total number of members of the second chamber in statute.

13.26 Responsibility for setting the overall size of the chamber should fall to the Appointments Commission. It should also be required, in consultation with the Leader of the House and the other party leaders in the second chamber, to keep under review the workload of the chamber, levels of attendance and the implications of those factors for the total number of members required. Such reviews should be conducted on a regular basis. An initial assessment should be made by the interim Appointments Commission as soon as possible, to inform other preparatory work.

13.27 When considering models for determining the composition of the reformed second chamber, we have had to make an assessment of the likely number of members required. Our estimate (it can be no more than an informed guess at this stage) is that the second chamber would need to have in the region of 550 members.[6]

13.28 We have earlier recommended that the overall balance between the political parties in the second chamber should reflect the share of votes cast for each party at the previous general election. This will be achieved by appointing party-affiliated members to the various party groups in the numbers required to produce the appropriate balance. The Appointments Commission will have the central role in allocating the available places between the parties. Its task will be made easier by the fact that our other recommendations should ensure a sufficiently high turnover of members to enable the Commission to engage in these essential 'rebalancing' exercises without, in the great majority of circumstances, having to appoint an unduly large number of new members. In addition, the Commission will normally have in mind beforehand the names of a number of members of the main political parties who could be appointed at relatively short notice if the need arose. We do not, however, envisage the necessary rebalancing exercises taking place within days, or even necessarily weeks or months, of the results of any general election being declared. The Appointments Commission must be given considerable leeway in deciding how quickly to rebalance the new House and how arithmetically precise any rebalancing needs to be. It will always be the case that no one party will have an overall majority, even among the party-affiliated members, and that the Government of the day, even a newly elected Government, will have enough members to ensure that its business can be managed efficiently.

Recommendation 91: The size of the second chamber should not be fixed in statute, but should be set by the Appointments Commission. The Appointments Commission should regularly review the total number of members required, taking account of the chamber's workload, levels of attendance and the need to achieve or maintain a balance between the political parties in the second chamber that reflects their shares of the votes cast at the previous general election.

---

[6] Made up of 65 (Model A)/87 (Model B)/195 (Model C) regional members serving for three electoral cycles, and about 500/450/350 other members, including Law Lords and representatives of religious faiths (see Chapter 15). This would produce an average of about 33/30/24 vacancies to be filled by the Appointments Commission each year.

Gender and ethnicity

13.29 The second chamber should be broadly representative of British society. The Appointments Commission should, over time, seek to achieve gender balance and a fair representation for minority ethnic groups. It should therefore be required to encourage nominations from under-represented groups and to report regularly on progress in achieving an appropriate balance. This would be entirely consistent with its overall approach of working to achieve a second chamber which was balanced across a range of different dimensions.

> **Recommendation 92:** The Appointments Commission should encourage appointments and nominations from under-represented groups and report regularly on progress in achieving gender balance and a fair representation for minority ethnic groups.

Regional representation

13.30 At present (see chart), life peers from London, Scotland and the South East of England represent a significantly higher proportion of the membership of the current House of Lords than might be expected on the basis of regional populations. Our proposal that regional members be selected on the basis of votes cast for parties in each region should go some way to redress the balance. However, the Appointments Commission should also be under a general duty to ensure adequate representation for each of the nations and regions of the United Kingdom among the membership of the second chamber as a whole.

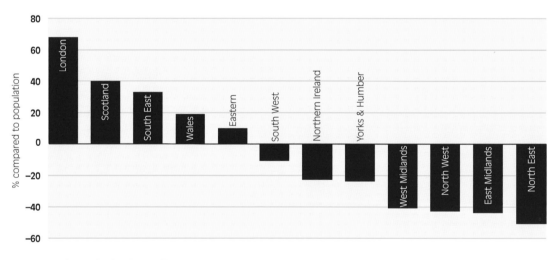

Regional distribution of life peers

(Life peers' regional affiliations have been assessed by reference to the territorial title they have taken.)

> **Recommendation 93:** The Appointments Commission should use its best endeavours to ensure that each of the nations and regions has an appropriate level of representation among the overall membership of the second chamber.

Making appointments

13.31 The Appointments Commission should have discretion in the appointment of all members of the second chamber, other than regional members, Lords of Appeal in Ordinary and any representatives of the Church of England as noted earlier (paragraph 13.5). This will require the Appointments Commission to:

- specify the characteristics members of the second chamber should possess;

- actively seek nominations;

- develop working relations with political parties; and

- vet nominations for propriety and security.

The Appointments Commission will need to ensure that the system it operates to carry out these functions is effective and so commands public confidence.

Specification of characteristics

13.32 The Appointments Commission should publish and keep up to date a statement specifying the broad characteristics which it would expect members of the second chamber, individually and collectively, to possess. This should build on our work, but it would be important to ensure that the Appointments Commission retained sufficient flexibility in determining the characteristics required that it could respond to changes in circumstances or in society as appropriate. Such a specification would be the foundation for any systems of inviting nominations or seeking out candidates and would also provide the benchmark against which individual appointments and the characteristics of the second chamber as a whole should be judged. The Appointments Commission's annual report should be used as a vehicle for setting out the characteristics for which it was looking and for reporting on the contribution which successive rounds of appointments had made to the achievement of that goal.

13.33 The proposed specification should therefore be couched in fairly general terms and should not be exhaustive. It should simply indicate the range of skills and interests across the whole of the community of the United Kingdom that the Appointments Commission would like to see represented in the second chamber. It should emphasise the Appointments Commission's intention to ensure that, at any one time, various broad sectors of society would have an appropriate voice in the second chamber, while avoiding any commitments which could create inflexibilities. It should also make the point that the various sub-sectors of society could not all be represented all the time and that appropriate balances would need to be struck, allowing for variations over time. The specification might need to bring out the importance of striking the right balance between the need for members of personal distinction and relevant expertise on the one hand and securing people representative of a broad cross section of British society on the other. The Appointments Commission should emphasise that no one should be ruled out from consideration, but that successful candidates would need to be able to make a contribution to the work of the second chamber.

13.34 The overall specification could be supplemented in the run-up to individual rounds of appointments by more specific descriptions of particular sets of characteristics which the Appointments Commission was particularly keen to strengthen at that time (e.g. to compensate for vacancies which had arisen). In considering what characteristics might need to be strengthened at a particular point in time, the Appointments Commission should take full account of the various characteristics of all the existing members of the second chamber, including regional members.

> **Recommendation 94**: The Appointments Commission should publish and keep up to date a statement specifying the broad characteristics it would expect members of the second chamber, individually and collectively, to possess.

Actively seeking nominations

13.35 The Appointments Commission should systematically develop its knowledge of, and relationship with, the main individuals and organisations in a wide range of vocational areas and other sectors of society (business organisations, trades unions, voluntary groups, interest groups, cultural organisations, sporting organisations, faith communities, etc) across the nations and regions of the United Kingdom. It should maintain close ties with those sectors of society likely to produce people with characteristics appropriate to the constitutional and human rights roles of the second chamber, for example practising and academic lawyers, and academics specialising in a range of relevant disciplines.

13.36 Such an approach would allow the Appointments Commission to identify potential candidates for appointment to the second chamber and to come to understand the considerations which might affect whether a particular appointment would be seen as appropriate and balanced. It would also give the various organisations the opportunity to suggest candidates.

> **Recommendation 95**: The Appointments Commission should systematically develop its knowledge of, and relationship with, a wide range of vocational areas and other sectors of society.

13.37 In addition to such direct contacts, the Appointments Commission should open up the nomination process to the widest possible range of candidates. We recognise that there might be some tension in doing this, given the reality that there will only be an average of about 20–30 vacancies per year. Nevertheless, the Appointments Commission should solicit nominations from members of the public and find imaginative ways of encouraging the emergence of candidates from unlikely quarters. As a minimum, it might advertise regularly and ensure that nomination forms were widely available, but some steps might need to be taken to avoid too many dashed expectations and too much nugatory work. In particular, people should be asked to substantiate their nominations against the broad criteria for membership and be reminded of the need to ensure that their candidates were willing to accept nomination and were in a position to make a contribution to the work of the second chamber.

> **Recommendation 96**: The Appointments Commission should open up the nomination process to the widest possible range of candidates.

13.38 The Appointments Commission should adopt a proactive approach to the identification of suitable appointees. It should do more than review the directly nominated potential candidates or those brought to its attention through its ongoing contacts with organisations and groups from various sectors of society. It should make specific efforts to identify and to encourage nominations or applications from suitable candidates with particular characteristics, for example from particular vocations or sectors of society.

13.39 Having drawn up a provisional list of likely appointees by reference to the original specification, the Appointments Commission should invite the people concerned to indicate whether they would be prepared, if appointed, to devote at least a reasonable minimum amount of time to the second chamber. Such a system would minimise the risk that potential appointees would be put off from applying: people would only be approached by the Appointments Commission about their readiness to stand once they had been provisionally selected. It would reduce the amount of nugatory work which would inevitably be involved in an application-based system and probably produce a better result. However, it would be essential to ensure that the process itself was open and transparent. The appointments would be widely advertised, the body making the selection would be independent and take its decisions against clear criteria, candidates in the provisional list would all be aware that their names were being considered and the Appointments Commission should have a broadly comparable range of information on every candidate. The system of selection would be entirely in accordance with the Nolan principles, but would avoid the cumbersome bureaucratic procedures sometimes associated with the practical implementation of the principles.

> **Recommendation 97:** The Appointments Commission should adopt a proactive approach to the identification of suitable appointees.

Relationship with the political parties

13.40 The second chamber, as part of the United Kingdom Parliament, will inevitably be a very political place. A large majority of members of the second chamber will be affiliated to a political party. It is therefore necessary to consider the Appointments Commission's role in filling these places.

13.41 While the political parties will have an important role in suggesting names to the Appointments Commission, we see no reason why they should have total control over the selection of party-affiliated members of the second chamber. When suggesting names to the Appointments Commission, the political parties should make a case for the appointment of each individual. The Appointments Commission should then make the final decision, in the light of its published criteria, its judgement of the suitability of each nominee and the needs of the chamber. It is highly likely that individuals proposed because, for example, they were required as Ministers or Front Bench spokesmen or women would be well qualified and would therefore be strong candidates for appointment, but every case should be considered on its merits.

13.42 The Appointments Commission should also be free to pursue the objective of a balanced second chamber, without being limited to the appointment of people who are politically neutral. Such a constraint would be artificial and might tempt people hoping for selection to suppress their political leanings. It might also require awkward questions to be asked about party affiliations, which could lead to the abrupt termination of the consideration of otherwise promising candidates, simply on the basis of their politics. We therefore recommend that the Appointments Commission should be responsible for making all discretionary appointments to the second chamber, not just Cross Bench appointments.

13.43 We regard it as a very important point of principle that the Appointments Commission should be able to appoint people regardless of their party affiliations in the interests of achieving wider balances within the second chamber. The political parties should not be able to secure the appointment of their own party nominees to the exclusion of the Commission's. Neither should they be in a position to veto Appointments Commission appointments, even of members of their own party. We recognise that ultimately the parties have the right to offer the party whip to, or withhold it from, individual members of the second chamber. There is therefore no sense in which party-affiliated appointees can be 'foisted' on a party group in the second chamber.

> **Recommendation 98:** The Appointments Commission should make all discretionary appointments to the second chamber and should make the final decision in all cases. The Appointments Commission should be able to appoint people with party affiliations, whether or not these have the support of their political party.

Propriety and security

13.44 We recommend that possession of a life peerage should be separated from membership of the second chamber (Chapter 18), but issues of propriety and security will continue to arise under an appointments system. At present, nominations for life peerages (like other political honours) are vetted for propriety by the Political Honours Scrutiny Committee. The issue of political donations and their connection with the award of places in the second chamber has attracted much attention recently. We therefore recommend that the Appointments Commission should vet all party nominations for propriety, following the practice established by the Political Honours Scrutiny Committee. Likewise, it would be appropriate that high-level security checks should be made on all candidates on the Appointments Commission's shortlist.

> **Recommendation 99:** The Appointments Commission should vet nominations for propriety and high-level security checks should be undertaken on all shortlisted candidates.

Approval of lists

13.45 We considered whether it would be appropriate for the Appointments Commission to seek Parliamentary approval for its recommendations. That, however, would carry with it the implication that Parliament had the right to reject either the list as a whole or individual names on it. It would be undesirable for the merits of individuals on the lists to be subject to debate, or for there to be scope for names to be added or removed. This would undermine the original selection process and might put pressure on the

Appointments Commission to tailor its lists in order to find favour with Parliament. The House of Commons has no role in approving its new members. The second chamber should equally have no role in approving the Appointments Commission's appointments.

> **Recommendation 100:** The Appointments Commission should not seek Parliamentary approval of its appointments.

Frequency of appointments

13.46 While it might be possible for the Appointments Commission to recommend a continuous trickle of appointments to the second chamber, such an approach would make its task of ensuring a balanced representation in the second chamber more difficult. A regular, perhaps half yearly cycle of appointments would be administratively easier. The Commission would be able to pursue particular themes in particular sets of appointments, which might make it easier to engage with relevant organisations or sectors of society in seeking suitable nominations. In making groups of ten or more appointments at a time, the Commission might also find it easier to demonstrate the achievement of a range of balances within the Chamber, than it would in making a series of individual nominations.

> **Recommendation 101:** The Appointments Commission should normally make appointments on a half-yearly cycle.

Conclusions

13.47 The recommendations made in this chapter would result in the establishment of an independent system for appointing members to the second chamber. This system would assess each nomination on its individual merits and select members by means of an open and transparent process, against criteria that were widely publicised. This would produce a membership that consisted of individuals who represented all parts of British society, and who possessed the breadth of experience and range of skills required for them to undertake effectively the functions we believe should fall to the second chamber. The system would also ensure that the chamber included a strong independent element and the political balance of its members matched that of the electorate. These are radical proposals and would, over time, produce a major change in the second chamber's composition.

Chapter 14 – The existing life peers

14.1   As at 1 December 1999 there were 552 life peers[1] in the House of Lords. It is probable that more will be created before this report is published and yet more before its recommendations could be implemented.

14.2   We need therefore to consider whether the existing life peers, and those to be created between now and the implementation of our report, should continue to have a role in the reformed second chamber and, if so, on what basis they should serve. We are conscious that four members of this Commission are themselves life peers and therefore need, in that sense, to 'declare an interest'.

Characteristics of the life peers

14.3   Collectively, the existing life peers possess a great many, but not all, of the characteristics we would wish to see in the reformed second chamber. Many can offer the second chamber broad experience of public life. Many can offer expertise and experience outside politics. Many are men and women of distinction in their own right. Also, they have a reasonable expectation that they will be members of the second chamber for life. That was the understanding on which they decided to accept the offer of a life peerage. Many will have arranged their affairs on that basis, possibly to their financial disadvantage. Their right to sit in the House of Lords can only be extinguished by means of retrospective legislation.

14.4   Moreover, in practice, there will need to be a transitional period before the reformed second chamber is fully established, and some or all of the existing life peers could provide a solid foundation for the second chamber during that period, helping to maintain continuity and facilitating a smooth transition to the new arrangements. The Appointments Commission would have time to find its feet and establish a regular pattern of appointments, without being under pressure to appoint a very large number of members at the outset.

14.5   On the other hand, as we have said in previous chapters of this report, we believe the present House of Lords is in many ways insufficiently representative of the modern United Kingdom. It is also the case that the average age of the existing life peers is higher than we believe is desirable for the reformed second chamber, and there is a considerable imbalance in the age profiles of the Conservative and Labour life peers. Most significantly, their tenure is very different from what we are recommending for new members of the second chamber.

---

[1] 525 appointed under the Life Peerages Act 1958 and 27 appointed as Lords of Appeal in Ordinary under the Appellate Jurisdiction Act 1876 (as amended).

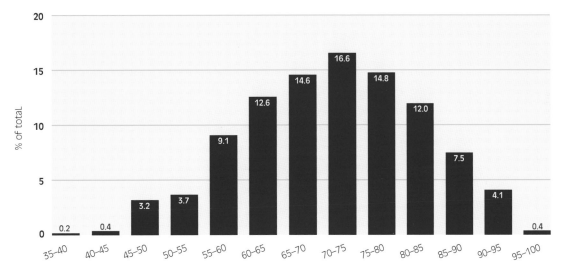

Age profile of life peers

The way ahead

14.6   The situation that the Commission faced is neither easy nor straightforward. In the best of all possible Parliaments, it would be preferable for all members of the second chamber to be there on the same basis, on the same terms and conditions and because they had been judged able to make a positive contribution to securing a second chamber with the characteristics we have set out. However, we have to face the situation as it exists, not as we would ideally like it to be. We considered three options:

- terminating the rights of the existing life peers to sit and vote in the House of Lords but at the same time inviting the Appointments Commission to consider appointing a proportion of them to provide a core of members for the reformed second chamber, for the normal 15-year term with the possibility of reappointment by the Appointments Commission for a further period of up to 15 years;

- giving existing life peers the *right* to continue to sit and vote in the reformed second chamber for 15 years, again subject to the possibility of reappointment; and

- giving all existing life peers the right to continue to sit and vote in the reformed second chamber, for life, coupled with arrangements to facilitate the departure of those no longer wish to make an active contribution.

14.7   The first option would represent a clean break with the past. The situation in which someone could be a member of the second chamber for life regardless of the quality of their contribution would, at a stroke, be ended. The new second chamber would be genuinely 'new', except to the extent that existing life peers were reappointed to it. Perhaps most important, all the appointed members of the new second chamber would be members of it on exactly the same basis. They would all have been appointed by the Appointments Commission for identical 15-year terms, and the Appointments Commission, in deciding whether or not to appoint existing life peers, would be in a position to make its decisions on the basis of individuals' personal contributions and also their contribution to creating the more representative second chamber that the Commission seeks.

14.8   Nevertheless, although the advantages of this option are obvious, the disadvantages are also obvious and the Commission unanimously recommends against it. Such a course of action, involving the extinction of the rights of the existing life peers, would require retrospective legislation. The simultaneous disappearance from the second chamber of some 525–75 existing life peers and the need to replace them would place an enormous – and probably insupportable – burden on the new Appointments Commission. Not least, such a course of action would maximise, and also greatly prolong, the uncertainty about its future that is already a problem for the existing House of Lords. If we recommended the removal of all the life peers, and given that the relevant legislation is unlikely to come into force until 2002 or 2003 at the earliest, we would be creating a situation in which every individual life peer, uncertain about his or her future, would be to some extent a 'lame duck' for a number of years to come and in which, worse, the whole House of Lords would come to be seen, and come to see itself, as a lame-duck chamber. The creation of uncertainty on this scale would be impossible to justify.

14.9   Some members of the Commission would, however, support the second option, which would guarantee a large measure of continuity from the present House of Lords and avoid most of the damaging uncertainty inherent in the first option while signalling an end to the anachronistic practice of allowing people to sit in the second chamber for life irrespective of their health or the quality of the contribution they would be making. It also has the advantage that, from the outset, all members of the reformed chamber would be serving terms of the same length.

14.10   However, we recommend, by a majority, that under the legislation necessary to implement our recommendations those existing life peers who wish to take up the opportunity should be deemed to have been appointed to the reformed second chamber, and for life rather than for a 15-year term.[2]

14.11 In addition to the general arguments summarised in paragraphs 14.3 and 14.4, the main reasons for adopting this third option are:

■ to avoid retrospective legislation which would inevitably be contentious and which many would see as unjust;

■ to avoid a potential 'cliff edge' at a point 15 years after the reformed second chamber has been established, with a large proportion of members leaving at one time; and

■ to avoid perpetuating the uncertainty which has been a problem for the House of Lords in recent months.

---

[2] Serving Lords of Appeal in Ordinary should be automatically deemed to be appointed to the reformed second chamber; but former Lords of Appeal in Ordinary should be given the same option as other life peers.

14.12 It is worth pointing out that, whichever of the latter two options were adopted, the practical effects, in terms of the second chamber's actual membership, would probably be quite similar. By the time any reforms have been enacted and a further 15 years have passed, only about 45 of the existing life peers will be under the age of 75 and not all of those would necessarily want to continue to play an active role. Under either option, the phasing out of the existing life peers is likely to be substantially complete by, at the latest, 2020.

> **Recommendation 102:** Under the legislation necessary to implement the second stage of Lords reform, those life peers created before the publication of this report who wish to take up the opportunity should be deemed to have been appointed to the reformed second chamber, for life.

14.13 The Government and the Parliamentary Draftsman would need to consider how best to achieve this result, whether by extinguishing the rights of existing life peers under the Life Peerages Act 1958[3] and providing equivalent rights under the new legislation; or by preserving those rights with some adaptations (as set out below).

New life peers

14.14 The above recommendation does not apply to life peers created between the publication of this report and the commencement of the relevant provisions. They would have accepted their peerages in full knowledge of our recommendations and they should therefore only be deemed to be appointed to the reformed second chamber for a period totalling 15 years from the award of their life peerage.

> **Recommendation 103:** Life peers created between the publication of this report and the enactment of the legislation necessary to implement the second stage of Lords reform should be deemed to have been appointed to the reformed second chamber for a period totalling 15 years from the award of their life peerage.

Provision for retirement

14.15 Our recommendation is also based on the understanding that steps would be taken to facilitate the departure of those life peers who wish to take no further part in the work of the second chamber. At the point at which the reformed second chamber comes into existence, all existing life peers should be asked whether they would like to stay on and only those who express a wish to continue to sit and vote in the reformed second chamber should be deemed to be appointed to it. If necessary, the Life Peerages Act 1958[3] should be amended to enable life peers to renounce their right to sit and vote in the second chamber. That would also provide a means for life peers to retire from the second chamber at a later point if they wished to do so. If they had been deemed to be

---

[3] and the Appellate Jurisdiction Act 1876.

appointed to the reformed second chamber under the new legislation they would of course be able to retire like any other member. Indeed, we recommend that, like other members, those life peers remaining in the second chamber should be reminded of their right to retire towards the end of each session. We expect that, in time, most will wish to take up this option and stand aside in favour of new members who could make a more active contribution.

> **Recommendation 104**: People appointed as life peers under the Life Peerages Act 1958 or the Appellate Jurisdiction Act 1876 and who remain in the reformed second chamber should be able to renounce their entitlement to sit and vote in the second chamber, or otherwise be able to retire from the second chamber under new legislation.

14.16 We considered whether the requirement proposed in Chapter 12, that members of the second chamber should be precluded from being elected to the House of Commons for a period of 10 years from the point at which their term of membership comes to an end, should apply to the existing life peers. We believe that it should. Existing life peers would have known, in accepting their peerage, that it would prevent them from ever seeking membership of the House of Commons and that, unlike hereditary peers, they could not renounce it. In introducing the right for life peers to retire from the second chamber, we think it right that, like other members of the chamber, they should be precluded from being elected to the House of Commons for 10 years after the point at which they leave the second chamber.

> **Recommendation 105**: Life peers who renounce their right to sit and vote in the second chamber, or otherwise retire from it, should, like other members of the reformed second chamber, be precluded from being elected to the House of Commons within the following 10 years.

Transition

14.17 Meanwhile, it would obviously be helpful for the independent Appointments Commission, in planning its work, to know how long the remaining life peers intended to serve for. Those life peers who chose to remain as members of the second chamber should be encouraged to indicate for approximately how long they would expect to make a continuing contribution to the work of the second chamber. This need not represent a binding commitment, and the position of individual members need not be publicised but it would help to structure expectations and provide a firm foundation for the Appointments Commission's work.

> **Recommendation 106**: The life peers who remain members of the second chamber should be encouraged to reach an informal understanding with the Appointments Commission about how long they intend to serve.

14.18 We envisage that the number of people who were members of the second chamber by virtue of being an existing life peer would decline as the number of members appointed by the Appointments Commission built up. We would be surprised if, within 20 years of the commencement of the legislation necessary to implement our recommendations, there were more than a handful of members sitting in the second chamber by virtue of a life peerage.

Chapter 15 – The representation of religious faiths

15.1   The present House of Lords is unique in the democratic world in providing seats in the national legislature for representatives of an established church. The Archbishops of Canterbury and York, the Bishops of London, Durham and Winchester and the 21 other most senior diocesan bishops of the Church of England are members of the House of Lords by virtue of their office, ceasing to be members of the House of Lords when they retire from their bishoprics.[1] The origins of the bishops' role as members of the House of Lords go back to the early Middle Ages, when they, along with abbots, represented some of the most powerful landed interests in the country and were among the Monarch's chief advisers. Until the Reformation, the Lords Spiritual usually outnumbered the lay members of the House of Lords. They remained a significant minority of the House of Lords until the mid 19th century, when their number was capped at 26 and the number of new lay peerages soared. This trend has continued and was reinforced by the introduction of life peerages in 1958. In the interim House of Lords, the Lords Spiritual make up some 4 per cent of the total membership.

15.2   In considering whether there is a place for Church of England bishops in the reformed second chamber, an important question to ask is whether it is appropriate to provide *any* distinct *explicit* representation for religious bodies in the second chamber. If the answer to the question were affirmative, it would be necessary to consider whether the particular form of representation accorded to the Church of England remains appropriate and how representation might be extended to other denominations and faith communities in the United Kingdom. The Church of England is of course only one denomination of one faith, active in only one part of the United Kingdom.

15.3   In its White Paper,[2] the Government announced that it did not intend to make any change to the representation of the Church of England in the interim House of Lords. It did, however, acknowledge "the importance of the House of Lords reflecting more accurately the multicultural nature of modern British society in which there are citizens of many faiths and none" and said it would be "looking for ways of increasing the representation in the Lords of other religious traditions", albeit "not [in] the form of providing regular representation such as is enjoyed by the Church of England".[3] In an allusion to the problems associated with extending the concept of religious representation in the second chamber, the Government concluded by encouraging the Royal Commission to consider "if there is a way of overcoming the legal and practical difficulties of replicating that regular representation for other religious bodies".

---

[1] Recently appointed bishops must retire at 70 and they usually do so between the ages of 65 and 70. In practice it is customary to offer retired archbishops life peerages under the Life Peerages Act 1958.

[2] Chapter 7, paragraphs 21 and 22.

[3] Other denominations and faiths have in the past been given representation in the House of Lords through the appointment of individual religious leaders as life peers. Examples include the late Lord Jakobovits, the former Chief Rabbi; Lord Eames, the Church of Ireland Archbishop of Armagh; and the late Lord Soper, a former Convenor of the Methodist Conference.

Sources of philosophical, moral or spiritual contributions

15.4   In considering whether the faith communities should have specific, explicit representation, we do not in any way imply that they are the sole source of philosophical, moral or spiritual insight or that their insights are necessarily more valuable than those contributed by people without a religious faith. In the reformed second chamber, as in the present House of Lords, individual members will bring their own deepest convictions to bear, whether their basis is religious or secular. Any formal representation for religious bodies should be seen as an acknowledgement that philosophical, moral and spiritual insights are a significant factor in many debates and that a variety of such contributions is welcomed.

15.5   Religious belief, however, is an important part of many people's lives and it is desirable that there should be a voice, or voices, in the second chamber to reflect that aspect of people's personalities and with which they can identify. It would be consistent with our overall views on the composition of the reformed second chamber that it should be in a position to view public policy issues from a range of points of view, including, specifically, the philosophical, moral and spiritual. Several submissions brought out the force of this point but the implication was not that members of religious bodies were the only people who could articulate such considerations. A particularly striking example was the submission from the Chief Rabbi, Professor Jonathan Sacks, in which he argued that, "In a plural society, by definition, moral authority does not flow from a single source. Instead it emerges from a conversation in which different traditions (some religious, some secular) bring their respective insights to the public domain." He identified a number of questions which were important to a society that is diverse and undergoing rapid change and argued that such an "ongoing moral conversation [was] fundamental to the long term project of society". He identified the need for a public arena "in which our several moral and spiritual traditions meet and share their hopes and concerns. The health of a free and democratic society is measured not by representative institutions alone. It is measured also by the strength and depth of the public conversation about the kind of social order we seek." His conclusion was that, in view of its role as a deliberative second chamber, the appropriate arena for this kind of conversation in the United Kingdom was the House of Lords.

15.6   We are sympathetic to much of this analysis and recommend that the reformed second chamber should continue to include people capable of articulating a range of philosophical, moral and spiritual viewpoints, both religious and secular. The Appointments Commission should have regard to this requirement and seek to identify people, whether religious leaders, moral philosophers or other secular thinkers, who can make a particular contribution to such 'moral conversations' alongside the general contributions of other members of the reformed second chamber. Furthermore, we hope the Commission will appoint people who not only have specific expertise in different areas, for example of scientific and medical advance, but who have thought deeply about these issues from philosophical and spiritual points of view.

Recommendation 107: The reformed second chamber should continue to include people capable of articulating a range of philosophical, moral and spiritual viewpoints, both religious and secular.

An explicit role for religious bodies

15.7   That said, there remains a question over the explicit role of the Church of England in the second chamber and the possibility of extending that role to embrace the representation of other Christian denominations and other faiths. Some of us would be opposed to going beyond the recommendation set out above, arguing that to do so would be inconsistent with the principle of neutrality between those who adhere to a faith and those who do not.

15.8   Those of us who would be prepared to go further are conscious of the historical fact of the Church of England's representation in the House of Lords and its unique place in English society and the wider constitutional framework of the country. Some 50 per cent of the population of England are baptised members of the Church of England and it is the Christian denomination to which they claim to belong and with which they identify, regardless of the regularity of their church attendance. The Church serves the whole of England through 13,000 parishes. It runs 5,000 primary schools (accounting for 25 per cent of all primary school children) and some 200 secondary schools. It is also the established Church in England, connected in a variety of ways to the Queen, who is its Supreme Governor, and to Parliament. The Church of England may legislate in respect of certain issues, although its Measures are subject to approval by both Houses of Parliament. While there is no direct or logical connection between the establishment of the Church of England and the presence of Church of England bishops in the second chamber,[4] their removal would be likely to raise the whole question of the relationship between Church, State and Monarchy, with unpredictable consequences.

15.9   More generally, a majority of us acknowledge that the presence of the Church of England bishops in the House of Lords has served a wider purpose than simply protecting or recognising the established status of the Church of England. The Church of England bishops' position as Lords of Parliament reflects the British history and culture of seeking to heal religious conflict and promoting ever greater religious tolerance and inclusiveness. The way in which the Church of England's representation in the House of Lords has been manifested over at least the past 100 years has served to acknowledge the importance of philosophical, moral and spiritual considerations – not just religious ones – in the conduct of public affairs. And that representation has been acknowledged by leaders of other Christian denominations and faith communities as providing a voice in Parliament for religion in general, not simply for the Church of England. A majority of us accept the force and the continuing validity of these points. For some of us, the presence of the Lords Spiritual is a sign that Governments are in the end accountable not only to those who elect them but also to a higher authority. Subject to the general caveat in paragraph 15.4, a substantial majority of us consider that there should continue to be formal religious representation in the second chamber. The time has come, however, to broaden and deepen the nature of that representation to embrace other Christian denominations in all parts of the United Kingdom, and other faith communities.

> **Recommendation 108:** The Church of England should continue to be explicitly represented in the second chamber, but the concept of religious representation should be broadened to embrace other Christian denominations, in all parts of the United Kingdom, and other faith communities.

---

[4] The Church of Scotland is also established but has no representation in the House of Lords and the Church in Wales was disestablished in 1919 with no observable ill-effects.

Broadening religious representation

15.10 The Church of England bishops, although they claim to speak in the House of Lords "not just for the Church of England but for its partners in other Christian churches, and for people of other faiths and none",[5] are not representative of the broad spectrum of religious opinion in the United Kingdom. By definition, they represent only the Anglican Church, in one part of the United Kingdom. That is the foundation of our majority view that it would be desirable to broaden the basis of explicit religious representation in the second chamber.

15.11 To achieve broader religious representation in the reformed second chamber, a number of obstacles would need to be overcome.

■ Not all denominations and faiths have a hierarchical structure, like that of the Church of England, which would lend itself to the identification of particular post holders who could be invited to serve in the second chamber on an *ex officio* basis.

■ Many of the other Christian denominations and faiths active in the United Kingdom have relatively loose structures with individual congregations or gatherings having a significant degree of independence.

■ In the United Kingdom there is a multiplicity of faiths, denominations and sects, making it difficult to identify those which could be considered truly 'representative'.

■ There is a risk that, in seeking to give adequate representation to each broad shade of religious opinion, the number of people who were members of the second chamber by virtue of their membership of a religious body would become disproportionate.

■ Members of some religious bodies would have practical and theological concerns about any suggestion that they should be 'represented' in the second chamber. The evidence we received from the Church of Scotland, for example, referred to the 'tension' which arises from the fact that "while the Church of Scotland is a National Church, whose life is, and has been for centuries, bound up with the life of the nation, it is also a Church which asserts its spiritual independence of the State, an independence which, moreover, the State recognises and guarantees by statute."[6]

15.12 On a related issue, it is clear that several religious bodies would find it difficult to agree to an arrangement in which the process of nominating someone to 'represent' them lay outside the control of their own authorities.

15.13 A specific concern raised by the evidence from the Roman Catholic Bishops' Conferences in England and Wales and in Scotland was the implications of the Canon Law of the Catholic Church[7] which forbids clerics from assuming "public office whenever it means sharing in the exercise of civil power". Both Bishops' Conferences clearly share the view that the presence of Roman Catholic representatives in the second chamber would be to the overall common good, but both mentioned the Canon Law bar. The Scottish Bishops' Conference took the view that this would require any Catholic representation to be undertaken by lay Catholics. The England and Wales Bishops'

[5] Church of England's submission to the Royal Commission, paragraph 4.
[6] Church of Scotland's submission, Part Two, paragraph 7.2.
[7] Code of Canon Law, 1983, canon 285, paragraph 3.

Conference was prepared to entertain the possibility that Roman Catholic representation in the second chamber could be undertaken by Roman Catholic bishops, but acknowledged that, once the role of the reformed second chamber and the proposed arrangements for securing representation in it were clearer, the Holy See would need to be consulted.

15.14 In proposing a way forward, we deal first with the representation of non-Christian faiths in the second chamber and then with the representation of the various Christian denominations throughout the United Kingdom, including the representation of the Church of England.

Non-Christian faiths

15.15 It is clearly not possible to find a way in which all other faith communities could be formally represented on any kind of *ex officio* basis. None of them has a suitable representative body. Even if a case could be made that the United Synagogue could in some sense act for Judaism (though this would be contested), there is nothing comparable for Islam or Hinduism. The only way, therefore, of providing a voice for other faith communities would be to place a duty on the Appointments Commission to appoint individuals who would be perceived as broadly representative of the different faith communities. A substantial majority of us so recommend.

15.16 Non-Christian faith communities in the country form between 5 and 6 per cent of the population. In our view, their explicit representation ought to be commensurate with this, in order to demonstrate a desire to give appropriate recognition to such communities. Religious belief is of course an important part of the identity of many minority ethnic or cultural groups. The Appointments Commission should therefore aim to ensure that at any one time there were at least five members of the second chamber specifically selected to represent the various non-Christian faith communities.

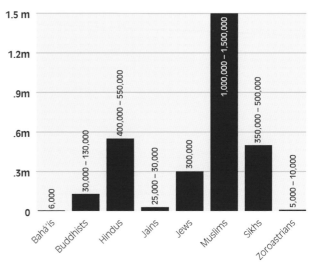

Number of members of non-Christian faith communities in the United Kingdom

15.17 The Appointments Commission should make clear to the various faith communities that it is open to receive nominations from them. It should consult the main inter-faith organisations but would ultimately have to make its own decisions on the basis of individual nominees' personal standing. The Appointments Commission would not be able to strike an exact balance at any one time, but through a series of nominations, over time, it should be able to ensure an appropriate level of representation for the main faith communities in the country. In achieving the necessary balances, it should also be able to take account of the spread of religious views among the members of the second chamber, including, in particular, those of members from minority ethnic groups.

Recommendation 109: The Appointments Commission should ensure that at any one time there are at least five members of the second chamber specifically selected to be broadly representative of the different non-Christian faith communities.

Christian denominations

15.18 As regards the representation of the various Christian denominations throughout the United Kingdom, we do not believe it would be right to increase the total number of such representatives beyond 26, the current number of Church of England bishops sitting as Lords Spiritual in the House of Lords. We believe they should be distributed according to the size of the population in each of the nations which comprise the United Kingdom.

Recommendation 110: The total number of places in the reformed second chamber for members formally representing the various Christian denominations throughout the United Kingdom should be 26. Taking into account the relative size of the population in each of the nations which comprise the United Kingdom, 21 of these places should go to members representing the Christian denominations in England and five should go to members representing the Christian denominations in Scotland, Wales and Northern Ireland.

15.19 For England, we recommend that the allocation of places to representatives of the various denominations should be done on the basis of the number of baptised members of each denomination rather than on levels of regular Sunday attendance. For virtually all Christian denominations, baptism is *the* mark of membership and it reflects the basis on which people identify their religious beliefs. With nearly 25 million baptised members, the Church of England accounts for nearly 80 per cent of the total church membership in England.

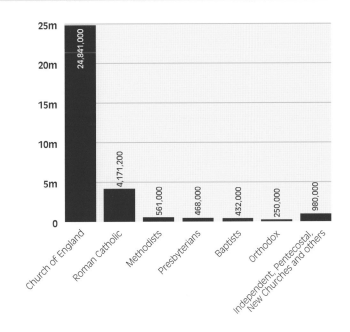

Distribution of baptised members of churches in England

Source: *Religious Trends* No 1, 1998/9, Dr Peter Brierley (ed). Christian Research, Paternoster Press.

Recommendation 111: Of the 21 places available for members of Christian denominations in England, 16 should be assigned to representatives of the Church of England and five to members of other Christian denominations in England.

15.20 In view of the considerations which arise from the Church of England's place in the life of the nation, we further recommend that the allocation of its 16 places to particular individuals should be done on a basis which provides considerable continuity from the present arrangements and is developed in consultation with the Church of England authorities. We return to this point below. As discussed in Chapter 13, the formal appointment of the Church of England's representatives as members of the second chamber should be the responsibility of the Appointments Commission.

15.21 So far as the five seats available to other Christian denominations in England are concerned, we recommend that the ultimate responsibility for appointing these members should rest with the Appointments Commission, but that it should consult extensively with the relevant ecumenical instrument, Churches Together in England (CTE). CTE and its equivalents in Wales, Scotland and Ireland are legally authorised instruments to promote co-operation and a common approach between the different Christian denominations.[8] They have no distinct theological position of their own: they exist to facilitate the closer working together of the Christian churches. We believe that they could play a useful part in helping the Appointments Commission to identify appropriate people to represent the various Christian denominations. They could also assist the Commission in striking the right balance, over time, between the claims of the different denominations active within the nations concerned. A convention might develop that, when nominations were requested by the Appointments Commission, whatever names were put forward by the ecumenical instrument would normally be accepted.

> **Recommendation 112:** The Appointments Commission should have the ultimate responsibility for appointing individuals to the five places available for members of Christian denominations in England other than the Church of England. But, in doing so, it should consult extensively with the relevant ecumenical instrument, Churches Together in England.

15.22 We have recommended that five places should be available to representatives of the Christian denominations in Scotland, Wales and Northern Ireland. The ultimate responsibility for making appointments to these five places should also rest with the Appointments Commission. Again we believe it should consult extensively with the relevant ecumenical instruments, Action of Churches Together in Scotland, Cytûn and the Irish Council of Churches.

15.23 Extending the logic of using a population basis for the allocation of these five places would point to drawing two members from denominations based in Scotland, one or two from denominations based in Wales and one from Northern Ireland. Given the nature of the community in Northern Ireland, however, we recommend that there should generally be two representatives of religious bodies from Northern Ireland. The precise distribution of all these seats should be the overall responsibility of the Appointments Commission and we believe it should be able, over time, to ensure appropriate representation for the various Christian denominations in all parts of the United Kingdom. There are two further complications connected with Northern Ireland. First, we understand that the

---

[8] Similar instruments exist in each county and most localities in England, and Churches Together in Britain and Ireland performs a similar role covering the whole of the British Isles.

Roman Catholic Church in Ireland has chosen to take 'observer' status only on the relevant ecumenical instrument. Second, the main Christian denominations in Northern Ireland operate on an all-Ireland basis. We do not consider that either complication represents an insuperable obstacle to the participation of the Irish Council of Churches in the kind of consultative arrangements we have recommended. We are confident that all concerned would demonstrate due sensitivity in putting nominations forward for consideration.

Recommendation 113: The Appointments Commission should have the ultimate responsibility for appointing individuals to the five places available for members of Christian denominations in Scotland, Wales and Northern Ireland, but it should consult extensively with the relevant ecumenical instruments.

15.24 Three further points should be made. First, our proposals for securing broader religious representation assume the need to identify appropriate individuals to take up the seats concerned and on a basis which involves an active role for the various denominations through their representation on the relevant ecumenical instrument. It would therefore be open to the various denominations and faiths to reach their own decision on whether to recommend clerical or lay members for appointment. This should, for example, give the Church of Scotland and the Roman Catholic Bishops' Conferences scope to reflect on the extent and nature of their participation in the reformed second chamber. They would be able to alter their positions over time, if appropriate, in the light of experience of the role and work of the reformed second chamber and of the machinery for identifying and appointing members of religious bodies.

Lambeth Palace

15.25 Second, under these proposed arrangements it would become easier than is currently the case for women and members of minority ethnic groups to secure places in the second chamber as representatives of religious organisations. They could do so as representatives of other faiths or of the smaller Christian denominations, as lay representatives or as ordained members of those Christian denominations which have women ministers.

15.26 The recommendations we have made in this chapter are based on current information about population and the numbers of people expressing some identification with religious bodies. Clearly, any demographic changes or changes in the level of adherence to particular sets of religious beliefs would need to be kept under review and appropriate adjustments made to the pattern of representation which we have proposed.

> **Recommendation 114:** Demographic changes and changes in the level of adherence to particular sets of religious beliefs should be reflected in adjustments to the pattern of religious representation which we have proposed.

15.27 Finally, we appreciate that our recommendations will create considerable difficulties for the Church of England. A reduction from 26 to 16 in the number of Church of England representatives entitled to sit in the second chamber will have some awkward consequences that could significantly alter the role of the diocesan bishop. At present a diocesan bishop (excluding the two Archbishops and the Bishops of London, Durham and Winchester) can expect to become a member of the House of Lords within about five years of taking up office and will normally serve as such for about ten years. The Church of England bishops have been effective members of the House of Lords, partly because their diocesan responsibilities have given them a valuable insight into a range of social and regional issues. On the other hand, the geographical spread of Church of England dioceses and the heavy workloads associated with being a diocesan bishop have meant that, individually, they are often relatively infrequent attenders. That is not a criticism, and we would not necessarily expect representatives of any religious bodies to be full-time members of the second chamber. But our recommendations will require the Church of England to think carefully about the nature of its formal representation in the reformed second chamber.

15.28 Unless the number of eligible bishoprics were reduced, or the basis of Church of England representation in the second chamber were altered, bishops would in future need to wait for up to ten years before becoming members of the second chamber and could then only expect to serve for three or four years. It would be difficult for them to make a significant contribution in such a short time and their tenure would be substantially different from that of other members of the second chamber. We hope that future Church of England representatives in the second chamber would also serve 15-year terms. Rather than attempt to provide a detailed answer to these complex questions, we think that the Church of England should take the lead in finding a satisfactory basis for determining how its representatives, whether bishops or not, should be identified. Similarly, the Church should lead in considering arrangements for reducing the number of bishops in the second chamber and liaising with the Appointments Commission about the timing for bringing ten members of other Christian denominations into the reformed chamber.

Recommendation 115: The Church of England should review the options for providing formal Church of England representation in the reformed second chamber. Their detailed recommendations should be made to the Government in time for incorporation into whatever legislation is required to implement our own recommendations.

Chapter 16 – Procedures

16.1   The most important influences on the effectiveness of the reformed second chamber will be its *powers*, the *characteristics* of its members and the perceived *legitimacy* of its overall membership. Nevertheless, the ability of the chamber to fulfil its remit will be greatly affected by the *procedures* by which it conducts its business.

16.2   The procedures followed by the House of Lords have developed over centuries, in response to changes in the composition and in the nature of the chamber. The further evolution of these procedures must be a matter for the reformed second chamber to determine, as the effects of changes in its functions and membership become apparent. It would not, therefore, be appropriate for us to make recommendations on procedural details, other than the few specific points made in earlier chapters. We do, however, make some general points about whether the reformed second chamber should seek to continue the House of Lords' tradition of open procedures, which give considerable freedom to individual members.

Open procedures

16.3   Until the end of the 19th century, the conduct of business in the two Houses of Parliament had many similarities. All stages of Bills were debated on the floor of both Houses, with any member able to move and speak to amendments, and there was no selection or obligatory grouping of amendments. In addition, Government business enjoyed no formal preference and any member could raise any issue, speaking without time limits and calling for votes as desired.

16.4   In the Commons, the growth of party feeling and the obstructionist tactics of Irish Nationalist MPs led to the rights of individual MPs being progressively restricted to ensure that the Government's business was processed. The guillotine, time limits, selection and grouping of amendments, and controls on opportunities for debate were the main tools employed. As a result, the Speaker was granted substantial powers, including responsibility for controlling debate and the conduct of MPs in the chamber. The only major aspect of the chamber not under the Speaker's authority is the business of the House, which remains in the hands of the Leader of the House of Commons on behalf of the Government. Similar trends have been observed in lower chambers around the world.

16.5   It is, however, a feature of second chambers, including, for example, the French Sénat and the United States Senate, that their members retain considerable procedural freedoms. That is certainly true of the House of Lords, where 19th century and earlier practice has largely been retained. The House cannot meet unless the Speaker or a deputy is present, but beyond that the Speaker has minimal powers: Standing Order 18[1] states that the Speaker may do nothing "without the consent of the Lords first had" and that any difference of opinion among the Lords is to be put to the vote. The Speaker's only role is to put the question. That the office is held by the Lord Chancellor, a Minister of the Crown, rather than by an impartial officer of the House, is therefore of no practical concern. Having no Speaker with powers of order, the House of Lords is self-regulating,

[1] Dated 27 March 1621.

working on the basis of consensus, guided by the Leader of the House. As the *Companion to the Standing Orders* notes, the Leader "advises the House on matters of procedure and order and has the responsibility of drawing attention to transgression or abuse". However, the Leader of the House has no formal authority either and his or her advice usually reflects the wishes of all sides. Responsibility for the maintenance of order therefore lies with the House itself. For example, when two peers stand up to speak at the same time, it is for the other members to make clear who should speak first.

16.6   The freedom given to individual members of the House of Lords is an important element in its ability to scrutinise legislation and hold the Government to account. With the Government unable to insist on its business having priority, and the Speaker having no powers of order, the chamber can linger over important issues, even if the Government would rather it did not. Any member who wishes to raise a point has the opportunity to do so. Such procedures are particularly suited to a revising chamber, whose main role is to improve the quality of legislation, rather than to sustain a Government in office. Several submissions pointed out that a number of professional bodies or organisations have found it more effective to raise their concerns with a peer than with an MP, on account of these greater rights. We therefore recommend that the second chamber should seek to continue the House of Lords' tradition of open procedures.

> **Recommendation 116:** The second chamber should seek to continue the House of Lords' tradition of open procedures.

16.7   One consequence of the variation in procedural styles adopted by the two Houses is that they may reach different decisions on procedural matters with regard to legislation. For example, in the Commons, the decision whether a proposed amendment is relevant or should be called for debate is the Speaker's alone. In the Lords, the relevance of amendments is decided by the House as a whole, while the member moving an amendment can insist on it being debated and decided separately. As a result, an amendment ruled out of order in the Commons may be debated and passed in the Lords. Similarly, while the rules as to whether a Bill is hybrid[2] are the same in both Houses, the Government can use its majority in the Commons to dispense with the relevant Standing Order, and so treat the Bill as if it were not hybrid. The Government cannot rely on being able to do this in the Lords.[3] Although these features may appear somewhat inconsistent, they are an inevitable consequence of the different approaches to procedure taken by the two Houses. The benefits for the work of the second chamber flowing from open procedures are such that inconsistencies of this sort are a relatively minor price to pay.

16.8   This approach to procedure provides for a more relaxed pace of business and allows greater time for detailed consideration and reflection than does the more hurried and regulated approach generally adopted by first chambers. It does, however, increase the risk of filibustering. The absence of any mechanism to ensure that Government business is dealt with within a reasonable time frame can result in deadlock, such as is regularly experienced in the United States Congress. In the case of the second chamber, it is necessary that the freedoms associated with open procedures should be tempered with

---

[2] A public Bill is considered to be hybrid, and special procedures therefore apply to it, when it "affects a particular private interest in a manner different from the private interest of other persons or bodies of the same category or class." *Erskine May*, p.554.

[3] In the case of the Aircraft and Shipbuilding Industries Bill 1976/77, the Government was by this means forced to remove the hybridising provisions.

an acknowledgement of political reality. Most legislation is proposed by a Government which has a majority in the House of Commons, the pre-eminent House of Parliament, that is based upon its victory in a general election. As we have noted in earlier chapters, it would not be appropriate in these circumstances for the second chamber to seek to delay Government business purely by procedural means. Therefore, while the benefits of open procedures are significant, we reaffirm our earlier recommendation (Chapter 4) that it is essential they be accompanied by a convention that all Government business be considered within a reasonable time.

Pressures on open procedures

16.9   It is necessary to consider, however, whether the time pressures on the reformed second chamber may in due course reach the point where the current approach of self-regulation, guided by advice from the Leader of the House, will no longer be sufficient to ensure the smooth and fair conduct of business.

16.10 The growing workload of the House of Lords has led to progressive restrictions on its members. These have usually been in the form of 'guidance' rather than a formal reduction in rights. The number of Questions for Written Answer that a peer can table is now limited to six per day, while the number of Starred (Oral) Questions which each peer is entitled to ask has been reduced from two per day: each peer is now permitted only one on the Order Paper at any one time. A limit of 30 minutes is also observed at Question Time. Numerous other examples exist, covering all aspects of members' involvement in the business of the House. Even where formal restrictions have not been imposed, the guidance has become firmer in tone and the scope and detail significantly expanded. The *Companion to the Standing Orders*, for example, has grown from 30 pages in 1955 to 247 pages today, while the Leader of the House has had to intervene more frequently to arbitrate between those competing for the floor. In short, there appear to be significant pressures on the existing system of conventions and procedures governing members' behaviour.[4] While recognising these pressures, the value of the current system of open procedures is such that any restrictions which become necessary should be designed to preserve the essential character of what exists at present.

> **Recommendation 117:** Any restrictions to the rights of members of the second chamber should be designed to preserve the essential character of what exists at present.

16.11 The self-regulatory nature of the House of Lords is a distinctive feature, shared with several other second chambers overseas. It is entirely in keeping with the maturity which members of a second chamber should be expected to show. It is also consistent with the relative lack of political passion, which we hope the reformed second chamber will display. Accordingly, we would regard it as a retrograde step if any pressures on the second chamber were to lead to a breakdown in its ability to be self-regulating and so require the introduction of a Speaker with powers of order. Indeed, it may be the absence of such a Speaker that encourages the Lords to conduct their business with courtesy. If members could rely on the Speaker to enforce order, they might feel less responsible themselves

---

4 The March 1999 report of the Group on Procedure in the Chamber (HL34) felt it necessary to remind peers of the importance of adhering to the existing conventions on procedure if these were to be maintained without further restrictions.

to behave in an orderly fashion and be more likely to push at the limits of behaviour in order to secure party political advantage. The proceedings of the second chamber would consequently become more like those in the House of Commons, which would be in complete contrast to the nature of the second chamber we would like to emerge from our work. Although this is a matter for the second chamber itself to settle, we recommend that every effort should be made to maintain an approach to the conduct of business which would allow the second chamber to remain self-regulating.

Presiding over the House of Lords

Recommendation 118: The second chamber's approach to the conduct of business should be such as to allow the chamber to remain self-regulating.

Chapter 17 – Resources

17.1   Our recommendations on the composition of the reformed second chamber are designed to produce a second chamber with the expertise and authority to fulfil the role and functions that we believe it should carry out. But it is not sufficient just to have the right people. They also need to have adequate resources.

17.2   The range and quality of the facilities and support available to members of the House of Lords have been improved significantly over the last 40 years. Expenses incurred in attending the House are refunded up to specified limits and the Library provides a valuable reference and research service. In recent years, the House has embraced modern information and communications technology. Computers are provided to members who wish to have them and all House of Lords papers, reports and debates are posted on the Internet.

17.3   Nevertheless, the support available to members of the House of Lords is still well below the standards enjoyed by members of the House of Commons and other legislatures. The number of desks available to members is insufficient, despite the cramped conditions resulting from an average of four desks being packed into every room. In addition, the modest level of expenses which are refundable for office support means that most members receive little if any support in scrutinising the mass of documents laid before Parliament and responding to the correspondence which this and other Parliamentary business generates. Finally, members receive no payment for the time they devote to their Parliamentary duties, nor recompense for the income that they may lose as a direct consequence.

17.4   A system of office support and expenses that relied upon members having a substantial private income may have been appropriate in the days when the House of Lords was both amateur and voluntary and the inheritance of a peerage may have carried with it substantial financial resources. Such a system would not be appropriate for a second chamber with the workload and membership we have proposed in this report. Members of the reformed second chamber will require adequate support if they are to meet the demands placed upon them.

17.5   It is the responsibility of the Review Body on Senior Salaries (SSRB) to determine the level at which allowances and other payments available to members of the second chamber should be set. We need do no more than set out some broad principles which we believe should be applied.

17.6   The support required by members falls into three categories:

■   recompense for time devoted to Parliamentary duties and lost income;

■   office and secretarial support; and

■   travel and overnight costs.

Recompense for time and lost income

17.7 Members of the present House of Lords receive no payment for the time they devote to their Parliamentary duties. If they are to attend more than infrequently, members have to supplement any expenses they may claim with income from other sources. Many are able to do this because they are retired from their former employment and receive an occupational pension. Others are able to arrange their outside employment around their Parliamentary duties. However, this is effectively restricted to those working in London in senior positions, or those in certain very limited professions. Members living away from London or who are in full-time employment find it extremely difficult to take an active part in the House and many suffer considerable financial loss as a result of taking their Parliamentary duties seriously. As a consequence, the active membership of the House is currently heavily skewed towards retired people based in the South East of England. One outcome of our recommendations for the composition of the reformed second chamber would be to broaden representation and provide a voice for the nations and regions. It is therefore essential that the financial arrangements which apply to members of the reformed second chamber should support their active involvement.

> **Recommendation 119:** The financial arrangements which apply to members of the second chamber should make regular attendance economically viable for people who live outside the South East of England and who do not have a separate source of income.

17.8 While there are many areas of public service where people give their time without payment, for example as school governors, these tend to be local posts and operate on the basis that the people concerned should be able to fit their commitments around a full-time job, rather than *vice versa*. Even so, they often receive a basic allowance plus payment for each meeting attended, as is the case with local councillors, in addition to expenses. By contrast, active membership of the second chamber may leave minimal time available for other employment, yet no payment for time is made. This has particular relevance for those based outside London, since they may have to add considerable travelling time to the already long hours the House sits.

17.9 In 1911, when proposing MPs should be paid for their attendance, Lloyd George argued that this was essential "to enable men to come here, men who would render incalculable service to the State, and whom it is an incalculable loss to the State not to have here, but who cannot be here because their means do not allow it." We believe the same considerations apply in principle to members of the reformed second chamber and that payment should be made to compensate for the time members devote to their Parliamentary duties.

> **Recommendation 120:** Payment should be made for the time members of the second chamber devote to their Parliamentary duties.

17.10 Current arrangements for defraying the expenses of members of the House of Lords are related to daily attendance. This is consistent with the fact that many members attend on a part-time basis, or not at all, and that the principle behind the arrangements has been to meet expenses rather than to pay an allowance. The question that arises now is whether any payment made in recognition of the time which members of the reformed second chamber devote to their Parliamentary duties should be related to attendance, or paid in the form of a salary regardless of attendance. We think it is desirable that the reformed second chamber should contain a significant proportion of people who will contribute on a less than full-time basis, allowing them to remain active in other walks of life. We were also very struck by the widespread concern expressed during our consultation exercise that the second chamber should not become a forum for yet another layer of salaried politicians. It must be emphasised that the core function of members of the reformed second chamber will be to make a contribution *in Parliament*. In particular, we would be concerned to avoid anything which might be misinterpreted as implying that members of the second chamber had duties 'at large' on behalf of individual members of the public. That is the function of constituency MPs. For all these reasons we recommend that financial support for members of the reformed second chamber should be related to attendance in Parliament.

> **Recommendation 121:** Financial support for members of the reformed second chamber should be related to attendance in Parliament.

17.11 The SSRB will need to consider what cumulative total of payments made for time and lost income would be appropriate if a member of the second chamber were to attend every sitting in an average year. Given the absence of constituency duties, we believe that over an average session payment should certainly be less than the basic salary of an MP.[1] As it would be an allowance, rather than a refund of expenses, it would be taxable.

> **Recommendation 122:** Total payments made to members for time and lost income should be less than the basic salary of an MP over an average session.

17.12 While we agree that the second chamber should not be a forum for salaried politicians, a number of members of the chamber will have significant additional duties over and above those of other members. These include the Chairman of Committees and the Principal Deputy Chairman of Committees, who is also Chairman of the European Union Committee. These office holders currently receive salaries in respect of their duties[2] and we recommend that this should continue to be the case. We also recommend that salaries should be payable to those members who take on the burden of chairing other significant Committees of the second chamber.

> **Recommendation 123:** Chairmen of significant Committees of the second chamber should receive a salary in respect of their additional duties.

---

[1] Currently £47,008 per year.

[2] Since they receive salaries, they are not eligible to claim expenses for subsistence and overnight accommodation.

17.13 Our recommendation that membership of the second chamber should be for a fixed term makes it necessary to consider, for the first time, arrangements for members leaving the chamber. Although we expect many members of the reformed second chamber will attend part-time and will keep contact with their outside occupation, the loss of income resulting from active membership is likely to have a long-term effect on individuals, even after they have left the chamber. Former members may not immediately be able to replace from other sources the income from their former Parliamentary duties and may have a reduced pension entitlement from their main occupation. We note that MPs have access to severance payments and a pension scheme and invite the SSRB to consider these matters in respect of the second chamber.

Recommendation 124: The SSRB should consider the issue of severance payments and pension arrangements for members of the reformed second chamber.

Office and secretarial support

17.14 Members of the current House of Lords have access to the Library, a computer, a desk (usually in a room shared with others), and an allowance of £35.00 per day for secretarial support. This allowance may be claimed only for days on which members attend the House, and for a maximum of 30 additional days per year. A member attending every one of the 160 sitting days in an average Session could therefore claim a maximum of £6,650 per year, sufficient only to employ a part-time assistant. This is a far cry from the allowances available to each MP,[3] although the tasks they perform are very different from those undertaken by members of the second chamber. Whereas an important role of MPs is to act as roving representatives of the people, taking up a wide range of cases on behalf of their constituents, the focus for members of the second chamber should be on their role in Parliament itself.

The House of Lords library

17.15 Our recommendation therefore is that additional office and secretarial resources should be made available to the reformed second chamber corporately, rather than to individual members. These resources might be targeted in particular at the various Committees of the House, ensuring that members of those Committees collectively have suitable assistance in carrying out their responsibilities. Some additional space is already available following the departure of most of the hereditary peers and more will be available by summer 2001. In addition the existing Parliamentary Data and Video

---

[3] A maximum of £54,155, including an element for staff pension costs, payable in addition to the member's annual salary.

Network is being extended. Although office space will still be limited, these factors should make it possible for each member to be assigned a desk with a computer and have access to staff, employed by the second chamber, who would provide the support necessary to enable Committees and individual members to fulfil their Parliamentary duties more effectively. This arrangement should allow more extensive office support to be provided in a cost effective and appropriate manner.

> **Recommendation 125:** The second chamber should provide additional office and secretarial resources to enable Committees and individual members to fulfil their Parliamentary duties more effectively.

17.16 Members may find it necessary to employ office support additional to that provided centrally. The allowance for such costs should be maintained at broadly the current level, such that it would not encourage or enable members to take on any 'constituency' work.

Travel and overnight costs

17.17 Attendance at the House of Lords requires members to be in Central London, often until late at night. For those members living outside London, this may involve substantial amounts of travel and many nights spent away from home. It seems likely that the same will be true for members of the reformed second chamber. The current arrangements for reimbursing expenses incurred as a result of attendance are somewhat inflexible and cause many members to suffer financial difficulties or lead them to subsidise their participation in the work of the House. We have earlier argued that the financial arrangements which apply to members of the second chamber should make regular attendance by people who live outside the South East of England economically viable. We understand that the SSRB considered these issues in their 1996 report on House of Lords allowances,[4] but that its recommendations were not adopted. We would therefore invite the SSRB to review once again the rules governing the payment of expenses incurred by members of the second chamber in the course of their Parliamentary duties, with a view to ensuring that these rules support our overall objective.

> **Recommendation 126:** The SSRB should review the rules governing the payment of expenses incurred in respect of travel and overnight costs by members of the second chamber in the course of their Parliamentary duties with a view to ensuring that regular attendance is economically viable for people who live outside London.

[4] Review Body on Senior Salaries, *Report no. 38: Review of Parliamentary Pay and Allowances* (Cm 3330-I) (4 July 1996), Chapter 4.

Conclusion

17.18 If the SSRB's recommendations reflect these principles, we believe they will enable members to participate more effectively in the work of the second chamber. We suspect that this will involve an increase in the costs of the second chamber. We make no apology for this and reject the notion that this country can have a Parliament 'on the cheap'. In practice, the increase in costs would not be inordinate. As its latest annual report shows, the total cost per member of the House of Lords – £38,000 – was less than one tenth that of the House of Commons.[5] The reduction in the number of members from 1,213 in the 1998/99 Session to the level we have proposed is such that, even were the cost per active member to double, the effect on the overall cost of the second chamber would be an increase of no more than £5–6 million per year. This would still leave the annual budget of the second chamber under £50 million, less than one fifth of the £260 million spent each year on the House of Commons. An effective second chamber at this price represents extremely good value for money.

---

[5] *House of Lords: Annual Report and Accounts 1998–99*, HL104 (July 1999).

Chapter 18 – Titles and name

18.1   Our task is to make recommendations to improve the effectiveness of the second chamber as a part of our national Parliament. Would the recommendations made earlier in this report be supported or undermined if the automatic link between the peerage and membership of the second chamber were broken or if the name of the second chamber and the titles by which its members are known were changed?

Links with the peerage

18.2   Our recommendations envisage a chamber of appointed and regional members, all serving terms of three electoral cycles or 15 years. They will all be chosen on the basis of the contribution they can make to the second chamber, not as a reward or mark of approval for past achievements.

18.3   This contrasts strongly with the perceptions associated with peerages. While many peerages, particularly life peerages, have been awarded to so-called 'working peers' in the expectation that they will contribute to the work of the present House of Lords (normally on behalf of one of the main political parties), they are also often seen as a recognition of past service and merit. Many life peers treat their peerages as essentially honorary and do not acknowledge any associated public service obligation to participate in the work of the second chamber. The perception that peerages are honours is reinforced by the fact that, like other honours, they are awarded by the Crown and for life.

18.4   It is already the case that most hereditary peers are no longer members of the second chamber.[1] It would be anachronistic and confusing to perpetuate the automatic link between membership of the second chamber and the possession of a peerage. This would be particularly true if some members of the second chamber were to be directly elected, as proposed in Models B and C (Chapter 12). Also, receiving a lifelong honour as a prior requirement for fixed-term membership of the second chamber would, in itself, be inconsistent. We therefore recommend that the automatic link between the peerage and membership of the second chamber should be broken.

---

[1] Irish peers and, before 1963, some Scottish peers were not able to sit and vote in the House of Lords, but they were relatively few in number.

18.5   New members of the reformed second chamber will enter through appointment by the independent Appointments Commission, whether by virtue of selection as a regional member or by the Appointments Commission itself, or by virtue of appointment as a Lord of Appeal in Ordinary or as a representative of the Church of England. Possession of a peerage should no longer be a necessary qualification for membership of the second chamber, and new members should not be offered a peerage in that connection.

18.6   The future of the peerage itself is not a matter on which we need express a view. However, we would expect that it would remain open to the Prime Minister to recommend award of a peerage in recognition of a person's merit and achievements. Possession of a peerage should not be a bar to membership of the reformed second chamber and members of the chamber should not be precluded from accepting peerages; but the two should be completely distinct.

> **Recommendation 127**: Possession of a peerage should no longer be a necessary qualification for membership of the second chamber, and new members should not be offered a peerage in that connection.

Titles of members

18.7   The decision to sever the automatic link between the peerage and membership of the chamber means that a new title for members will be required. This is not a central issue, but the title adopted will symbolise the nature and style of the new institution and its members.

18.8   Some have suggested that members of the reformed second chamber should adopt the suffix LP (Lord/Lady of Parliament) and the courtesy title 'Lord/Lady'. This option would signal and symbolise the elements of continuity from the present House of Lords, which we believe should be sustained. It would also reflect the fact that for at least the first few years of its existence, until new members came to outnumber the remaining life peers, the reformed second chamber would continue to have a majority of Lords (and Ladies) among its members. There would be no need to change the name of the chamber and many of the formal usages could be left unaltered. While there might be a risk of confusion with the title 'Lord of Parliament' held by Church of England bishops and some members of the Scottish peerage, the numbers involved are sufficiently small as to suggest this would be a minor issue.

18.9 Others have proposed that a fresh chamber needs a fresh start. A change of title could clarify the changed nature of entry to the reformed second chamber and its separation from the peerage. They suggest that there would be a considerable risk of confusion between the Lords/Ladies of Parliament who were members of the second chamber but not peers, the Lords/Ladies who were peers but not members of the second chamber and, potentially, the Lords/Ladies who were peers and might be elected to the House of Commons. Alternative titles would be 'State Counsellor' and 'Senator'/'Senator of Parliament'. The former has little to commend it and could easily be confused with local government 'councillor'. By contrast, 'Senator' has the great advantage of being generally understood as referring to a member of a country's second chamber.

Name of the chamber

18.10 Should members of the second chamber be known as Lords/Ladies of Parliament, this would allow many of the traditions and usages of the current House of Lords to continue and would not require any change in the name of the chamber. A change would be required, however, if members of the reformed second chamber were to receive the title Senator/Senator of Parliament. In this country, we are accustomed to our two national legislative chambers being 'Houses' of Parliament. This would imply that the reformed second chamber should be known as the House of Senators.

Conclusion

18.11 These issues are not central to the successful reform of the second chamber and there are arguments in favour of each of the options canvassed above. We consider that the situation should be left to evolve. Parliament should determine whether, in time, the reformed second chamber should be called something other than the House of Lords and its members given a new title.

Recommendation 128: The question of the name of the second chamber and the titles of its members should be left to evolve.

Chapter 19 – Implementing this report

19.1   We began this report by saying that we did not want it to gather dust in a pigeonhole. If our recommendations win support and are accepted by the Government, they could be implemented quickly. We see no reason why the various preparatory steps could not be taken in time for the first selection of regional members to take place at the time of the next general election, within 2½ years, or the next European Parliament election in 2004, depending on which model of composition is adopted. Meanwhile the independent Appointments Commission which the Government intends to establish during the interim stage of Lords reform could be equipped and prepare itself to take on the wider role envisaged in this report.

Follow-up action

19.2   The Government is committed "to [making] every effort to ensure that the second stage of reform has been approved by Parliament by the time of the General Election".[1] It may wish to promote the establishment of a Joint Committee of both Houses of Parliament to review some aspects of our recommendations before it reaches final conclusions of its own. It will certainly be necessary for the appropriate authorities in the interim House of Lords to reach a view on the size, structure and inter-relationship of the various new Committees we have proposed. They should also consider the implications of our recommendations for the workload and the overall size of the reformed second chamber. The Church of England would also need to decide how the 16 members of the second chamber to be drawn from its own ranks should be selected.

Legislation

19.3   If our recommendations are agreed, legislation would be required to bring them into effect. A Bill would be needed to:

■ make provision for the choice of regional members;

■ put the independent Appointments Commission on a statutory basis;

■ make the single, limited amendment to the Parliament Acts which we propose in Chapter 5;

■ amend the Statutory Instruments Act 1946 on the lines suggested in Chapter 7;

■ make provision for existing life peers to be deemed to have been appointed to the reformed second chamber;

[1] See the penultimate paragraph of the Executive Summary to the White Paper *Modernising Parliament: Reforming the House of Lords.*

- amend the Life Peerages Act 1958 to:

  - make provision for life peers to be created without entailing any right to sit and vote in the reformed second chamber; and

  - (if necessary) enable life peers to renounce their entitlement to sit and vote in the second chamber;

- amend the Appellate Jurisdiction Act 1876 to provide that Lords of Appeal in Ordinary should be formally appointed as members of the second chamber by the Appointments Commission; and

- amend the Bishoprics Act 1878 to:

  - limit the number of Church of England bishops with *ex officio* seats in the second chamber to 16; and/or

  - make any necessary provision for whatever system of selection the Church of England recommends should be put in place.

There is no need for primary legislation to secure the removal of the remaining hereditary peers from the second chamber, as the so-called 'Weatherill 92' are there by virtue of a Standing Order of the House of Lords. It might be convenient, however, to settle the point beyond doubt by incorporating it in the relevant Bill.

The first regional members

19.4   The timetable for implementing our recommendations and selecting the first regional members will depend on which of the models set out in Chapter 12 is adopted.

- Under *Model A*, if the necessary legislation can be enacted before the forthcoming general election, the first set of regional members could be appointed, using the system of 'complementary' election, in the immediate aftermath of that election. As there is no requirement under this model to introduce a separate election process, we believe that the necessary practical steps could easily be taken in the time available.

- Under *Models B and C*, legislation might be enacted during the first or second session of the next Parliament to enable the practical steps to be taken in time for the first round of elections of regional members to take place in association with the next European Parliament election (June 2004).

19.5   Under *Models A and B*, we recommend that regional members should be appointed or elected in respect of *every* region in the country at the *first* relevant election, so that the reformed chamber has a full complement of regional members from the outset. Under *Model C,* we envisage that the first tranche of 65 regional members would be elected at the first (European Parliament) election and the rest at the two subsequent European Parliament elections. The alternative of electing 195 regional members in one go by 'partially open' list PR would cause some of the ballot papers to become unwieldy. Also, the influx of such a large number of new regional members at an early stage in the life of the reformed second chamber would be too great to be easily accommodated and make the chamber over-large.

19.6 Whichever model is chosen, we envisage that the 92 remaining hereditary peers would leave the second chamber at the time the first regional members are selected, so that the overall size of the second chamber would not be significantly affected. Some of those hereditary peers, or indeed some of the other hereditary peers whose entitlement to sit and vote in the present House of Lords has already been removed, might well decide to stand for election (or put themselves forward for nomination) as regional members of the second chamber. A number of hereditary peers have strong regional links and considerable relevant experience of working in the second chamber and so might be strong contenders.

19.7 Under *Model C,* the full complement of regional members would build up over three European Parliament elections, reaching 195 by 2014. Regional members would then be replaced by new regional members as their terms came to an end. Under *Models A and B,* it would be necessary to be clear at the time of the first relevant election that those selected to serve as regional members for one third of the regions would serve for only one electoral cycle, and those chosen to serve as regional members for a further third of the regions would serve for only two electoral cycles. The regions concerned could be selected by lot or determined on a basis which produced a geographically and numerically balanced outcome. On that basis, the regions might be grouped as follows:

Group 1	Group 2	Group 3
Greater London	South East	North West
West Midlands	Eastern	East Midlands
Yorkshire and The Humber	North East	Scotland
Northern Ireland	Wales	South West

19.8 As an exception to the recommendation we made in Chapter 12, any members elected under Model B at the first election of regional members to serve for less than the full term should be eligible to stand for *re-election* as regional members for a full 15-year term at the end of their first period of membership. Equivalent arrangements would be required for the regional members selected under Model A.

Recommendation 129: Depending on which of the models (set out in Chapter 12) for selecting regional members is adopted, we recommend the following:

Model A

At the first general election after the passage of the necessary legislation, 65 regional members should be selected using a system of 'complementary' election, so that every region has its full complement of regional members from the outset. Those selected for one-third of the regions should serve for one Parliamentary term, and those selected for a further third of the regions should serve for two Parliamentary terms: exceptionally (as a transitional measure) all of these regional members should be eligible for reselection at the point at which their membership would otherwise lapse. At the second and all subsequent general elections, regional members would be selected by 'complementary' election in respect of the relevant one-third of the regions.

Model B

At the first European Parliament election after the passage of the necessary legislation, 87 regional members should be elected by whatever method of election is in use to elect MEPs so that every region has its full complement of regional members from the outset. Those elected for one-third of the regions should serve for one European Parliament term, and those elected for a further third of the regions should serve for two European Parliament terms: exceptionally (as a transitional measure) all these members should be eligible for re-election at the point at which their membership would otherwise lapse. At the time of the second and all subsequent European Parliament elections, regional members should be elected by the relevant one-third of the regions.

Model C

At the first European Parliament election after the passage of the necessary legislation, 65 regional members should be elected by 'partially open' list PR, so that each region has one-third of its eventual complement of regional members. A further 65 regional members should be elected in the same way at the time of each of the next two European Parliament elections.

Recommendation 130: The remaining hereditary peers should cease to be entitled to sit and vote in the second chamber at the point at which the first regional members join the second chamber. They, and other hereditary peers, would be eligible to seek nomination as regional members, or offer themselves for appointment by the Appointments Commission.

The interim Appointments Commission

19.9   The independent Appointments Commission, even prior to its formal establishment in legislation, should prepare to carry out the wider role we envisage. It should develop and publish a clear and comprehensive statement of the characteristics which the reformed second chamber should possess and the balances which it should strike. It should conduct an audit of the expertise and experience of the members of the interim House of Lords

and identify the areas which need reinforcing. This work would of course be informed by the outcome of its private dialogue with individual life peers about the length of the contribution they would expect to make. It should result in the preparation of a report identifying those characteristics which the Appointments Commission wished to strengthen immediately, in order to provide a firm foundation for the early rounds of appointments.

19.10   Meanwhile, we would expect the Appointments Commission to establish the necessary contacts with and knowledge of the organisations and individuals active in all the appropriate sectors of society. It would then be in a position to identify potential appointees who would enable the second chamber as a whole to display the full range of desired characteristics. It might bear in mind the fact that some hereditary peers with extensive experience in the House of Lords could well have characteristics which would make them well-suited for appointment to the second chamber, on merit.

> **Recommendation 131:** Pending its formal establishment as a statutory body, the independent Appointments Commission which will be responsible for nominating Cross Bench members of the interim House of Lords and vetting political nominations for propriety, should prepare to take on the wider role we envisage it discharging as part of the 'second stage' of Lords reform.

19.11 It will be for the Government to decide whether the Appointments Commission should be given responsibility for achieving and maintaining the appropriate party balance within the second chamber as from the date of the next general election. The Government could also give the Commission power to nominate party-affiliated as well as Cross Bench members of the interim House of Lords from the outset. It might conclude, however, that these developments should be deferred until the Commission has been formally established in primary legislation. In the latter case, we recommend that the Prime Minister of the day should be guided by the principles of composition we have recommended in settling the number of nominations to be made in respect of each political party and by the Appointments Commission. We also recommend that the Prime Minister and the other party leaders should accept, even during the remainder of the interim stage of Lords reform, that all party nominations should be consistent with the gender and ethnic minority requirements we have proposed and be endorsed by the Appointments Commission, rather than being made directly by the Prime Minister or the other leaders of political parties.

> **Recommendation 132:** Even prior to the formal establishment of the Appointments Commission as a statutory body, the Prime Minister of the day should be guided by the principles of composition we have recommended in settling the number of nominations (for life peerages) which each party and the Appointments Commission should make; and all party nominations should be consistent with the gender and ethnic minority requirements we have proposed and be endorsed by the Appointments Commission, rather than made directly by the party leaders.

Envoi

20.1   We were not set a simple question and this report does not provide a simple answer. Our recommendations are a coherent response to the challenge of devising a second chamber which has a vital role to play at the heart of the United Kingdom's system of Parliamentary democracy but must avoid a number of dangers – some obvious, some less so. We have explained our thinking. We have not rejected other approaches lightly. We believe our recommendations provide a solid basis for the successful long-term reform of the House of Lords. They would produce a reinvigorated second chamber which would work with the House of Commons to hold the Government more effectively to account and thus produce better government.

20.2   Of course, the many submissions we received and the public hearings in which we engaged revealed a wide variety of views on how a reformed second chamber should be constituted, some of them totally incompatible. Our recommendations are not in line with any individual set of proposals that were put to us. Our method was to go back to first principles and ask about the kind of second chamber we need and the qualities required amongst its members before going on to consider how these could best be achieved through particular methods of composition.

20.3   The Queen's Speech at the opening of the present session of Parliament included these words: "My Government are committed to further long-term reform of the House of Lords". We very much hope that it will prove possible to move rapidly to the second stage of reforming the House of Lords. But if interested parties choose to hold out for what they would ideally like, the opportunity may pass for another generation, maybe another century. If they are prepared, however, like us, to go back to first principles and ask the same questions, we believe they will recognise the force of our recommendations and that these will provide a firm foundation on which to build a House for the Future – authoritative, confident and broadly representative of the modern United Kingdom.

Summary of Conclusions and Recommendations

Chapter 3 – The overall role of the second chamber

Recommendation 1: The new second chamber should have the capacity to offer counsel from a range of sources. It should be broadly representative of society in the United Kingdom at the beginning of the 21st century. It should work with the House of Commons to provide an effective check upon the Government. It should give the United Kingdom's constituent nations and regions, for the first time, a formally constituted voice in the Westminster Parliament. (Paragraph 3.30.)

Chapter 4 – Making the law

Recommendation 2: The House of Commons, as the principal political forum, should have the final say in respect of all major public policy issues, including those expressed in the form of proposed legislation. Equally, the second chamber should have sufficient power, and the associated authority, to require the Government and the House of Commons to reconsider proposed legislation and take account of any cogent objections to it. (Paragraph 4.7.)

Conclusion: Other ways of resolving disputes between the two chambers of Parliament which have been considered in the past, or which are used in other countries, do not seem to offer any significant advantages over the suspensory veto. (Paragraph 4.11.)

Recommendation 3: The second chamber should continue to have a suspensory veto of the present length in respect of most primary legislation. (Paragraph 4.12.)

Conclusion: The technical weaknesses of the Parliament Acts have not given rise to any real difficulty in practice and there would be no point in seeking to tackle them unless wider substantive changes were proposed. (Paragraph 4.15.)

Recommendation 4: No attempt should be made to impose a time limit on the second chamber's consideration of 'Parliament Act' Bills in the second session. (Paragraph 4.17.)

Recommendation 5: The scope of the Parliament Acts should not be extended to cover Bills which are introduced into the second chamber, unless the Acts are to be subjected to a radical overhaul. (Paragraph 4.19.)

Recommendation 6: The reformed second chamber should maintain the House of Lords' convention that all Government business is considered within a reasonable time. (Paragraph 4.20.)

Recommendation 7: The principles underlying the 'Salisbury Convention' remain valid and should be maintained. A version of the 'mandate' doctrine should continue to be observed: where the electorate has chosen a party to form a Government, the elements of that party's general election manifesto should be respected by the second chamber. More generally, the second chamber should be cautious about challenging the clearly expressed views of the House of Commons on any public policy issue. It is not possible to reduce this to a simple formula, particularly one based on manifesto commitments. The second chamber should pragmatically work out a new convention reflecting these principles. (Paragraph 4.24.)

Recommendation 8: The two chambers should consider whether the current informal conciliation procedures could usefully be supplemented by the establishment of a Joint Committee designed to facilitate agreement between the two chambers over Bills. (Paragraph 4.29.)

Recommendation 9: Pre-legislative scrutiny of draft Bills should become an established feature of Parliamentary business. (Paragraph 4.34.)

Recommendation 10: The Delegated Powers and Deregulation Committee's role could evolve to include making recommendations which would encourage greater flexibility in the use of delegated powers, making it easier to strike an appropriate balance between primary and secondary legislation. (Paragraph 4.45.)

Recommendation 11: The reformed second chamber should consider whether the practice of deferring votes until Report Stage, which has been a feature of the use of Grand Committees off the floor of the House to consider certain Bills, should be extended to conventional Committee Stages. (Paragraph 4.47.)

Recommendation 12: Reviewing the quality of the statute book and keeping the law up to date should not be a primary function of the second chamber. However, if any specific aspects of the law on a particular issue were identified as meriting detailed consideration, it might well be appropriate for the second chamber to establish an *ad hoc* Committee for that purpose. (Paragraph 4.48.)

Recommendation 13: The current arrangements for dealing with Consolidation Bills should continue. (Paragraph 4.49.)

Recommendation 14: The reformed second chamber should consider what steps might be taken to expedite the Parliamentary consideration of law reform Bills proposed by the Law Commissions. (Paragraph 4.51.)

Conclusion: The characteristics of the reformed second chamber may make it appropriate for a larger proportion of private Bills to be considered first by the second chamber. (Paragraph 4.52.)

Conclusion: There is no distinctive role for the second chamber in post-legislative scrutiny. (Paragraph 4.53.)

Chapter 5 – Protecting the constitution

Recommendation 15: One of the most important functions of the reformed second chamber should be to act as a 'constitutional long-stop', ensuring that changes are not made to the constitution without full and open debate and an awareness of the consequences. (Paragraph 5.4.)

Conclusion: Increasing the powers of the second chamber in respect of any particular category of legislation would be inconsistent with maintaining the position of the House of Commons as the pre-eminent chamber of Parliament. (Paragraph 5.7.)

Recommendation 16: The second chamber should not be given additional powers in respect of a list of designated constitutional legislation. (Paragraph 5.8.)

Recommendation 17: The second chamber should not be given additional powers in respect of constitutional *issues*. There is no satisfactory basis on which this could be done and no suitable machinery for adjudicating on whether a particular Bill raised constitutional issues. (Paragraph 5.11.)

Recommendation 18: The second chamber should not be given additional powers over constitutional or human rights issues or legislation. (Paragraph 5.12.)

Recommendation 19: The Parliament Acts should be amended to exclude the possibility of their being further amended by the use of Parliament Act procedures. (Paragraph 5.15.)

Recommendation 20: The second chamber's veto over any Bill to extend the life of a Parliament should be reinforced. Our previous recommendation would achieve that. (Paragraph 5.16.)

Recommendation 21: The second chamber should establish an authoritative Constitutional Committee to act as a focus for its interest in and concern for constitutional matters. (Paragraph 5.22.)

Recommendation 22: There should be a mechanism, at least in the second chamber, for looking behind Ministerial statements of compatibility under Section 19 of the Human Rights Act 1998 and checking that all provisions of a Bill really are compatible with the ECHR. (Paragraph 5.30.)

Recommendation 23: The second chamber should establish a Committee with a wide-ranging remit in relation to human rights. (Paragraph 5.31.)

Recommendation 24: The second chamber should consider whether the proposed Constitutional Committee should establish a Human Rights Sub-committee to serve as the focus for the second chamber's interest in human rights. That Sub-committee might also provide the second chamber's members of the proposed Joint Committee on Human Rights. (Paragraph 5.33.)

Chapter 6 – Giving a voice to the nations and regions

Recommendation 25: The reformed second chamber should be so constructed that it could play a valuable role in relation to the nations and regions of the United Kingdom whatever pattern of devolution and decentralisation may emerge in future. (Paragraph 6.5.)

Recommendation 26: The reformed second chamber should be, and be seen to be, a chamber which serves the interests of the whole of the United Kingdom. (Paragraph 6.7.)

Recommendation 27: At least a proportion of the members of the second chamber should provide a direct voice for the various nations and regions of the United Kingdom. (Paragraph 6.8.)

Recommendation 28: The second chamber should not become a 'federal legislature', supporting a 'federal' government. (Paragraph 6.10.)

Recommendation 29: The reformed second chamber should not become a forum for inter-governmental liaison. Liaison between the Government and the executive authorities in Scotland, Wales and Northern Ireland is most appropriately and effectively carried on outside Parliamentary institutions. (Paragraph 6.12.)

Recommendation 30: While it would clearly be desirable to promote the development of links between the various legislatures across the United Kingdom, none of the members of the various devolved assemblies should be automatically entitled to sit in, or nominate others to join, the second chamber. (Paragraph 6.19.)

Recommendation 31: The role of the reformed second chamber in relation to the nations and regions of the United Kingdom should not be to provide a vehicle by which the devolved institutions themselves could be represented in Parliament. Its primary role in this context should be to provide a voice in Parliament for all the nations and regions of the United Kingdom. (Paragraph 6.20.)

Recommendation 32: The reformed second chamber should consider establishing a Committee to provide a focus for its consideration of the issues raised by devolution, possibly as a further Sub-committee of the proposed Constitutional Committee. (Paragraph 6.25.)

Recommendation 33: The reformed second chamber as a whole should not meet outside London but it should consider whether Committees, perhaps particularly any 'Devolution' Committee, should meet in the various regional centres from time to time. (Paragraph 6.27.)

Recommendation 34: The Overseas Territories should not be formally represented or given a voice in the second chamber; but individuals from the Territories might be offered membership on a personal basis in the light of the closer ties that may develop. (Paragraph 6.30.)

Chapter 7 – Scrutinising statutory instruments

Recommendation 35: There is a strong case for enhanced Parliamentary scrutiny of secondary legislation. The reformed second chamber should make a strong contribution in this area. (Paragraph 7.6.)

Recommendation 36: The Delegated Powers and Deregulation Committee should encourage the practice of publishing particularly significant Statutory Instruments in draft so that they can be subjected to detailed comment by interested parties and members of both Houses of Parliament before being formally laid before Parliament. Ministers and Departments should consider doing so wherever that would be beneficial. (Paragraph 7.22.)

Recommendation 37: A 'sifting' mechanism should be established to look at the significance of every Statutory Instrument subject to Parliamentary scrutiny; call for further information from Departments where necessary; and draw attention to those Statutory Instruments which are important and those which merit further debate or consideration. (Paragraph 7.23.)

Recommendation 38: A joint Committee should be established to sift Statutory Instruments. Alternatively, the second chamber should consider setting up machinery to sift Statutory Instruments, perhaps inviting the Delegated Powers and Deregulation Committee to take on the task. (Paragraph 7.26.)

Recommendation 39: Neither chamber should consider a Statutory Instrument until the JCSI has reported on it. The Statutory Instruments Act 1946 should be amended to extend the statutory 'praying time' in respect of negative resolution instruments from 40 days to 60 days. (Paragraph 7.28.)

Conclusion: There is no case for making it possible to amend Statutory Instruments once they have been formally laid before Parliament. (Paragraph 7.29.)

Recommendation 40: The reformed second chamber should adopt an open-minded, flexible and innovative approach to the consideration of Statutory Instruments within the present procedural arrangements. (Paragraph 7.30.)

Recommendation 41: Where the second chamber votes against a draft instrument, the draft should nevertheless be deemed to be approved if the House of Commons subsequently gives (or, as the case may be, reaffirms) its approval within three months. (Paragraph 7.37.)

Recommendation 42: Where the second chamber votes to annul an instrument, the annulment should not take effect for three months and could be overridden by a resolution of the House of Commons. (Paragraph 7.37.)

Recommendation 43: In both cases the relevant Minister should publish an Explanatory Memorandum, giving the second chamber an opportunity to reconsider its position and ensuring that the House of Commons is fully aware of all the issues if it has to take the final decision. (Paragraph 7.37.)

Conclusion: Changing the nature of the second chamber's powers in relation to Statutory Instruments would actually strengthen its influence and its ability to cause the Government and the House of Commons to take its concerns seriously. (Paragraph 7.38.)

Chapter 8 – Holding the Government to account

Recommendation 44: It should continue to be possible for Ministers to be drawn from and be directly accountable to the second chamber. (Paragraph 8.6.)

Recommendation 45: A mechanism should be developed which would require Commons Ministers to make statements to and deal with questions from members of the second chamber. (Paragraph 8.7.)

Recommendation 46: The current complementary system of scrutiny of European Union business by the two Houses of Parliament should be maintained and improved. (Paragraph 8.16.)

Recommendation 47: The reformed second chamber should consider making additional staff and other resources available to the European Union Committee. (Paragraph 8.16.)

Recommendation 48: No one should become a member of the second chamber by virtue of being a United Kingdom MEP. (Paragraph 8.20.)

Recommendation 49: The reformed second chamber should consider what steps it could take to make United Kingdom MEPs feel more welcome at Westminster. It should also consider how it might provide greater opportunities for United Kingdom MEPs to contribute to the development of Parliament's understanding of and approach to EU issues. (Paragraph 8.21.)

Recommendation 50: The House of Commons European Scrutiny Committee is best placed to assess the extent to which European Union proposals comply with the principle of subsidiarity but the European Union Committee should co-operate fully in that task. (Paragraph 8.23.)

Recommendation 51: The reformed second chamber should set aside a regular time for dealing with Questions for Oral Answer on EU matters. (Paragraph 8.24.)

Recommendation 52: The second chamber should continue to play its part in developing inter-parliamentary contact and co-operation within the EU, both with the European Parliament and with the national parliaments of EU Member States. (Paragraph 8.26.)

Recommendation 53: The reformed second chamber should continue to provide a distinctive forum for national debate. (Paragraph 8.27.)

Recommendation 54: Specialist committee work should continue to be an important function of the reformed second chamber. (Paragraph 8.29.)

Recommendation 55: Parliament should continue to scrutinise the Government's general conduct in making public appointments, but there is no distinctive role for the second chamber in this area. (Paragraph 8.36.)

Recommendation 56: The Liaison Committee should consider the establishment of a Select Committee to scrutinise international treaties into which the Government proposed to enter. (Paragraph 8.42.)

Chapter 9 – The Law Lords and the judicial functions of the second chamber

Conclusion: There is no reason why the second chamber should not continue to exercise the judicial functions of the present House of Lords. (Paragraph 9.5.)

Recommendation 57: The Lords of Appeal in Ordinary should continue to be *ex officio* members of the reformed second chamber and carry out its judicial functions. (Paragraph 9.7.)

Recommendation 58: The terms for which Lords of Appeal in Ordinary can be appointed to the second chamber under the Appellate Jurisdiction Act 1876 should be amended to bring them into line with those of other members of the second chamber, subject to automatic reappointment for as long as they are entitled to sit on the Appellate or Appeal Committees. (Paragraph 9.8.)

Recommendation 59: The Lords of Appeal should set out in writing and publish a statement of the principles which they intend to observe when participating in debates and votes in the second chamber and when considering their eligibility to sit on related cases. (Paragraph 9.10.)

Chapter 10 – Characteristics of the reformed second chamber

Recommendation 60: The reformed second chamber should be authoritative. That authority could be derived from a number of sources, but should not be such as to challenge the ultimate democratic authority of the House of Commons. (Paragraph 10.7.)

Recommendation 61: The reformed second chamber should be sufficiently confident and cohesive to use its powers effectively and appropriately. (Paragraph 10.9.)

Recommendation 62: The reformed second chamber should be broadly representative of British society as a whole. (Paragraph 10.13.)

Recommendation 63: The reformed second chamber should contain a substantial proportion of people who are not professional politicians, who have continuing experience in a range of different walks of life and who can bring a broad range of expertise to bear on issues of public concern. Accordingly, part-time membership of the second chamber should continue to be facilitated and even encouraged. There should be no minimum attendance requirement. (Paragraph 10.18.)

Recommendation 64: The reformed second chamber should include members with the knowledge and skills necessary to enable it to discharge effectively its roles in relation to constitutional matters and human rights issues. (Paragraph 10.20.)

Recommendation 65: The reformed second chamber should continue to include people who can help it to maintain a philosophical, moral or spiritual perspective on public policy issues. (Paragraph 10.21.)

Recommendation 66: The reformed second chamber should contain people of considerable personal distinction who have established reputations in various walks of life and can make a positive contribution to its work. (Paragraph 10.22.)

Recommendation 67: The reformed second chamber should not be capable of being dominated by any one political party and its members should be encouraged and enabled to deal with issues on their merits. (Paragraph 10.28.)

Recommendation 68: The reformed second chamber should preserve the relatively non-polemical style of the present House of Lords. (Paragraph 10.30.)

Conclusion: Members of the reformed second chamber should have a long-term perspective and the chamber should have a reasonable degree of continuity of membership from one period to another. (Paragraph 10.32.)

Chapter 11 – Principles of composition

Conclusion: We cannot recommend:

- a wholly or largely directly elected second chamber;

- indirect election from the devolved institutions (or local government electoral colleges) or from among British MEPs;

- random selection; or

- co-option. (Paragraph 11.36.)

Recommendation 69: Our broad overall recommendations on composition are that an independent appointments system should be supplemented by an arrangement which would give the regional electorate a voice in the selection of regional members and that the political balance in the reformed second chamber should match that of the country as expressed in votes cast at the most recent general election. (Paragraph 11.36.)

Recommendation 70:

(a) An Appointments Commission, independent of the Prime Minister, Government and the political parties, should be responsible for all appointments to the second chamber.

(b) A significant minority of the members of the second chamber should be 'regional members' selected on a basis which directly reflects the balance of political opinion within the regional electorates, to provide a voice for the nations and regions of the United Kingdom.

(c) The Appointments Commission should ensure that at least 20 per cent of the members of the second chamber are not affiliated to one of the major parties.

(d) The Appointments Commission should exercise its own judgement in selecting appointees who are affiliated to political parties. It should of course have regard to nominations made by the political parties, which it would also vet for propriety.

(e) In making appointments, the Appointments Commission should be required to ensure that members of the second chamber are broadly representative of British society on a range of stated dimensions. They should possess a variety of expertise and experience and various specific qualities appropriate to the role and functions of the reformed second chamber.

(f)   It should be under a statutory duty to ensure that a minimum of 30 per cent of new members of the second chamber should be women, and a minimum of 30 per cent men, with the aim of making steady progress towards gender balance in the chamber as a whole over time. It should also be required to use its best endeavours to ensure a level of representation for members of minority ethnic groups which is at least proportionate to their presence in the population as a whole. It should also play a role in ensuring appropriate representation for religious faiths (see Chapter 15).

(g)   One of the tasks of the Appointments Commission in making appointments to the second chamber should be to achieve or maintain an overall balance among all those members affiliated to political parties (both regional members and directly appointed members) which matches the distribution of votes between the parties at the most recent general election.

Chapter 12 – Composition: specific proposals and practicalities

Recommendation 71: All members of the second chamber should so far as possible serve the same terms, benefit from the same allowances and facilities and be treated in all respects identically, in order to minimise the risk of 'mixed membership' problems. There are also more practical reasons for believing that our specific proposals would not give rise to 'mixed membership' problems. (Paragraph 12.6.)

Recommendation 72: Regional members, whatever the precise means of their selection, should serve for the equivalent of three electoral cycles and appointed members should serve for fixed terms of 15 years. (Paragraph 12.15.)

Recommendation 73: There should be no minimum age for members of the reformed second chamber. (Paragraph 12.17.)

Recommendation 74: Both regional and directly appointed members should be eligible for reappointment, at the discretion of the Appointments Commission, for further periods of up to 15 years. Regional members should not be eligible for reselection on a regional basis. (Paragraph 12.18.)

Recommendation 75: Members of the reformed second chamber should be able to retire. (Paragraph 12.20.)

Recommendation 76: Members of the reformed second chamber should not be eligible for election to the House of Commons until ten years after their term of membership ends, whether or not they serve out their full term. (Paragraph 12.21.)

We present three possible models for the selection of regional members. Each model has the support of different members of the Commission. Model B has the support of a substantial majority of the Commission.

Model A   The regional members should be selected on the same day as a general election, using a system which we have called complementary voting. Under this system the votes cast for the parties' general election candidates would be accumulated at regional level and the parties would secure a number of regional members for each region proportional to their share of the vote in that region.

There would be 65 regional members, who would be selected on a staggered basis, with the complementary voting system being applied in one-third of the twelve nations and regions at each general election. (Paragraphs 12.26–12.32.)

Model B   There should be a total of 87 regional members, elected by thirds at the same time as each European Parliamentary election (with one-third of the nations and regions voting for regional members at each European election). The system of election should be the same as that used for electing United Kingdom MEPs, although a majority of those supporting this model would prefer the 'partially open' list system of proportional representation (PR). (Paragraphs 12.33–12.38.)

Model C   The regional members should be directly elected on a regional basis, using a form of 'partially open' list PR. Sixty-five regional members would be elected at the same time as each European Parliament election and serve for three terms, giving a total of 195 regional members in the reformed second chamber. (Paragraphs 12.39–12.42.)

Recommendation 77: The reformed second chamber should establish a procedure for expelling members whose continued presence would otherwise bring the chamber into disrepute. (Paragraph 12.45.)

Recommendation 78: Vacancies among the regional members arising within the first electoral cycle after they join the second chamber should be filled by offering the vacant place to the next person on the relevant party list. Under Models A and B, consideration should be given to introducing a system of co-option where a vacancy arises some time after the original selection. (Paragraph 12.46.)

Recommendation 79: The arrangements for selecting regional members should be kept under review, in the light of experience and taking account of any changes which flow from devolution or from the emergence of new structures in the English regions. (Paragraph 12.47.)

Chapter 13 – The Appointments Commission

Recommendation 80: The Appointments Commission should be charged by the Crown with a general duty to appoint members to the second chamber and empowered to appoint individual members on its own authority. (Paragraph 13.3.)

Recommendation 81: The independent Appointments Commission should be the only route into the second chamber, whether individuals reach this point through selection as a regional member, through selection by the Commission, or through appointment as a Lord of Appeal in Ordinary or representative of the Church of England. (Paragraph 13.4.)

Recommendation 82: The Appointments Commission should have no discretion over the appointment to the second chamber of regional members, Lords of Appeal in Ordinary, or any representatives of the Church of England. (Paragraph 13.6.)

Recommendation 83: The Appointments Commission should be established by primary legislation. (Paragraph 13.13.)

Recommendation 84: There should be eight Appointments Commissioners. Three should be nominees from the main political parties, one a nominee of the Convenor of the Cross Benchers and four should be independents, of whom one should be the chairman. (Paragraph 13.14.)

Recommendation 85: The independent members of the Appointments Commission should be selected according to the Nolan principles. (Paragraph 13.15.)

Recommendation 86: A number of Appointments Commissioners, though not a majority, should be members of the second chamber. None should be an MP. (Paragraph 13.16.)

Recommendation 87: Appointments Commissioners should be appointed by the Queen following an Address, on a motion moved by the Leader of the second chamber following the normal consultation with the leaders of the other party groupings and the Convenor of the Cross Benchers. (Paragraph 13.18.)

Recommendation 88: Appointments Commissioners should hold office for no more than ten years. (Paragraph 13.19.)

Recommendation 89: Removal of an Appointments Commissioner should require a resolution of the second chamber. (Paragraph 13.20.)

Recommendation 90: The Appointments Commission should make an annual report to Parliament. This report should set out the characteristics required of members of the second chamber and the Commission's strategy for ensuring that there is an appropriate balance of members from all parts of society and between the political parties. The report should also provide a detailed breakdown of the composition of the chamber, in terms of party, gender, ethnicity, age and region and the extent to which the chamber's membership as a whole reflects the characteristics set out in the Appointments Commission's published specification. (Paragraph 13.23.)

Recommendation 91: The size of the second chamber should not be fixed in statute, but should be set by the Appointments Commission. The Appointments Commission should regularly review the total number of members required, taking account of the chamber's workload, levels of attendance and the need to achieve or maintain a balance between the political parties in the second chamber that reflects their shares of the votes cast at the previous general election. (Paragraph 13.28.)

Recommendation 92: The Appointments Commission should encourage appointments and nominations from under-represented groups and report regularly on progress in achieving gender balance and a fair representation for minority ethnic groups. (Paragraph 13.29.)

Recommendation 93: The Appointments Commission should use its best endeavours to ensure that each of the nations and regions has an appropriate level of representation among the overall membership of the second chamber. (Paragraph 13.30.)

Recommendation 94: The Appointments Commission should publish and keep up to date a statement specifying the broad characteristics it would expect members of the second chamber, individually and collectively, to possess. (Paragraph 13.34.)

Recommendation 95: The Appointments Commission should systematically develop its knowledge of, and relationship with, a wide range of vocational areas and other sectors of society. (Paragraph 13.36.)

Recommendation 96: The Appointments Commission should open up the nomination process to the widest possible range of candidates. (Paragraph 13.37.)

Recommendation 97: The Appointments Commission should adopt a proactive approach to the identification of suitable appointees. (Paragraph 13.39.)

Recommendation 98: The Appointments Commission should make all discretionary appointments to the second chamber and should make the final decision in all cases. The Appointments Commission should be able to appoint people with party affiliations, whether or not these have the support of their political party. (Paragraphs 13.42 and 13.43.)

Recommendation 99: The Appointments Commission should vet nominations for propriety and high-level security checks should be undertaken on all shortlisted candidates. (Paragraph 13.44.)

Recommendation 100: The Appointments Commission should not seek Parliamentary approval of its appointments. (Paragraph 13.45.)

Recommendation 101: The Appointments Commission should normally make appointments on a half-yearly cycle. (Paragraph 13.46.)

Chapter 14 – The existing life peers

Recommendation 102: Under the legislation necessary to implement the second stage of Lords reform, those life peers created before the publication of this report who wish to take up the opportunity should be deemed to have been appointed to the reformed second chamber, for life. (Paragraph 14.12.)

Recommendation 103: Life peers created between the publication of this report and the enactment of the legislation necessary to implement the second stage of Lords reform should be deemed to have been appointed to the reformed second chamber for a period totalling 15 years from the award of their life peerage. (Paragraph 14.14.)

Recommendation 104: People appointed as life peers under the Life Peerages Act 1958 or the Appellate Jurisdiction Act 1876 and who remain in the reformed second chamber should be able to renounce their entitlement to sit and vote in the second chamber, or otherwise be able to retire from the second chamber under new legislation. (Paragraph 14.15.)

Recommendation 105: Life peers who renounce their right to sit and vote in the second chamber, or otherwise retire from it, should, like other members of the reformed second chamber, be precluded from being elected to the House of Commons within the following 10 years. (Paragraph 14.16.)

Recommendation 106: The life peers who remain members of the second chamber should be encouraged to reach an informal understanding with the Appointments Commission about how long they intend to serve. (Paragraph 14.17.)

Chapter 15 – The representation of religious faiths

Recommendation 107: The reformed second chamber should continue to include people capable of articulating a range of philosophical, moral and spiritual viewpoints, both religious and secular. (Paragraph 15.6.)

Recommendation 108: The Church of England should continue to be explicitly represented in the second chamber, but the concept of religious representation should be broadened to embrace other Christian denominations, in all parts of the United Kingdom, and other faith communities. (Paragraph 15.9.)

Recommendation 109: The Appointments Commission should ensure that at any one time there are at least five members of the second chamber specifically selected to be broadly representative of the different non-Christian faith communities. (Paragraph 15.17.)

Recommendation 110: The total number of places in the reformed second chamber for members formally representing the various Christian denominations throughout the United Kingdom should be 26. Taking into account the relative size of the population in each of the nations which comprise the United Kingdom, 21 of these places should go to members representing the Christian denominations in England and five should go to members representing the Christian denominations in Scotland, Wales and Northern Ireland. (Paragraph 15.18.)

Recommendation 111: Of the 21 places available for members of Christian denominations in England, 16 should be assigned to representatives of the Church of England and five to members of other Christian denominations in England. (Paragraph 15.19)

Recommendation 112: The Appointments Commission should have the ultimate responsibility for appointing individuals to the five places available for members of Christian denominations in England other than the Church of England. But in doing so, it should consult extensively with the relevant ecumenical instrument, Churches Together in England. (Paragraph 15.21.)

Recommendation 113: The Appointments Commission should have the ultimate responsibility for appointing individuals to the five places available for members of Christian denominations in Scotland, Wales and Northern Ireland, but it should consult extensively with the relevant ecumenical instruments. (Paragraph 15.23.)

Recommendation 114: Demographic changes and changes in the level of adherence to particular sets of religious beliefs should be reflected in adjustments to the pattern of religious representation which we have proposed. (Paragraph 15.26.)

Recommendation 115: The Church of England should review the options for providing formal Church of England representation in the reformed second chamber. Their detailed recommendations should be made to the Government in time for incorporation into whatever legislation is required to implement our own recommendations. (Paragraph 15.28.)

Chapter 16 – Procedures

Recommendation 116: The second chamber should seek to continue the House of Lords' tradition of open procedures. (Paragraph 16.6.)

Recommendation 117: Any restrictions to the rights of members of the second chamber should be designed to preserve the essential character of what exists at present. (Paragraph 16.10.)

Recommendation 118: The second chamber's approach to the conduct of business should be such as to allow the chamber to remain self-regulating. (Paragraph 16.11.)

Chapter 17 – Resources

Recommendation 119: The financial arrangements which apply to members of the second chamber should make regular attendance economically viable for people who live outside the South East of England and who do not have a separate source of income. (Paragraph 17.7.)

Recommendation 120: Payment should be made for the time members of the second chamber devote to their Parliamentary duties. (Paragraph 17.9.)

Recommendation 121 : Financial support for members of the reformed second chamber should be related to attendance in Parliament. (Paragraph 17.10.)

Recommendation 122: Total payments made to members for time and lost income should be less than the basic salary of an MP over an average session. (Paragraph 17.11.)

Recommendation 123: Chairmen of significant Committees of the second chamber should receive a salary in respect of their additional duties. (Paragraph 17.12.)

Recommendation 124: The SSRB should consider the issue of severance payments and pension arrangements for members of the reformed second chamber. (Paragraph 17.13.)

Recommendation 125: The second chamber should provide additional office and secretarial resources to enable Committees and individual members to fulfil their Parliamentary duties more effectively. (Paragraph 17.15.)

Recommendation 126: The SSRB should review the rules governing the payment of expenses incurred in respect of travel and overnight costs by members of the second chamber in the course of their Parliamentary duties with a view to ensuring that regular attendance is economically viable for people who live outside London. (Paragraph 17.17.)

Chapter 18 – Titles and name

Recommendation 127: Possession of a peerage should no longer be a necessary qualification for membership of the second chamber, and new members should not be offered a peerage in that connection. (Paragraph 18.6.)

Recommendation 128: The question of the name of the second chamber and the titles of its members should be left to evolve. (Paragraph 18.11.)

Chapter 19 – Implementing this report

Recommendation 129: Depending on which of the models (set out in Chapter 12) for selecting regional members is adopted, we recommend the following:

Model A
At the first general election after the passage of the necessary legislation, 65 regional members should be selected using a system of 'complementary' election so that every region has its full complement of regional members from the outset. Those selected for one-third of the regions should serve for one Parliamentary term, and those selected for a further third of the regions should serve for two Parliamentary terms: exceptionally (as a transitional measure) all of these regional members should be eligible for reselection at the point at which their membership would otherwise lapse. At the second and all subsequent general elections, regional members would be selected by 'complementary' election in respect of the relevant one-third of the regions.

Model B
At the first European Parliament election after the passage of the necessary legislation, 87 regional members should be elected by whatever method of election is in use to elect MEPs so that every region has its full complement of regional members from the outset. Those elected for one-third of the regions should serve for one European Parliament term, and those elected for a further third of the regions should serve for two European Parliament terms: exceptionally (as a transitional measure) all these members should be eligible for reelection at the point at which their membership would otherwise lapse. At the time of the second and all subsequent European Parliament elections, regional members should be elected by the relevant one-third of the regions.

Model C
At the first European Parliament election after the passage of the necessary legislation, 65 regional members should be elected by 'partially open' list PR, so that each region has one-third of its eventual complement of regional members. A further 65 regional members should be elected in the same way at the time of each of the next two European Parliament elections. (Paragraphs 19.4–19.8.)

Recommendation 130: The remaining hereditary peers should cease to be entitled to sit and vote in the second chamber at the point at which the first regional members join the second chamber. They, and other hereditary peers, would be eligible to seek nomination as regional members, or offer themselves for appointment by the Appointments Commission. (Paragraph 19.6.)

Recommendation 131: Pending its formal establishment as a statutory body, the independent Appointments Commission which will be responsible for nominating Cross Bench members of the interim House of Lords and vetting political nominations for propriety, should prepare to take on the wider role we envisage it discharging as part of the 'second stage' of Lords reform. (Paragraph 19.10.)

Recommendation 132: Even prior to the formal establishment of the Appointments Commission as a statutory body, the Prime Minister of the day should be guided by the principles of composition we have recommended in settling the number of nominations (for life peerages) which each party and the Appointments Commission should make; and all party nominations should be consistent with the gender and ethnic minority requirements we have proposed and be endorsed by the Appointments Commission, rather than made directly by the party leaders. (Paragraph 19.11.)

The full text of our report is available at **www.lords-reform.org.uk**, and at **www.official-documents.co.uk/document/cm45/4534/4534.htm**

ALL OF WHICH WE HUMBLY SUBMIT FOR YOUR MAJESTY'S GRACIOUS CONSIDERATION

The Rt Hon Lord Wakeham
(Chairman)

The Rt Hon Gerald Kaufman MP

**The Rt Hon Baroness Dean
of Thornton-le-Fylde**

The Rt Hon Lord Hurd of Westwell,
*Member of Your Order of the Companions of Honour,
Commander of Your Most Excellent Order of the
British Empire*

Lord Butler of Brockwell,
*Knight Grand Cross of Your Most Honourable
Order of the Bath, Commander of Your
Royal Victorian Order*

**The Rt Reverend Richard Harries,
Lord Bishop of Oxford**

Sir Michael Wheeler-Booth,
*Knight Commander of Your Most Honourable
Order of the Bath*

Kenneth Munro

Professor Anthony King

Ann Beynon

William Morris

Professor Dawn Oliver

David Hill *(Secretary)*

Dr Martin Samuels *(Deputy Secretary)*

Royal Commission on the Reform of the House of Lords
4 Central Buildings, Matthew Parker Street, London SW1H 9NL

Appendix A – Consultation process

Analysis of submissions

A.1   We received a total of 1,734 pieces of written evidence.[1] These were mainly sent in response to the consultation paper, but many were stimulated by our public meetings and through wider media publicity.

A.2   Members of the public were responsible for sending in the largest number of submissions, over 76 per cent of the total. Members and former members of the House of Lords submitted 127 pieces of evidence, 7.3 per cent of the total. The other evidence was submitted by a wide range of organisations and individuals, providing a good cross section of background information, views and suggestions on the wide range of complex issues we had to consider.

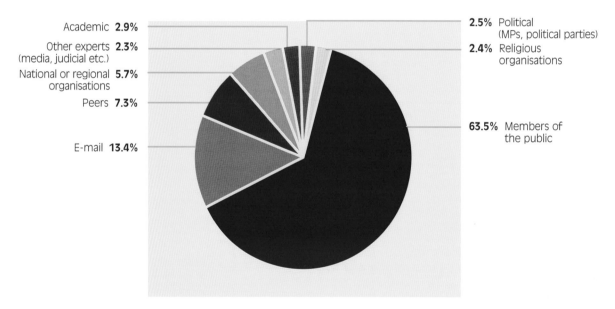

Academic **2.9%**
Other experts **2.3%** (media, judicial etc.)
National or regional **5.7%** organisations
Peers **7.3%**
E-mail **13.4%**

2.5% Political (MPs, political parties)
2.4% Religious organisations
63.5% Members of the public

Submissions by originator type

---

[1] This figure includes 233 pieces of evidence submitted through our website.

A.3 By far the largest percentage of responses was received from individuals and organisations based in London and the South East. These two areas accounted for over 46 per cent of the total number of responses. Other responses were received from across the whole of the UK, the rest of Europe, Australia, Canada, Hong Kong and the United States of America.

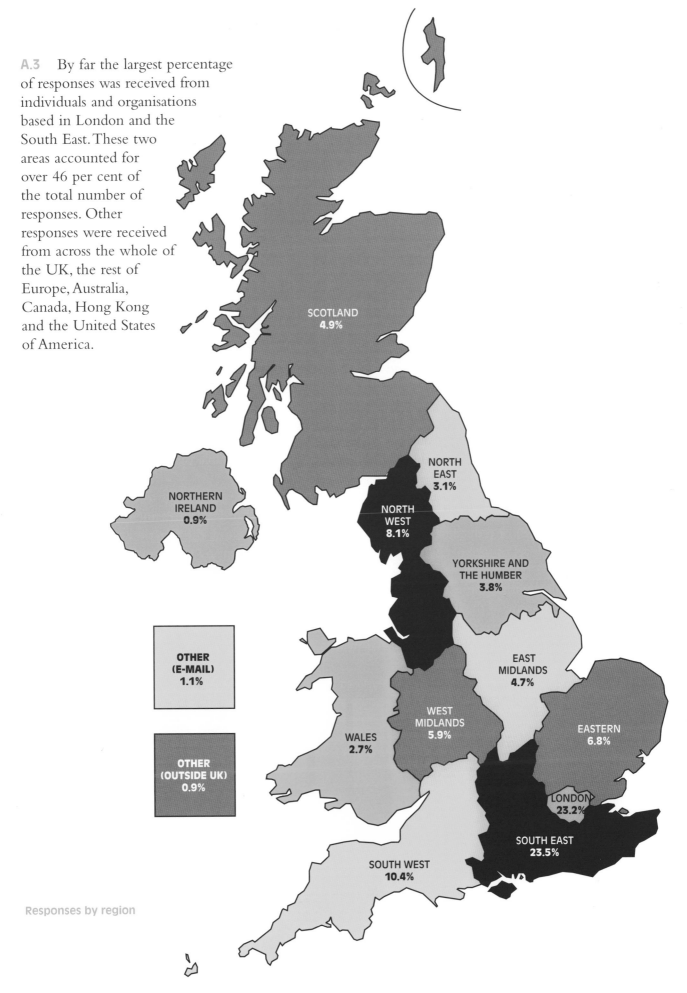

SCOTLAND
4.9%

NORTH EAST
3.1%

NORTHERN IRELAND
0.9%

NORTH WEST
8.1%

YORKSHIRE AND THE HUMBER
3.8%

EAST MIDLANDS
4.7%

OTHER (E-MAIL)
1.1%

WEST MIDLANDS
5.9%

EASTERN
6.8%

WALES
2.7%

OTHER (OUTSIDE UK)
0.9%

LONDON
23.2%

SOUTH EAST
23.5%

SOUTH WEST
10.4%

Responses by region

Analysis of questionnaires

A.4   We held a total of 21 sessions of public hearings to take oral evidence from witnesses. These were attended by 1,026 people. Over 58 per cent of those attending completed questionnaires to help us gauge public opinion on some of the major issues affecting the reform. The adjacent table gives a breakdown of the number of people who attended each public hearing, and the number of questionnaires completed at each.

Location of hearing	Number of attendees	Number of completed questionnaires	Response rate	% of total number completed
London (May)	140	105	75.0%	17.5%
Exeter	82	40	48.8%	6.7%
Peterborough	26	19	73.1%	3.2%
Newcastle	52	35	67.3%	5.8%
Manchester	105	69	65.7%	11.5%
Birmingham	100	42	42.0%	7.0%
Edinburgh	64	42	65.6%	7.0%
Cardiff	113	47	41.6%	7.9%
London (July)	344	200	58.1%	33.4%
Total	1,026	599	58.4%	100.0%

Public Hearing statistics

A.5   In addition to the questionnaires from the public hearings, we also received 340 responses to the copy of the questionnaire which was available on our website.

A.6   The following chart indicates the extent to which respondents to the questionnaire wanted the various functions of the present House of Lords to be maintained (and/or developed) or reduced. The chart has been arranged to show the function areas in order of the level of support which they attracted. Thus, the scrutiny function attracted most support (91 per cent), while only 27 per cent supported a function relating to organised religion within the reformed chamber. The large number of 'no comment' responses against some of the functions listed in the questionnaire suggests that a considerable proportion of respondents were uncertain as to the possible role of the second chamber in those areas, notably international treaties, devolution and major public appointments.

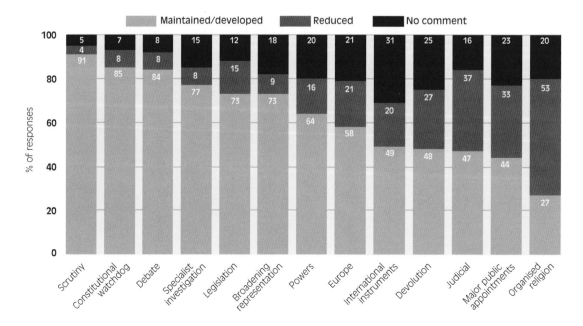

Responses to questionnaires – functions

A.7   The charts on this page summarise the results of the questions regarding the composition of a reformed second chamber and the method or methods which should be used to select members. The responses are again shown in order of the support they gained. Direct election received most support: nearly half the respondents favoured this method. Life peers selected by an independent Appointments Commission were supported by nearly 40 per cent, compared to only 16 per cent who thought they should be chosen by party leaders. Over one-third indicated support for a mixed chamber. In addition, some respondents chose more than one method of selection without specifying that the chamber should be mixed. Random selection received the support of only 13 per cent.

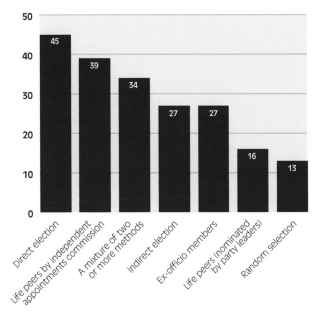

Responses to questionnaires – selection systems

Responders could select more than one option. Consequently, the figures do not sum to 100 per cent.

A.8   On composition, 67 per cent of the respondents wanted to include independent/experienced people in the second chamber. Nearly half indicated that they would like to see representatives of the nations and regions of the United Kingdom. At the other end of the scale, representation for British MEPs received the support of only 20 per cent of respondents, although this rose at the London hearings. Perhaps curiously, in view of the low level of support for a role concerning organised religion, almost one-third of respondents favoured including Church of England bishops in the membership – more than favoured political nominees.

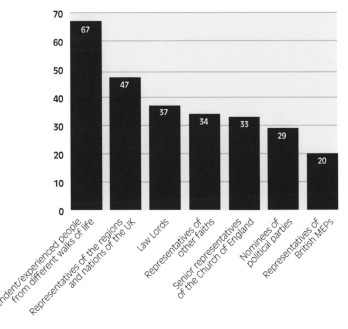

Responses to questionnaires – composition

Responders could select more than one option. Consequently, the figures do not sum to 100 per cent.

Appendix B – List of submissions

The following individuals and organisations submitted evidence to the Royal Commission as part of its consultation exercise. Copies of all the submissions are included on the attached CD-ROM, except for those few where the individuals concerned requested that their evidence be treated as confidential.

To view evidence from CD-ROM click on names below.

Parliamentarians and Political Parties

The Alliance Party of Northern Ireland
The Conservative and Unionist Party
The Co-operative Party
Democratic Party
The Green Party of England and Wales
The Labour Party
Liberal Democrats
Plaid Cymru – The Party of Wales
Scottish Conservative and Unionist Party
Scottish National Party
Welsh Liberal Democrats

The Rt Hon Lord Aberdare KBE DL
Lord Acton
Lord Alexander of Weedon QC, Delegated Powers
    and Deregulation Committee
Lord Annan OBE
Lord Ashburton KG KCVO DL

Richard Balfe MEP
The Rt Hon Lord Barnett
The Rt Hon Tony Benn MP
Gerald Bermingham MP
Lord Bethell
The Rt Hon Lord Bingham of Cornhill
The Rt Rev Lord Bishop of Blackburn
Lord Blake FBA JP
The Rt Hon Lord Blaker KCMG
Lord Bowness CBE DL
The Rt Hon Lord Brightman
Lord Bruce of Donington
His Grace the Duke of Buccleuch & Queensberry KT
Richard Burden MP
Lord Butterfield OBE FRCP
John Butterfill MP

The Rt Hon Lord Callaghan of Cardiff KG
Lord Campbell of Alloway ERD QC
Dennis Canavan MP MSP
The Rt Hon Baroness Chalker of Wallasey
Lord Christopher CBE
The Rt Hon Lord Cledwyn of Penrhos CH
Lord Clifford of Chudleigh DL
Lord Cobbold DL
Lord Coleraine
Lord Cooke of Thorndon KBE

Richard Corbett MEP
Earl of Cork and Orrery DSC VRD
Lord Craig of Radley GCB OBE

Lord Dahrendorf KBE FBA
Lord Derwent LVD DL
Professor Lord Desai
Earl of Devon DL
The Rt Hon Lord Diamond
Viscount Dilhorne
Lord Dixon-Smith DL
The Rt Hon Lord Donaldson of Lymington

Michael Elliott MEP
Louise Ellman MP, Parliamentary Labour Party
    Regional Government Group
Lord Elton TD

The Rt Hon Eric Forth MP

Roger Gale MP
Christopher Gill RD MP
The Rt Hon Lord Goff of Chieveley FBA
Lord Gordon of Strathblane CBE
Teresa Gorman MP
Baroness Gould of Potternewton
Lord Gray
Dominic Grieve MP
Jane Griffiths MP

The Rt Rev and The Rt Hon Lord Habgood
Earl of Halsbury FEng FRS
Lord Harding of Petherton
Lord Hardinge of Penshurst
Lord Hardy of Wath DL
The Earl of Harrowby TD
Lord Haskel
Lord Hazlerigg MC TD DL
John Healey MP
The Rt Hon Sir Edward Heath KG MBE MP
Lord Hemingford
The Rt Hon Douglas Hogg QC MP
The Rt Hon Lord Hope of Craighead
The Rt Hon Lord Howe of Aberavon CH QC
Lord Hylton

Lord Inglewood ARICS DL

Robert Jackson MP
The Rt Hon Lord Jauncey of Tullichettle
The Rt Hon Lord Jenkin of Roding
Lord Judd

The Rt Hon Lord Keith of Kinkel GBE
Lord Kennet
Lord Kilmarnock

Lord Lester of Herne Hill QC
The Rt Rev Lord Bishop of Lichfield
The Rt Rev Lord Bishop of Lincoln
The Rt Hon Lord Lloyd of Berwick DL
Lord Lucas of Crudwell and Dingwall
Earl of Lytton

John McAllion MP
Anne McIntosh MP
The Rt Hon John MacGregor OBE MP
The Rt Hon Lord Mackay of Clashfern KT
Fiona Mactaggart MP
The Rt Hon John Major CH MP
Seamus Mallon MP, Northern Ireland Assembly
Dr John Marek MP
Lord Marlesford DL
The Rt Hon Lord Marsh
Graham Mather MEP, European Policy Forum
The Rt Hon Lord Merlyn-Rees
Lord Middleton MC DL
Lord Monson
Viscount Montgomery of Alamein CBE
Lord Mottistone CBE
Viscount Mountgarret

The Rt Hon Lord Naseby
Lord Nathan
Lord Northbourne DL
Prof Lord Norton of Louth, University of Hull
Lord Nunburnholme

The Earl of Onslow

The Rt Hon Lord Patten
Roy Perry MEP
Lord Peston
Baroness Platt of Writtle CBE DL

Anita Pollack MEP
Gordon Prentice MP
Peter Price MEP, European Strategy Counsel
Lord Puttnam CBE

Earl of Radnor
Lord Rea
The Rt Hon Lord Renton KBE QC TD DL
The Rt Hon Lord Richard QC
The Rt Hon Lord Rodgers of Quarry Bank
Viscount Runciman of Doxford

Lady Saltoun of Abernethy
Earl of Sandwich
Lord Selsdon
The Rt Hon Lord Shore of Stepney
The Rt Hon Lord Simon of Glaisdale DL
The Rt Hon Lord Slynn of Hadley (on behalf of
   the Lords of Appeal in Ordinary)
Clive Soley MP
Tom Spencer MEP
Sir Michael Spicer MP
Lord Stone of Blackheath
Baroness Strange
Desmond Swayne MP

Lord Tanlaw
The Rt Hon Baroness Thatcher LG OM FRS
Gareth Thomas MP
Lord Thomas of Swynnerton
Andrew Tyrie MP

Lord Vinson LVO DL

The Rt Hon Lord Waddington GCVO DL QC
Lord Walton of Detchant TD
Baroness Warnock DBE
Phillip Whitehead MEP
The Rt Hon Lord Wilberforce CMG OBE
The Rt Rev Lord Bishop of Winchester
The Rt Hon Lord Windlesham CVO
David Winnick MP
Nicholas Winterton MP
Phil Woolas MP
The Rt Hon Lord Woolf
Rev Lord Wrenbury
Dr Tony Wright MP

Expert witnesses

Stephen Alambritis, Federation of Small Businesses
Lord Alexander of Weedon QC, JUSTICE
Lincoln Allison, Warwick University
Prof Antony Allott
Bob Armitage, Cheshire Association of Town and
    Parish Councils
Dr Mac Armstrong, British Medical Association
Robert Ashby, British Humanist Association
His Eminence Hazrat Allama Qamaruzzama Azmi,
    West Midlands Racial Equality Forum

Rev Dr Peter Baines, Baptist Union of Wales
Rev Canon Robin Baker
The Very Rev Dr R D Bakere
Dr Nicholas D J Baldwin, Wroxton College of
    Fairleigh Dickinson University
Prof James P Barber
Anthony Barnett, Demos
Michael Bartlett, Religious Society of
    Friends (Quakers)
Prof David Beetham, Leeds University
Hon Michael Beloff
Nigel Bennett, Barnardos
Prof Robert Blackburn, King's College London
Prof Donald Bligh
Sir Louis Blom-Cooper QC
Prof Vernon Bogdanor CBE, Oxford University
Frances Bolton, Society of Conservative Lawyers
Dr Martyn Bond
Sir Wilfrid Bourne
Billy Bragg
Rev Marcus Braybrooke, World Congress of Faiths
Prof Rodney John Brazier, University of Manchester
A J E Brennan CB
Dr John Bridge, One North East
Peter Briggs, British Association for the
    Advancement of Science
Brian Briscoe, Local Government Association
David Brown, North Cornwall District Council
Rev A Burnham, The United Reform Church
David Butler CBE, Hansard Society

The Campaign for a Northern Assembly
Celia Capstick, National Board of Catholic Women
Hon Mr Justice Carnwath CVO, Law Commission
David Chapman, Democracy Design Forum
Rev David Coffey, Baptist Union of Great Britain
Dr M J Collins
Patrick Coyle, Guild of Catholic Doctors
Rev Jeremy Cresswell
Prof Bernard Crick
Sir Brian Cubbon
Mark Curtis, Action Aid

Graham Dale, Christian Socialist Movement
Philip Daniel, Catholic Union
Prof John Davis
John Day, Independent Methodist Churches
Sir Robin Day
Prof Brice Dickson, Northern Ireland Human
    Rights Commission
Shelagh Diplock OBE, Hansard Society
Rev Sheila Douglas, International Ministerial
    Council of Great Britain
Martin Drury, The National Trust
Phillip Dry, The Law Society of Scotland
Rev John Dunlop, Presbyterian Church in Ireland
Dr David Dyke, University of Birmingham

Rev Aled Edwards, Churches' National
    Assembly Centre
Liz Edwards, Local Governance Review Group
Richard A Edwards, Southampton Institute
Cllr F A J Emery-Wallis DL FSA Hon FRIBA
    Hon FLA, Hampshire County Council
Steven Everts, Centre for European Reform

Matthew Farrow, CBI Scotland
Dr M A Fazal, Nottingham Trent University
Helen Ferguson, Carers' National Association
    Northern Ireland
Prof P Fidler MBE, University of Sunderland
Susan Forscey-Moore, The Campaign for a
    Fair Hearing
Pat Frankish, The British Psychological Society

David R S Gallagher PhD, Methodist Church
    in Ireland
Chris Garner, Nuffield College
Philip Giddings, University of Reading
Pam Giddy, Charter 88
Dr L Goldstone, The Institute of Electrical Engineers
Sir Nicholas Goodison, Lloyds TSB Group Plc
Cllr E Goodman, Reigate and Banstead
    Borough Council
John Gouriet, Freedom In Action
Prof William Gray DPH (Soc) Ect
Dr John Greenaway, University of East Anglia
Sally Greengross, Age Concern England

G Hale, North East Constitutional Convention
Lawrence Hall, Charter 88, Brighton & Hove
Sir David Hannay
Martin Havenhand, Yorkshire Forward
David G Henshaw, SOLACE
Ros Hepplewhite, General Dental Council
Rev Canon Roger Hill
Jonathan Hirst QC, The General Council of the Bar
Derek Hodgson, Communication Workers Union
Barry Horne, East Midlands Regional Assembly
Carole Hudson, North West Regional Chambers

Dr T D Inch BSc PhD DSc CChem FRSC,
  Royal Society of Chemistry
Sir Bernard Ingham
Canon David Ison, Diocese of Exeter

Dr Joseph Jaconelli, University of Manchester
Stephen Jakobi, The Fair Trials Abroad Trust
Simon Jenkins, The Times
Nevil Johnson, Nuffield College
Cllr Johnstone, Harrogate District Council
Afron Jones, The Evangelical Alliance, Wales
Audrey Jones, Wales Assembly of Women
Prof George Jones, School of Economics &
  Political Science
Cllr Robert Jones, East Midlands Regional Local
  Government Association

Gavin Kelly, Fabian Society
Rev John Kennedy, The Methodist Church
Liz Kerry, Regional Assembly for Yorkshire
  and Humberside
Venerable Ajahn Khemadhammo, Abbot,
  Santidhamma Forest Hermitage
Lord Kilmaine, Irish Peers Association
Alison King, Norfolk County Council
Cllr Sir Richard Knowles, Birmingham City Council

Philip Leach, Liberty
Uwe Leonardy MA
Sir Michael Lickiss, RDA (South West)
J M Lloyd, Ubley Parish Council
Ian Loveland, Brunel University

Rev Finlay Macdonald MA BD PhD, General
  Secretary, Church of Scotland
Prof Amyan Macfayden
Prof Iain McLean, Oxford University
Ian MacNicol, Country Landowners Association
Dr Richard Marquis-Hirsch MA PhD FRSA FRGS
Malcolm Marsh, Justices' Clerks' Society
Philip Mawer, General Secretary, The Church
  of England
Rev David Megson
Dr Jeremy Mitchell, The Open University
Neill Mitchell, Plymouth Chamber of Commerce
  and Industry
Sir Michael Moore KBE LVO, Institute of
  Mechanical Engineers
Philip Moran, Committee for the Protection of
  the Constitution
Rowland Morgan, University of Bristol

Neville Nagler, Board of Deputies of British Jews
National Board of Catholic Women
Richard North, The Social Affairs Unit

John Oliver, Commoners

Prof Edward Page, University of Hull
Sir Dick Pantlin CBE
Susie Parsons, Commission for Racial Equality
The Rt Hon Christopher Patten CH
Prof Sir Alan Peacock DSC FBA FRSE, The
  David Hume Institute
Brian Pearce, The Inter Faith Network for the
  United Kingdom
Samantha Peters, The British Youth Council
Derek Phillips, Church of Ireland
Sid Platt, West Midlands LGA
Gill Pope, National Federation of Womens' Institutes
K Porteous Wood FCCA, The National
  Secular Society
John Pratt, Centre for Citizenship
Julian Priestley, European Parliament
Prof Peter Pulzer, Oxford University

Prof John Radford
D N P Radlett, Mid Kent College of Higher and
  Further Education
John Ritblat, The British Land Company Plc
Rev P D Richards, Free Church Federal Council
Ken Ritchie, Electoral Reform Society
Colin Robertshaw, Eastern Region Local
  Government Conference
The Rt Rev Mgr Arthur Roche, General
  Secretary, Catholic Bishops' Conference of
  England and Wales
Rev Geoffrey Roper, The Free Churches' Council
Prof William D Rubinstein, University of Wales
Alan Rusbridger, The Guardian
Prof Michael Rush, University of Exeter

Prof Jonathan Sacks, The Chief Rabbi
M Sanders, Oldham Metropolitan Borough Council
Peter Sanguinetti, Common Sense for Lords Reform
Prof Roger Scruton
Vicky Seddon, Sheffield Charter 88
S E Sharpe LLB, Royal Pharmaceutical Society of
  Great Britain
Prof N Sheppard
Malcolm Shirley, The Engineering Council
Cllr Mike Simpson, Tandridge District Council
Prof Alfred P Smyth, Interfaith Foundation
Sister Isabel Smyth, Churches Agency for Inter
  Faith Relation in Scotland
Linda Spence, Wear Valley District Council
Frank Spencer, Equal Opportunities Commission
Rev Graham St John Willey BSc MA
Mary Ann Stephenson, Fawcett Society
Dr Robert Stevens, Pembroke College
The Rt Rev Dr Kenneth Stevenson
Simon Still, Northern Business Forum
Prof A K Stock
Peter Stothard, The Times
Tim Symonds, Shevolution (Project Parity)

Pamela Taylor, Water UK
Prof Alastair Thomas, Charter 88 North West
Lord Thomas of Macclesfield, RDA (North West)
Brian Thompson, University of Liverpool
Lesley Thornley, The Industrial Society
Prof Leonard Tivey
Thomas Toward, Durham Association of Parish and
   Town Councils
The Rt Rev Howard Tripp, Chairman, Bishops'
   Committee for Public Life, Catholic Bishops'
   Conference of England and Wales
G Tubb, SEERA
Susan Tubey, Yate Town Council

Dr Scott Veitch, University of Glasgow

Prof Sir William Wade QC LLD FBA
Martin Wainwright
Prof Clive Walker, University of Leeds
Shona Wallace, Evangelical Alliance UK

P M Walsh LLB, Harrogate Borough Council
Dr Jenny Watts
Nicholas J Way, Country Landowners Association
Stuart Weir, The Democratic Audit
Dr Paul Weller, University of Derby
Robin Wendt, The National Association of
   Local Councils
Matthew West, Corpus Christi College
Clare Whelan, Tory Reform Group
R D Whiteman, Scottish Episcopal Church
Dr Neil Wigglesorth, Lancaster University
John Wilkins, The Tablet
Alan Willett, SEEDA
Prof Sir Dillwyn Williams, British Medical
   Association
Archbishop Thomas J Cardinal Winning, Roman
   Catholic Bishops of Scotland
Prof Michael Winter, University of Notre Dame
Prof Diana Woodhouse, Oxford Brookes University
Rev Dr Janet Wootton

Others

Richard Abott
E K Abrahall
David Ackerman
David Acland
Prof Christopher John Adams
   MA(Oxon) D Phil C Chem
   FRSC IChemE
John Adams
Keith Adams
Patrick Adams
Sheila Adams
Sally Adamson
Alison Adcock
J M Agar
Maureen Ahmadi
Martin Aitken
Phil Alderton
Maureen Aldridge
Nicholas Aleksander
H J Alexander
Peg Alexander
Titus Alexander, Learning
   Initiatives
Graeme J Allan
H Allan
Nick Allan
Paul Allard
R L F Alley
C N Anderson
Gareth Anderson
J Douglas Anderson
Michael Anderson
Philip Anderson
D M Annett

J Antchings
Derek Antrobus
Dr Richard Appleton
Christopher Arnander
P D Arthur
J Ashcroft
Graham Ashley
Richard Askwith
Adrian Atkins
Bryan Atkinson
George Atkinson
Tom Aubrey
M L G Aubrey-Cound

Margaret Bailey
G C Baines
Stephen Baker
Walter Baker
Paul Balaam
Sir Peter Baldwin
Peter L Baldwin
Keith Ball
R H W Ban
R C Banham
Ashley Banks, The New
   Frontier Club
Mr Bannister
Stephen Barber
P L Barden
Sir Brian Barder
G G Barfield
Robert Bargery
H K Barker
P J Barker

Ruth Barker
Mr & Mrs Barnard
Anne Barne
R L Barraclough
B Barrett
D H Bartholomew
Dr Jeremy Bartlett
Donald Barton
Dr & Mrs A J Barwood
M J Batchelor
Mark Batchelor
P J Bates
R L Batty
John Bausor
Tim Baynes, Charter 88
T W Beamond
Peter Beauchamp FRSA
D Beaumont
Harry Beckhough
David Bell
Lionel Bell
M Hilary Bell
P D Bell
Peter Bell
Anthony Bellringer
Derek Bennett
Richard Bennett
Stephen Bennett
Francis Bennion
M D Berkin
Israel Berkovitch
Prof David Berry
Randall Bevan
Dr Richard Bewley

Eric Biddulph
Jennifer W Biggs
Richard Biggs
P Biglin
Saul Billingsley
V N Bingham
Dennis Bird
Joan Bird
John Bird
R H Bird
R V Bird
Ann Black, Oxford East
    Constituency Labour Party
John Black
Sian Blaine
Dr George Blair
Leslie Blake
David W Blomeley, Tideway
    Consultancy Services Ltd
Michael Blumenthal
S W Blunt
Cora W Blyth de Portillo
Nigel Boddy
Richard Bomford
Jean Bond
Roger Boniface
Philip Booth
R Botterill
John Bourke
Derek Bourne-Jones
Edgar Bowden
Selwyn Bowen
Margretta R W Bowstead
Dr Adrian Bowyer
Robert Boyd
Arthur Boyd Phillips
C Boyle
Grace Boyle
John Bradley JP
G Bradshaw
Christopher Braganza
Kevin Branch
Mr & Mrs Branigan
Earl Brannigan
Peter Bratt
J R Brettell
H K Brew
D Briggs
R C H Briggs
Daniel Brittain-Catlin
Chris Britton
C J Brockhurst
Howard Brooksbank
Jessie Brown
W K Brown
Matthew J Browning,
    The British Israel World
    Federation
Rebecca Bryant

M W Buchanan
Nicholas Buckley
Dominic Buckwell
Elinor Buddle
M A Bull
Kevin Bullimore
Michael Bullock
Mark Bunting
Philip Burbidge
Dr Eric A Burkitt
John Burton
M A Burton
Richard Butt
Andrew Paul Buxton
A N Byford

Nigel Calder
Christopher Campbell
Craig Campbell
David Campbell
Brian Candeland
Sarah Cann
F R Cannings
P Cannings
Simon Caplan
Ian Carney
Jamie Carnie
Beverly Carpenter
James Carruthers
John Cartledge
John S Cartwright
Ronald Cater
G Cathcart
Dr Peter Catterall
Darren Caunt
Ben Challis
Lee Chamberlain
Joyce Chamberlayne
Mike Chambers
Alan Chapman
David Chapman
Indar Charles
Lance Charlton
Rev Bernard Chart
Angele Chick
P K Chilvers
K Chongo
M D Choulton
R Chui
Dr Stephen G Clackson
A P Clark
Maggi Clark, Rotherham
    Constituency Labour Party
Elisabeth Clarke
Y B Clarke
Jason Clay
Amy Clements
Gillian Cleverley
Lewis Cligman

Andrew Close
Clive Coates
Jane Cobbald
Beryl Cobbing
E J Cobbing
Ollie Cochran
H Cockerman
G H Cole
A M Coleman
Gavin Coles
S J Collander-Brown
David Collier
Mike Collins
Andrew Colquhoun
Peter Colyer
R A Comaish
David Connah
Richard Cook
Susan Cook
Daniel Cooke
Captain D G Cooper RN Retd
David Cooper
Donald B Cooper
N J Cooper
Robert Cooper
Eric Copestake
B E B Copley
C H Copley
Ian Corfield
Shirley Corke
Peter Cornall
T M Corson
P Coughlan
P Coughlin
John Courouble
F M Courtney
Dixon Cowan
G Crawley
David Crease
Malcolm Crocker
M Cronin
George Crosby C Eng MIGE
Rev Canon Philip Crosfield
G M Crossman
Colin Crouch
George E Crowther
Ashley Crump
Gillian Cummins
Michael Cunningham
Paul Cunningham
David Currer
Mark Curry
John Cutcliffe
D Cutting

Mr & Mrs Dagley
Alison Dale
S J Dalton
J F Darycott

John Davies
R E Davies BA
R G Davies, The Royal Stuart
    Society
Robert Davies
Shona Davies
T E Davies
Barbara J Davis
Kathleen Davis
Pamela Davis
Sue Davis
W J Davis
Bernard Dawkins
S De Peyer
William de Salis
Rodolph de Salis
Peter Dean
Conrad Dehn QC
C G Delbridge
Simon Dennis Hart
Dharmaghosha
Sita Dickson
Tom Dix
G Dixon
C Donnison
Ron Dorman
Tom Dove
Dr R W Doy
Gavin Drake
Dr Joan Draper
B E Driscoll
S Duke

Ben Earnshaw-Mansell,
    Chichester Constituency
    Labour Party
Dr T M East
Anthony Edkins
Ali Edney
John Edward
J R Edwards
K Edwards
Alex Egerton
D A Eley
W R Elford
D L Elliott
B J Ellis
Harry Elsdale
W H Elvis
Rupert Emerson
Trevor England
Dr Mary P English
Louis Epstein
Jean Etridge
Elizabeth Evans
J D Evans
Matthew Evans
Meg Evans
Tom Everest

Chris Everett
Roger Evers
P Eyres

Mary Fagan JP
R W Falconer
Will Fancy
William Fane
John Faulder
Stephen Fawbert
Valerie Fawcett
Margaret M Feeny
Prof P B Fellgett
John Fenis
Group Captain J Fennell (Rtd)
Rev Dr John Fenwick
G A Fereday
Gordon Fergusson
Dr R P Fernando
T W Ferrers-Walker
Susan Feuch
Paul Fidler
J M Fieldier
John Fisher
David E Flavell
G A Fletcher
Paul Fletcher
Mr Flint
J S Florentin
Cllr Chris Foote Wood
J Forbes
Peter Ford
Nigel Fordham
C E Forrest
Robert Forrest
David Forster
Adrian Foster-Fletcher
Dr Richard Foulkes
E J Fowler
D Fox
S Francis
Patricia Frank
D B Franklin
John A Franks
Constance Fraser
James Fraser
John R Frears
G Freedman
Gill Freeman
Derek French
Richard Frey
J R Frost
Rob Fuller

Roy Galbraith
John Gallagher
J Gardiner
D E Gardner
Peter Garland

A Garside, Swanmore Parish
    Council
K H R Garton
R Gates
D Gay
Simon Gazelely
Neal Geach
M B Gerrard
Roger Gibbs
Dr E A Gibson
J C Gibson
J R D Gildea
Jack Gill
William Gill
Paul Gilmore
Keith Gimson
Ian Glegg
Anne Glyn-Jones
Paul Godden
John Godson
Douglas A Gohl
Anna Gokool
Joseph A Goldsmith
Alan Goodman
David Gorham
David Gorvett
Julian Gould
Nick Goulder
S J Gowar
Hon Jon-Paul Graham
Edgar J Grant
John Grant
S Grant
Edmund Gray
Jon Gray
Chris Grayling
J W Grayson
Lawrence Greaves
C J Green
D J Green
David Green
Norman Greenhil
Jane Greenlaw
J L Greenwood
Isabelle Gregory
Nigel P Gregory
P G M Greig
Colin J Grey
Philomena Grey
J H S Grieve
H G Griffiths
J Griffiths
James Griffiths
Natalie Griffiths
Harry Grove
David Gullick
R F Gunstone
E J Guy
P Guy

B W Hackman
Richard Hadden
James Hadfield
Valerie Hadley
R Hadman BSc PhD
Peter Hagle
Douglas Haines
Jim Halcrow
Rev J P Haldane-Stevenson
Barbara Hall
Fred Hall
John Hall
Dr L Hall
Michael Halliwell
Trevor Halvorsen
D R Hannay
Lady Fiona Hannon
Christian P Hansen
E Hardacker
David Harding
Dr John Harding Price
John Hardy
Martin Hardy
Paul Hardy
D H Harman
Roger Harper
W M Harper
J E Harris
Mark Harris
R Harris
J F Harrison
Mark Harrison
Peter T Harrison
Kevin J Hart
Roy Hart
Simon Hartfree
Oonagh M Hartnett
Dr Richard Harvey
R E Hastings
L H Hatcher
Leigh Hatts
Francis Hawkings
M M A Hay
N Hayes
M G Haymes
Francis Heald
David Heathfield
Paul Heaton
Terence Hegarty
Ben Hegedus
Richard Heller
Donald Henderson
Margaret L Henman
Joan Hennell
Teresa Hennell
Marc Henry
R J Herd
R Herman and A-Level Politics
    Group, St Bede's College

B Herring
Simon Hewin
P B Hewitt LCP M Phil
Arthur D Hewlett
Dr R Heyworth
David Hill
Rev Malcolm Hill BA
R J Hills
Nicholas Hinde
James Hiney
Aline Hinton
Arthur Hinton
Bernard Hiorns
A D Hoadley
M F H Hobbs
D J Holden
A J Holland
Neil Hollow
Joshua Holman
David Holmes
Stuart Honan
H Hook
Frank Hooley
Michael Hooper
Dr P D Hooper
C V Horie
John Horsfield
Nuala Horsham
D S Hoskins
Dr Houghton
A Houston
Monica Howes
Geoff Hoyle
D J Huddart
Michael G Hudgell
John Hudson
S M Hudson, Hampshire
    Association of Parish & Town
    Councils
M K Hughes
Colin Hull
J J Hull
Philip Humble
Dr Anthea Hume
G Humphrey
John Hunt
Robert L C Hunter
J A M Hutchinson
Simon Hutchinson
David Huxley, Joshua Ellis & Co

C K M Imrie BA LDS RCS
J Ingram
Martin Ingram
Peter Ireson
Adam Isaacs

A C Jackson
Martyn Jackson

I Jacobs
Sam Jacobs
Mr & Mrs James
Dr R James
Dr Michael Jarmulowicz
M J Jefferson
R G Jenkins
Caren Jennings
K R Jennings
Andy Jenns
Dr David Jessop
Andrew S Jessup-Bould
Kenneth Joel
Caroline John
Guy Johnson
C E Johnson
D Johnson-Laing
R C Johnston
John Johnstone
Andrew Jones
E C Jones
H G Jones
Keith Jones
Malcolm Jones
Pat Jones
Peter Jones
R L Jones
Sam Jones
Anthony Jordan
Edward Joyce
Christopher J Jukes

Dr Basil C Kahan
Amanda Kay
Raymond Kay
Chris Keating
D H Kedge
Yvonne Kedge
John Keenan
Bernard Kelly
Robbie Kelly
Alan J Kennard
A R Kennard
Lady Kennet
John Kenney
E A Kennington
Christopher M Kershaw
John Kershaw
David Keys
J Kidger
Gary Killick
Hamish Killip
Brian King
Stuart M King, Internet
    Business Solutions (UK) Ltd
Terence J King
Rene H Kinzett
Dr Linda Kirk
Martin Kirk

R C Kirk MIGD
M D St G Kirke
Bill Kirkman
Darren Kirkman
John Kirton
Alan Knight
Hugh Knight
Oliver J Knight
Amelia Knott

William La Chenal
S Lake
Anne Lamb
Rob Lancaster
Kenneth A Lane
Rob Lang
M M Langdom
Sir Michael Latham
Jon Latimer
Jack Lavety
Brian Lawrence
Doug Lawrence
Fred Lawson
Revd Brian Lay
Dr Paul Layman
M G F Le Blancq
Raymond Le Goy
Martin Le Jeune
Julie Leathwood
Les Lee
Keith Leed
Dennis I Leeds
W A Leighton
David Leonard
Jenny Leung
R Levene
David Lever
Linda Lever
C A Leversha, Crookham
    Village Parish Council
John Lewis
N M Lewis
Dr Grant Lewison
David Leyshon
Daniel Lightman
S W Lindsay
Stephen Linstead
H Elizabeth Little
Peter Littlewood
Dr Anne Lloyd-Thomas
B C Lloyd-Briden
Cllr Keith Lock
Keith Loney
Derek Long
A R Longley
Paul Louden
D Loveday PhD DIC BSc
Melissa Lovett
Bernard C Lowe

Peter B Lowe
Ian Lowe
J R Lucas
Martin Lucas-Smith
Christopher Luke
Richard Lung
K Lupton
John Lynch
I Lynch-Watson
Dr Christopher Lyons
Anthony Lyster

Kenneth MacArthur
Judy Maciejowska
Donald MacInnes
Ian & June Mackenzie
Marjory Mackenzie
B Mackenzie-Williams
W S Mackie
Dr Niall L MacKinnon
Nora Maclaren
Tom Maclean
Sean Mahoney
Christine Makin
Don Manhire
John Manning
J D Manson
Dr Paul Marett
M A Marfani
James Marginson
Steven Markham
Adam Marks
Matthew Marques
John P Marriot
R Marriott
Emily Marsden
M A Marshall
Peter Marshall
Teresa Marshall
Andrew Martin
Norman Mason
Dr Jack Massey
Sir Carol Mather
Anthony Matthews
Kingsley Matthews
Dinah May
Jandy May
Richard Mayer
Mr & Mrs Mayo
M McAleavy
Jim McCall
Roger McCallister
John D McCallum
Malcolm McCandless
Alexander McClintock
S McConnachie
Bryan McGee
Peter McGinty
James McGlynn

Richard McGrath
James McIlwraith
K M McIntosh
R Michael McKeag
I W McKendrick
Christopher McLaren
M J McLean
Norah McManus
James McNaughtie
John M Meade
Justin Meadows
J Meads
J C Meigh
Dr W J G Meldrum
S R Mellor
Ellen Meredith
David Metz
Stuart Middleton
David Millar
Dick Millard
Barry Miller
Roger Miller
Tim Miller
Piers Milne
Brian Minchin
M K Mindt
Roger Minshull
Brian Mitchell
G M Mitchell
Julie Mitchell
Mark Mitchell
Andrew Neil Mobbs
Hans-Martin Moderow
Keir Moilliet
David Monkton
Jonathan Monroe
Tom Montemarano
S M Mooney
A Moore
Dr A R Moore
D A Moore
John Moore
A E Morley
D E Morris
Norman Morris
Peter Morris, Wycombe
    Constituency Labour Party
R V Morris
Susan Morris, Wycombe
    Constituency Labour Party
Dr Clive Morrison
D W Morrison
M C T Morrison FRCS
N J B Morrison
Sir Jeremy Morse
W Mortimore
H P A Moser
Michael Mounteney
I E Munday

Geoffrey W G Munnery
Ian Murdoch
Susan J Murray
M Murray
The Rt Hon Lord Murray
S H Murray Wells
Ruth Muttlebury
Charles Mynor

Sir Patrick Nairne
Sir David Naish
M S R Napier
W Nash
Eric Naylor
Geoff Naylor
D A Needham
R Neill
Dr Peter G Nelson
Adele & Guy Nevill
Revd Canon Graham Neville
Jenny Newby, Charter 88
Christopher M Newell
R G Newton
Elizabeth Nicholas
David Nichols
Anthony Nixon
Sir Iain Noble OBE
Professor P Noble
Gerard Norris
Edward F Northcote
D C Nott
Jean Nutting

Peter O'Curry, Bucks County
    Labour Party
Barry O'Dwyer
Brian O'Gorman BA MA
Edward O'Hara
Luke O'Mahoney Magee
Adam Ogilvie-Smith
Fabian Olins
Becki Orford
T G Oswald
Fred Ottey
W Oxburgh

Anne Packington
Sir John Page
Eric Paine
Richard Palk
Anne Palmer
Andrew Papworth
Richard Paramor
Dudley Park
Ian J H Parker
J D Parkinson
Richard Parrish
Janet Pascoe
Indira Patel OBE

Guy Patterson
Val Pattie
Laura Pattison
Jean Peacy
S F Pearce
Euan F S Pearson
Keith B Pearson
Sarah Peet
Liam Pennington
Helene R Perriss
Beth Perry
J H Perry
James B Petrie
B Pettitt
Charles J L Pfeil
Andrew Phillips
Mary Phillips
R H Phillips
F W Philpot
P Pibley
David Pickering
Erica Pilliner
Severin E Pinder
Alderman F A C Pinney OBE
G L B Pitt
Stephen Plowden MA MCIT
Erin Polaschek
V R Pole
Allan Pond
Dr John Ponsonby
Brenda Pooley
M H Pope
Mary Porter
H A Potter
Kenneth E Pottle Carmen
Alex Potts
Dave Powicke
Paul Powter
Jason Preece
John Preston
Matt Prince
S K Prior
Stuart Pritt
B A Proctor
Byron Proffitt
H A Prowse
John Pruce
L M Pryor
Henry Pryor
R H Pullan
P M Puntis

Yon Quinn

Nicholas J Radcliffe
A G Raffield
Joan Rankin
L Rawling, Sir George Monoux
    A Level Govt & Politics Group

Malcolm Rawson
T S Rayt
Anthony H Read
Allan Redgrave
A H Reed
Robin Reed
Ben Rees
Ian Rees
Dr A Drummond Rees
Tim Reeves
Walter Reid
Edward Rhodes
Rhonda Riachi
James Richards
Victoria Richards
G Richards
Ian Richardson
J Ridgeway
Prof Robert Roaf
Geoffrey Robert-Pearce
Dave Roberts
Derek Roberts
Edward F Roberts
Janet L Roberts
P H Roberts
William Robertson
J Robinson
John Robinson
John Martin Robinson
M Robinson, Barton Peveril
    College
N K Robson
Peter Roche
Thomas Roedl
B J Rofe
J W Roger Lewis
Peter Rogers
Mark Rolfe
D A & P A Ross
Marjory Ross
Richard Rouse
Richard Rouse
Francis Routledge
Chris Rowley
Vice Admiral Sir John
    Roxburgh KCB CBE DSO
    DSC
G J Rudd
J E Russell
Bryan Russell
Bridget Russell
Martin R Rutter
Anne Ryan

J Sadler
Marilyn Saklatvala
John Samkey
M Samson
E R Samuel

Alec Samuels
Dr Sarah R Sanderson
Paul Sandford, St Philip's
    Church
Graham Sands
Alan J Sarfas
Dick Saunders
Suzanne Saunders
Michael Saundery
Ben Sawbridge
The Rev Graham Sawyer
A Schaefer
Damian Schofield
Anthony Scholefield
Helen Scoflin
Sam Scorer
Maurice L Scott
Peter D Scott
Peter Scrope
Helen Seaford
Robert Seaton
Miles Secker
Damian Sefton
David Selby
Derek Selby
Christine Seymour
John Shanks
Alderman James Shannon,
    Ards Borough Council
C A Sharp
Dave Sharp
Jonathan Sharp
Anthony Sharpe
Edward Sharpe
B L Shaw
Matthew Shaw
Audrey Shepherd
David Shepherd
Roger Shepherd
Matthew Shepherdson
Norman Shields
Simon Shields
Mark Shurville
D Simmonds
David Simmons
John G Simmons
Donald Simpson
Glenn Simpson
Peter Simpson, Hambleton
    District Council
G E Simpson
N A Sinclair
Nicole Sinclaire
M A Sinfield
Andy Sipple, Kettering
    Borough Council
Peter Slade
C L Smiley
Rev C H Smith

David Smith
David Smith
David F Smith
G Smith
Geoff Smith
George Smith
J Smith
John C Smith
John F H Smith
Katherine Smith
R A Smith
Stan Smith OBE
William Smith
Michael Smyth
Tim Snape
James Sneath
Gordon Snow
Penny Solomons
Andrew Soper
Nigel Spearing
Dave Spenceley
Bryan Spinks
D A Spry
J M Stabler
E Stanbank
P J Stanbridge
Peter Stanley
Simon Stanley
Frederic Stansfield
Dr Martin Stanton KLJ
Norman S Staveley
Tyler Stein
J R Stephenson
R L Stephenson
Jonathan T Sternberg
Andrew Stevens
Dorothy Stevens
Helen Stevens
Leila M Stevenson
Jean Stewart
Charles Stewart Main
Dr & Mrs Stokes
Dr John T Stopford, J S
    Consulting
Sir Richard Storey Bt CBE
Dr John Storr
John E Strafford, Campaign for
    Conservative Democracy
Ronald A Strank
Raymond F Strong
G Sturley
Patrick Sumner
J K B Sutherland
N G Sutton
M J Swain
Mary Swann
A Swindells
Dr & Mrs Sykesud
P Symmons

Jack Synom
Mike Sztanko

Richard Tabberer
Mark Taha
Guy Talbot
W R N Tapp
Jonathan Tapscott
Peter Tatton-Brown
A R Taylor
David J Taylor
F John Taylor
G W Taylor
Helen Taylor
John Taylor
M F Taylor
Martin Taylor
J T Teighe
G E Tew
Justin E Theed
Cllr Bransby Thomas
C M Thomas
Dr Graham G Thomas
R L Thomas
B H Thompson
Constance Thompson
Eric J Thompson CB
Graham Thompson
P M Thompson
W G Thompson
Neil Thomson
J E M Thornhill
Duncan Thorp
D J Thorpe
Phillip J Thorpe
James Thring
Martin Tither
Raymond Toney
Terry Tonks
Ian Tonothy
Keith Townend
J P Truman
R Tubman
Andrew Tucker
Mr Tudor
Anthony Tuffin
D Tufnell
A J Turner FRSA
C Turner
Chris Turner
Rev Garth Turner
J Turner
T B Turner
Bob Tutton
T E Tweed
Robert Twigg
D R Twist
B Underwood
Howard Underwood

D R Underwood
U.S.E.
Simon Usherwood

J A G Vear
Stevan Vernon-Brown
Colin Vesey
Edward Vickerman
Philip Vince
Simon Virr
C Vost

Jacqueline L Wachlarz
Alan M Waddington
C W Wade
Nigel Wade
J W Wagstaff
Martin Waldron BSc CEng
    MIEE
Angus Walker
F G F Walker
John de Vere Walker
Tina Walker
Elizabeth Wallace
Simon Wallace
Brian Wallis
Charles Walster
N A Walter
Nicolas Walter
Lee Walters
Barry Waltho
Everlin Ward
Martin Ward
Perry Ward
B S Wardman
D E Warren
Cynthea Warth
A G W Wash
Julian Washington
Lee Waters
N C Watkis AE DipM CMC
    MCIM MIMC

Harry Watson
Richard Watson
Robert Watson
William Watson
Peter Waugh
W J Webber
Philip Webster
Robert Weems
Dr Diarmid J G Weir
Dr Robert Welding
Derek A Wells
Gordon West
W C West
John E Wheeler
M H Wheller
Mr Whitaker
B A White
David White
J White
J W White
Rachel White
S White
David Whitfield
Tony Whiting
A M Whittaker
Brian Wichman
F N H Widdrington
Claire Wigg
Anthony Wilder
Joe Wiles
K W Wilkes
James Wilkinson
Mary E Wilkinson
A Wilks
Mr & Mrs Williams
A G Williams
David Williams
G Williams
Heather Williams
Michael Williams
Michael J Williams
Pru Williams

Zoe Williams
Andrew Williamson
Christina Williamson
I D Williamson
Adam Wilson
Dorothy V Wilson
J Wilson
J R Wilson
Jon Wilson
Michael Wilson
A J Wimbury LLB FCA
G C Winstone
Ron A Winwood
Allan Wisbey
John Withington
Dave Womersley
David Wood
M Wood
B Woodcare
Joyce I Woodhouse
Dr Eric Woodling
David Woodman
Philip F Wooller
Keith E H Woolley
Michael Woolsterholmes
Pat Woolven
F M Wouters
J H Wright
J M H Wright
Martin Wright
O A Wright
Parisa Wright
G T Wylie
John Wymer

Andrew Yale
J C Yandle
Sally Young

Select bibliography

About Japan Series. *The Diet, Elections, and Political Parties.* Foreign Press Centre/Japan.

Alexander, R. *The Voice of the People – A Constitution for Tomorrow.* London: Weidenfeld & Nicolson. 1997. ISBN 0 297 84109 2.

Bagehot, W. *The English Constitution.* Sussex Academic Press. 1997. ISBN 1 898723 71 0.

Baldwin, N. *Lawyers in Parliament.* In: Oliver, D. and Drewry, G. eds. *The Law and Parliament.* 1998. ISBN 0 406 98092 6.

Benn, T. and Hood, A. *Common Sense: A New Constitution for Britain.* Hutchinson. 1993. ISBN 0091773083.

Blackburn, R. and Plant, R., eds. *Constitutional Reform – The Labour Government's Constitutional Reform Agenda.* Longman. 1999. ISBN 0 582 36999 1.

Bogdanor, V. *The Monarchy and the Constitution.* Clarendon Press. 1995. ISBN 0 198277695.

Bogdanor, V. *Power and the People – A Guide to Constitutional Reform.* Cassell Group. 1997. ISBN 0 575 06491 9.

Bogdanor, V. *Devolution in the United Kingdom.* Oxford University Press. 1999. ISBN 0 19 289310 6.

Brazier, R. *Constitutional Reform – Reshaping the British Political System.* Oxford University Press. 1998. ISBN 0 19 876524 X.

Bryce, Viscount. *Conference on the Reform of the Second Chamber – Letter from Viscount Bryce to the Prime Minister (Cd 9038).* 1918.

Cabinet Office. *Modernising Government (Cm 4310).* 1999.

Cabinet Office. *Modernising Parliament – Reforming the House of Lords (Cm 4183).* 1999.

Cabinet Office. *Parliament Bill 1947 – Agreed Statement on Conclusion of Conference of Party Leaders (Cmd 7380).* 1948.

Cabinet Office. *House of Lords Reform (Cmnd 3799).* Her Majesty's Stationery Office. 1968.

Cabinet Office. *The Governance of Public Bodies: A Progress Report (Cm 3557).* The Stationery Office. 1997. ISBN 0 10 135572 6.

Cabinet Office. *Devolution: Memorandum of Understanding and Supplementary Agreements between the United Kingdom Government, Scottish Ministers and the Cabinet of the National Assembly for Wales (Cm 4444).* The Stationery Office. 1999.

Cabinet Office. *The Government's Response to the First Report from the Committee on Standards in Public Life (Cm 2931).* HMSO. 1995. ISBN 0 10 129312 7.

Carnarvon KCVO KBE, Earl of, et al. *Second Chamber – Some Remarks on Reforming the House of Lords.* Douglas Slater. 1998. ISBN 0 9526512 03.

Charter 88. *Policy Paper – Reform of the House of Lords.* 1998. ISBN 1873311 583.

Committee on Standards in Public Life. *Standards in Public Life: First Report (Cm 2850-I).* HMSO. 1995. ISBN 0 10 128502 7.

Committee on Standards in Public Life. *Standards in Public Life: Fifth Report, The Funding of Political Parties in the United Kingdom (Cm 4057-I).* The Stationery Office. 1998. ISBN 0 10 140572 3.

Constitution Unit. *Reform of the House of Lords.* 1996. ISBN 0 9527960 0 7.

Constitution Unit. *Constitutional Watchdogs.* Briefing. 1997.

Constitution Unit. *Reforming the Lords: A Step by Step Guide.* 1998.

Constitution Unit. *Rebalancing the Lords: The Numbers.* Briefing. 1998.

Constitution Unit. *Checks & Balances in Single Chamber Parliaments (Stage I).* 1998.

Constitution Unit. *Single Chamber Parliaments: a Comparative Study (Stage II).* 1998.

Constitution Unit. *The Impact of the Human Rights Act: Lessons from Canada and New Zealand.* 1999.

Constitution Unit. *A Transitional House of Lords: Balancing the Numbers.* 1999.

Cooke of Thorndon, Lord. *Unicameralism in New Zealand: Some Lessons.* In: *Canterbury Law Review – Volume 7.* 1999.

Cornes, R. *Constitutional Reform and the United Kingdom's Highest Courts.* The Constitution Unit. 1999.

Desai, Lord and Kilmarnock, Lord. *Destiny not Defeat: Reforming the Lords.* Fabian Society. 1997. ISBN 0 7163 3029 6.

Dickson, B. and Carmichael, P. *The House of Lords – Its Parliamentary and Judicial Roles.* Hart Publishing. 1999. ISBN 1 84113 020 6.

Dungey, J. and Newman, I., eds. *The New Regional Agenda.* Local Government Information Unit. 1999. ISBN 1 8979 5758 0.

Dunleavy, P. and Margetts, H. *Report to the Government Office for London: Electing the London Mayor and the London Assembly.* LSE Public Policy Group. 1998.

Dunleavy, P. and Margetts, H. *Report to the Independent Commission on the Voting System: The Performance of the Commission's Schemes for a New Electoral System.* LSE Public Policy Group. 1998.

Dunleavy, P., Hix, S. and Margetts, H. *Counting on Europe: Proportional Representation and the June 1999 Elections to the European Parliament.* LSE Public Policy Group. 1998. ISBN 0 7530 1225 1.

Electoral Reform Society. *Towards a Fairer Vote – The Submission of the ERS on the Independent Commission on Voting Systems.* 1998.

European Parliamentary Elections Act 1999.

Foreign and Commonwealth Office. *Partnership for Progress and Prosperity – Britain and the Overseas Territories (Cm 4264).* The Stationery Office. 1999.

Foreign and Commonwealth Office. *4th Report from the Foreign Affairs Committee: Gibraltar: Response of the Secretary of State for Foreign and Commonwealth Affairs.* The Stationery Office. 1999. ISBN 0101447027.

Garrett, J. *Westminster – Does Parliament Work?* Victor Gollancz Ltd. 1992. ISBN 0 575 04994 4.

Griffith, J.A.G. and Ryle, M. (with Wheeler-Booth, M.A.J.). *Parliament –Functions, Practice and Procedures.* Sweet and Maxwell. 1989. ISBN 0421 35280 9.

Hazell, R. *Re-inventing the Constitution: can the State survive?* CIPFA/Times Lecture. The Constitution Unit. Nov. 1998.

Hazell, R., ed. *Constitutional Futures – A History of the Next Ten Years.* Oxford University Press. 1999. ISBN 0-19-829801-3.

Heathcoat Amory, E. *Lords a' Leaping.* Centre for Policy Studies. 1998. ISBN 1 897969 79 1.

Hedges, A. and White, C. (with Seyd, B., Kahn, P. and Woodfield, K.). *New Electoral Systems: What Voters Need to Know.* Social & Community Planning Research. 1999. ISBN 0 904607 364.

Home of the Hirsel KT, Lord. *The House of Lords – The Report of the Conservative Review Committee.* 1978.

Home Office (UK). *Putting Rights into Public Service: The Human Rights Act 1998.* 1999.

Home Office (UK). *The Report of the Independent Commission on the Voting System (Cm 4090-I).* The Stationery Office. 1998. ISBN 0 10 140902 8.

Home Office (UK). *The Funding of Political Parties in the United Kingdom: The Government's Proposals for Legislation in Response to the Fifth Report of the Committee on Standards in Public Life (Cm 4413).* The Stationery Office. 1999. ISBN 0 10 144132 0.

House of Commons. *Select Committee on Procedure, Fourth Report: Delegated Legislation.* HMSO. 1996. ISBN 0 10 239896 8.

House of Commons. *Select Committee on Procedure, Fourth Report: The Procedural Consequences of Devolution.* The Stationery Office. 1999. ISBN 0 10 2331995.

House of Commons. *Public Service Committee, First Report: The Code of Practice for Public Appointments.* HMSO. 1996. ISBN 0 10 222796 9.

House of Commons. *Public Service Committee, Second Report: The Work of the Commissioner for Public Appointments.* HMSO. 1997. ISBN 0 10 212397 7.

House of Commons. *Foreign Affairs Committee, Fourth Report: Gibraltar.* The Stationery Office. 1999. ISBN 0 10 236899 6.

House of Commons. *Procedural Consequences of Devolution: Government Response to the 4th Report from the Committee.* The Stationery Office. 1999. ISBN 0102331995.

House of Commons. *Members' Pay, Pensions and Allowances.* Information Office Factsheet No. 17. 1998.

House of Commons Library. *Parliamentary Scrutiny of Deregulation Orders.* Research Paper. 94/116. 1994.

House of Commons Library. *Special Standing Committees in Both Houses.* Research Paper. 96/14. 1996.

House of Commons Library. *House of Lords Reform: Recent Proposals.* Research Paper. 97/28. 1997.

House of Commons Library. *The Commons Committee Stage of 'Constitutional' Bills.* Research Paper. 97/53. 1997.

House of Commons Library. *Aspects of Parliamentary Reform.* Research Paper. 97/64. 1997.

House of Commons Library. *Scotland and Devolution.* Research Paper. 97/92. 1997.

House of Commons Library. *Parliamentary Reform: The Commons 'Modernisation' Programme.* Research Paper. 97/107. 1997.

House of Commons Library. *Devolution and Europe.* Research Paper. 97/126. 1997.

House of Commons Library. *Government of Wales Bill: Operational Aspects of the National Assembly.* Research Paper. 97/132. 1997.

House of Commons Library. *The Scotland Bill: Some Operational Aspects of Scottish Devolution.* Research Paper. 98/2. 1998.

House of Commons Library. *The Barnett Formula.* Research Paper. 98/8. 1998.

House of Commons Library. *Regional Government in England.* Research Paper. 98/9. 1998.

House of Commons Library. *The Human Rights Bill: Some Constitutional and Legislative Aspects.* Research Paper. 98/27. 1998.

House of Commons Library. *Cabinets, Committees and Elected Mayors.* Research Paper. 98/38. 1998.

House of Commons Library. *House of Lords Reform: Developments since the General Election.* Research Paper. 98/85. 1998.

House of Commons Library. *Parliamentary Pay and Allowances: Current Rates.* Research Paper. 98/86. 1998.

House of Commons Library. *The European Parliamentary Elections Bill.* Research Paper. 98/102. 1998.

House of Commons Library. *Lords Reform: The Legislative Role of the House of Lords.* Research Paper. 98/103. 1998.

House of Commons Library. *Lords Reform: Background Statistics.* Research Paper. 98/104. 1998.

House of Commons Library. *Lords Reform: Recent Developments.* Research Paper. 98/105. 1998.

House of Commons Library. *Voting Systems: The Jenkins Report.* Research Paper. 98/112. 1998.

House of Commons Library. *Voting Systems – The Government's Proposals.* Research Paper. 98/113. 1998.

House of Commons Library. *The House of Lords Bill: 'Stage One' Issues.* Research Paper. 99/5. 1999.

House of Commons Library. *The House of Lords Bill: Options for 'Stage Two'.* Research Paper. 99/6. 1999.

House of Commons Library. *The House of Lords Bill: Lords Reform and Wider Constitutional Reform.* Research Paper. 99/7. 1999.

House of Commons Library. *Devolution and Concordats.* Research Paper. 99/84. 1999.

House of Commons Library. *The Procedural Consequences of Devolution.* Research Paper. 99/85. 1999.

House of Commons Library. *The House of Lords Bill: Lords Amendments.* Research Paper. 99/88. 1999.

House of Commons. *Joint Committee on Financial Services and Markets – First Report, Draft Financial Services and Markets Bill. Vols I and II.* 1999. HC 328 I and II.

House of Councillors. *The National Diet of Japan – House of Councillors.* Ministry of Finance (Japan). 1995.

House of Lords. *Freedom and Function: Report to the Leader of the House from the Group on Procedure in the Chamber.* The Stationery Office. 1999. ISBN 0 10 403499 8.

House of Lords. *Select Committee on Delegated Powers and Deregulation: Special Report for Session 1998-99 – The Committee's Work.* The Stationery Office. 1999. ISBN 0 10 411299 9.

House of Lords. *Reform and Proposals for Reform Since 1900.* Briefing paper. 1998.

House of Lords. *The Salisbury Doctrine.* Library Notes. LLN 97/004. 1997.

House of Lords. *Proposals for Reform of the Composition and Powers of the House of Lords, 1968-1998.* Library Notes. LLN 98/004. 1998.

House of Lords. *Peerage Creations, 1958-1998.* Library Notes. LLN 98/005. 1998.

House of Lords. *Membership of the House of Lords.* Library Notes. LLN 99/001. 1999.

House of Lords. *The House of Lords Bill 1998/99.* Library Notes. LLN 99/002. 1999.

Irvine of Lairg, Lord. *'Government's Programme of Constitutional Reform'*. Annual Constitution Unit Lecture. 1998.

Jaconelli, J. *The Parliament Bill 1910-1911: The Mechanics of Constitutional Protection*. In: *Parliamentary History, Vol 10*. 1991.

Jeffrey, C. *Electoral Reform: Learning From Germany*. In: *The Political Quarterly*. The Political Quarterly Publishing Co. Ltd. 1998.

Jenkins, R. *Mr Balfour's Poodle*. Collins. 1968.

Life Peerages Act. 1958.

Locabail (UK) Ltd v Bayfield Properties Ltd and another, Locabail (UK) Ltd and another v Waldorf Investment Corporation and others, 17 November 1999, www.courtservice.gov.uk/locabail

Lindbeck, et al. *Turning Sweden Round*. MIT Press, Cambridge. 1994. ISBN 0 262 12181 6.

Mackay of Clashfern KT, The Rt Hon The Lord, Chair. *The Report of the Constitutional Commission on Options for a new Second Chamber*. Douglas Slater. 1999. ISBN 0 9526512 11.

Marquand, D. *Populism or Pluralism? New Labour and the Constitution*. The Constitution Unit. 1999.

Mather MEP, G., Watson MEP, G. and Corbett MEP, R. *Brussels On Britain: The UK in Europe viewed from Brussels*. European Policy Forum. 1999.

May, E. (Limon, Sir D. and McKay, W. R., eds). *Parliamentary Practice*. 22nd ed. Butterworths. 1997. ISBN 0 406 89587 2.

Mitchell, A. *Farewell my Lords*. Politicos Publishing. 1999. ISBN 0192301439.

Mitchell, J. and Davies, A. *Reforming the Lords*. Institute for Public Policy Research. 1993. ISBN 1 872452 65 5

Mushwana, M.L. MP. *The National Council of Provinces (NCOP) – A Presentation*.

Narita, N. *Changing Japanese Politics*. Foreign Press Centre/Japan. 1999. ISBN 4 939030 04 0.

Norton, P. *National Parliaments and the European Union*. Frank Cass. 1996. ISBN 0 7146 4330 0.

Office of the Commissioner for Public Appointments. *Commissioner for Public Appointments: First Report 1995-1996*. 1996. ISBN 0 7115 0336 2.

Office of the Commissioner for Public Appointments. *Commissioner for Public Appointments: Second Report 1996-1997*. 1997. ISBN 0 7115 0351 6.

Office of the Commissioner for Public Appointments. *Commissioner for Public Appointments: Third Report 1997-1998*. 1998. ISBN 0 7115 0362 1.

Osmond, J. *Reforming the Lords and Changing Britain*. Fabian Society. 1998. ISBN 0 7163 0587 9.

Parliament Act(s). 1911 and 1949.

Parliament (No. 2) Bill. HMSO. 1968.

Patterson, S.C. and Mughan, A., eds. *Senates – Bicameralism in the Contemporary World*. Ohio State University Press. 1999. ISBN 0 8142 5010 6.

Peerage Act. 1963.

Political Quarterly. *Reforming the Lords*. Vol. 70 – Number 4 – October-December 1999. ISSN 0032-3179.

Reidy, A. *A Human Rights Committee for Westminster*. The Constitution Unit. 1999.

Richard, I. and Welfare, D. *Unfinished Business – Reforming the House of Lords*. Vintage UK. 1999. ISBN 0099289598.

Riddell, P. *Parliament Under Pressure*. Cassell Group. 1998. ISBN 0 575 06435 8.

Russell, M. *An Appointed Upper House: Lessons from Canada*. The Constitution Unit. 1998.

Russell, M. *A Directly Elected Upper House – Lessons from Italy & Australia*. The Constitution Unit. 1999.

Russell, M. *A Vocational Upper House? Lessons from Ireland*. The Constitution Unit. 1999.

Seyd, B. *'Democracy Day' – Planning for Referendums on PR and Lords Reform*. The Constitution Unit. 1999.

Shell, D. *The House of Lords*. 1992.

Shell, D. and Beamish, D. *The House of Lords at Work*. 1993.

Shell, D. and Giddings, P. *The Future of Parliament – Reform of the Second Chamber*. King-Hall Paper No. 8. The Hansard Society. 1999.

Shell, D. *Bicameralism Reconsidered*. Paper prepared for Third Workshop of Parliamentary Scholars and Parliamentarians, Wroxton College. 1998.

Sinclair, D. *Putting Our House in Order*. The Bow Group. 1998. ISBN 0861 29 149 2.

Spencer, S. and Bynoe, I. *A Human Rights Commission – The Options for Britain and Northern Ireland*. Institute of Public Policy Research. 1998. ISBN 1 86030 060 X.

Stevens, R. *The Final Appeal: Reform of the House of Lords and Privy Council 1867–1876*. In: *The Law Quarterly Review*, Vol. 80 July 1964.

Steyn, Rt Hon Lord. *The Constitutionalisation of Public Law*. The Constitution Unit.

Tyrie A. MP *Reforming the Lords: A Conservative Approach*. Conservative Policy Forum. 1998. ISBN 085070952.

Weller, P., ed. *Religions in the UK – A Multi-faith Directory*. 2nd ed. University of Derby. 1997. ISBN 0 901437 68 9.

Wyndham, W. *Peers in Parliament Reformed*. Quiller Press. 1998. ISBN 1 899163 43 3.

Commissioned papers

The following papers were specifically commissioned to assist the Royal Commission and are included on the attached CD-ROM. Some have subsequently been published by the relevant bodies.

Cornes, R. *The Role of the Law Lords*. The Constitution Unit. 1999.

Davie, G. *Religious Representation in the House of Lords*. University of Exeter. 1999.

Dunleavy, P. and Margetts, H. *Electing Members of the Lords (or Senate)*. LSE Public Policy Group. 1999. This is a merged version of papers presented in May, September and October 1999.

Foreign & Commonwealth Office. *Memorandum of Evidence to the Royal Commission: Approval of Treaties*.

Lewis-Jones, J. *House of Lords: The Role of the Bishops*. The Constitution Unit. 1999.

Martin, D. *Deposition on the Lords Spiritual in the Upper House*. 1999.

Reidy, A. *Reforming the House of Lords: Its role in a Human Rights Culture*. The Constitution Unit. 1999.

Reidy, A. and Russell, M. *Guardians of the Constitution and Protectors of Human Rights*. The Constitution Unit. 1999.

Russell, M. *Territorial Representation in the Upper Chamber: Lessons from Overseas*. The Constitution Unit. 1999.

Russell, M. *The Spanish Senate: A Cautionary Lesson for Britain*. The Constitution Unit. 1999.

Russell, M. *Second Chambers Overseas*. The Constitution Unit. 1999.

Russell, M. *Resolving Disputes between the Chambers*. The Constitution Unit. 1999.

Printed in the UK for The Stationery Office Limited
on behalf of the Controller of Her Majesty's Stationery Office
Dd 5069277 1/00 J0101687 474698 19585